HEAVEN IS UNDER OUR FEET

HENRY DAVID THOREAU

I went to the woods because I wished to live deliberately, to front only the essential facts of life, and see if I could not learn what it had to teach, and not, when I came to die, discover that I had not lived.

WALDEN
HENRY DAVID THOREAU

HEAVEN IS UNDER OUR FEET

Edited by Don Henley and Dave Marsh

BERKLEY BOOKS, NEW YORK

Jimmy Carter: Foreword © 1991; Don Henley: Preface/*How Civilized Are We?* © 1991; Edmund A. Schofield: *Introduction, Sand and Water, Fire and Ice* © *1991*; Edmund A. Schofield: *Walden, Symbol of Hope* © 1991; E.L. Doctorow: *Remarks at the Walden Woods Project Press Conference* © 1990; James Earl Jones: *Winter Ponds* © 1991; Edward M. Kennedy: *Remembering Thoreau and Preserving Walden Pond* © 1991; Martin J. Rosen: *A World of Waldens* © 1991; Thomas McGuane: *West Boulder Spring* © 1991; Bette Midler: *Out of Rot, All Good Things Cometh* © 1991; Don Johnson: *The End of More* © *1991*; Anne LaBastille: *Walden Woods* © 1991; Jim Harrison: *A Revisionist's Walden* © 1991; Robert Redford: *Taking It Personally* © 1991; Chester G. Atkins: *The Fabric of Thoreau Country* © 1991; Wesley T. Mott: *That "Dirty Little Atheist" Thoreau* © 1991; Ted Danson: *Environmental Ramblings* © 1991; Reverend Jesse Jackson: *A Tribute to Henry David Thoreau* © 1991; Richard F. Fleck: *Mountaineity* © 1991; Paula Abdul: *Little Green* © 1991; James Michener: *Of Living Creatures* © 1991; George T. Frampton, Jr.: *Toward a Land Ethic* © 1991; Tom Cruise: *I Can't See The Forest if There Are No Trees* © 1991; Garry Trudeau: *The Swim* © 1991; Alan H. Edmond: *On Spirit and Initiative* © 1991; John Nichols: *Yo Thoreau!*, © 1991 and *Conscience and Community* © 1986; Mike Farrell: *As Pogo Said . . .* © 1991; Bette Woody: *The Lessons of Walden* © 1991; John O'Connor: *The American Promise* © 1991; Jimmy Buffett: *A Boxful of Africa* © 1991; John Kerry: *Stewards of the Lake and the Woods* © 1991; Marian Thornton: *"I would fain drink a draught of Nature's serenity"* © 1991; Pat Riley: *Following Dreams* © 1991; Michael Kennedy: *Commerce & Community: The Natural Partnership* © 1991; John A. Hoyt: *In Wildness is the Preservation of the World* © 1991; Michael Dorris: *Three Yards* © 1991; Louise Erdrich: *Three Ponds* © 1991; John McAleer: *A Walk on the Gurnet* © 1991; Jack Nicholson: *Solar Electricity* © 1991; Kathi Anderson: *A River and a Pond* © 1991; Gregory Peck: *Walden Woods: A Sacred Trust* © 1991; Jim Hightower: *Back to the Grassroots* © 1991; Meryl Streep: *Children Are Our Future, Give Them Light and Let Them Lead the Way* © 1991; Arun Gandhi: *A Balance Between Our Need and Our Greed* © 1991; Paul C. Pritchard: *One Pond, Many Parks* © 1991; Mary Kay Place: *From the Big Chill to the Big Picture* © 1991; Robert Bly: *Seeing What Is Before Us* © 1991; Kirstie Alley: *The Romans, the Mad Hatters and . . . . . Walden 1991?* © 1991; Todd N. Tatum: *The New Call To Arms* © 1991; Diandra M. Douglas: *Deya—Change Comes to the Global Village* © 1991; Ed Begley, Jr.: *Live Simply So Others Can Simply Live* © 1991; Floyd Red Crow Westerman: *Note on Chief Seattle Speaks* © 1991; Arlo Guthrie: *Walled-In Beings* © 1991; Paul Tsongas: *Walden Our Living Heritage* © 1991; Whoopi Goldberg: *Talking Loud and Saying Nothing* © 1991; Edward T. McMahon: *Scenic America* © 1991; Sting: *Progress, The G.N.P. and The Naming of Things* © 1991; Kurt Vonnegut: *To Hell with Marriage* © 1991; Janet Jackson: *Listen* © 1991 (with Michael Churchill); Cesar Chavez: *Pesticides, Children and Cancer* © 1991; Tom Hanks: *Baby, You Can Drive My Hovercraft* © 1991; John DeVillars: *Earth Day, 1990* © 1991; Shigeyuki Okajima: *Thoreau & Qomolangma* © 1991; Priscilla A. Chapman: *Air Apparent* © 1991; Dave Marsh: *The Boll Weevil Song* © 1991; Carrie Fisher: *Reading By Lamplight* © 1991; Bill McKibben: *Thoreau Country—The Wild, Wild East* © 1991; Wallace Stegner: *Qualified Homage to Thoreau* © 1991. Map on endpapers © 1991, Thoreau Country Conservation Alliance. Reprinted by permission.

We gratefully acknowledge the use of "Mowing" by Robert Frost, courtesy of Henry Holt Publishers.

Printed on recycled paper.

This Berkley book contains the complete text
of the original hardcover edition.

HEAVEN IS UNDER OUR FEET

A Berkley Book / published by arrangement with
Longmeadow Press

PRINTING HISTORY
Longmeadow edition published 1991
Berkley trade paperback edition / December 1992

ISBN: 0-425-13546-2

A BERKLEY BOOK ® TM 757,375
Berkley Books are published by The Berkley Publishing Group,
200 Madison Avenue, New York, New York 10016.
The name "BERKLEY" and the "B" logo
are trademarks belonging to Berkley Publishing Corporation.

PRINTED IN THE UNITED STATES OF AMERICA

10 9 8 7 6 5 4 3 2 1

To all those
who love and respect the land,
the air, the water,
and all the creatures who dwell therein.

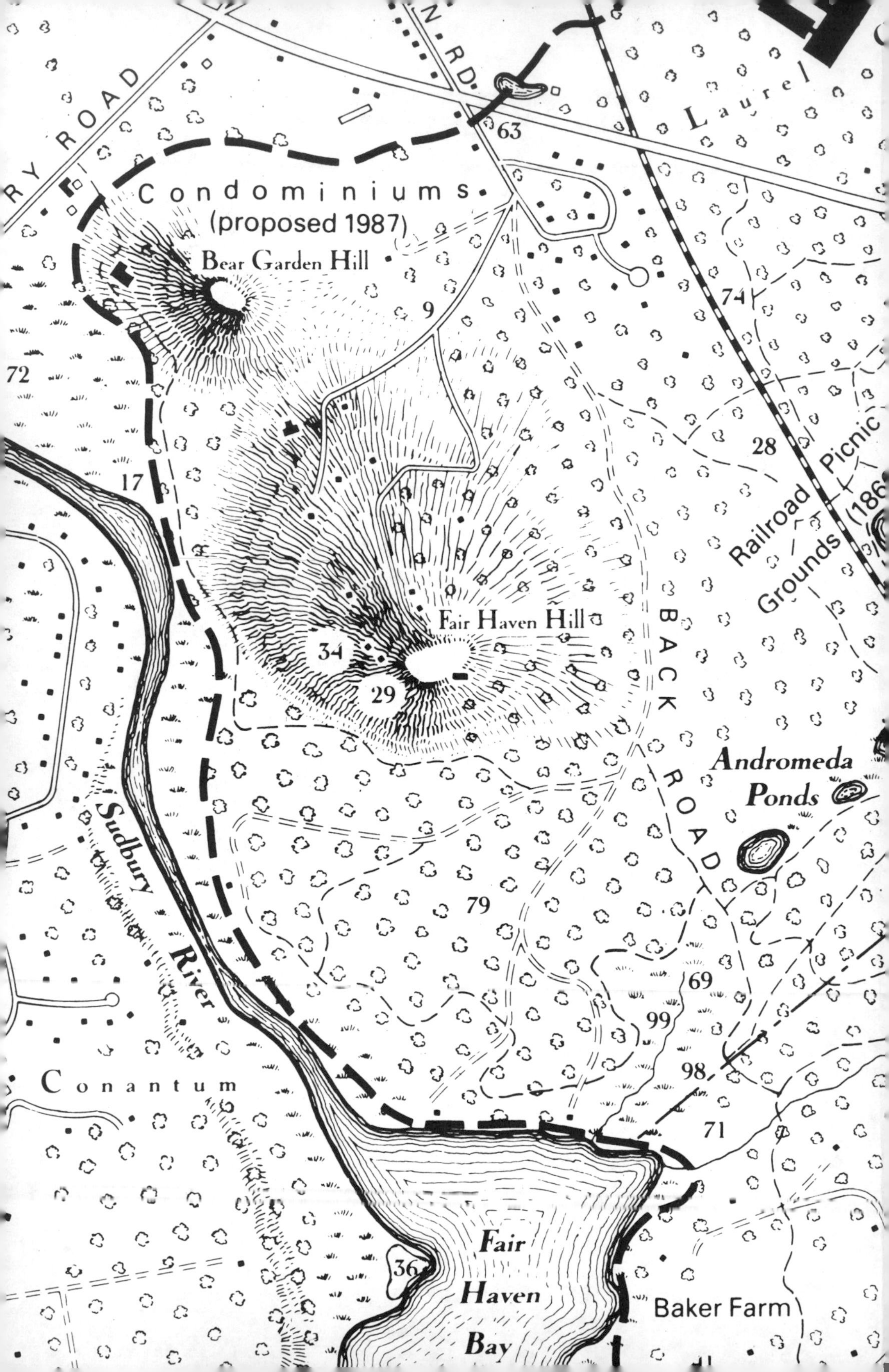

N. RD.

RY ROAD

Laurel

63

Condominiums
(proposed 1987)

Bear Garden Hill

9

74

72

28

17

Railroad Picnic Grounds (186

BACK ROAD

Fair Haven Hill

34

29

Andromeda
Ponds

Sudbury River

79

69

99

98

Conantum

71

Fair
Haven
Bay

36

Baker Farm

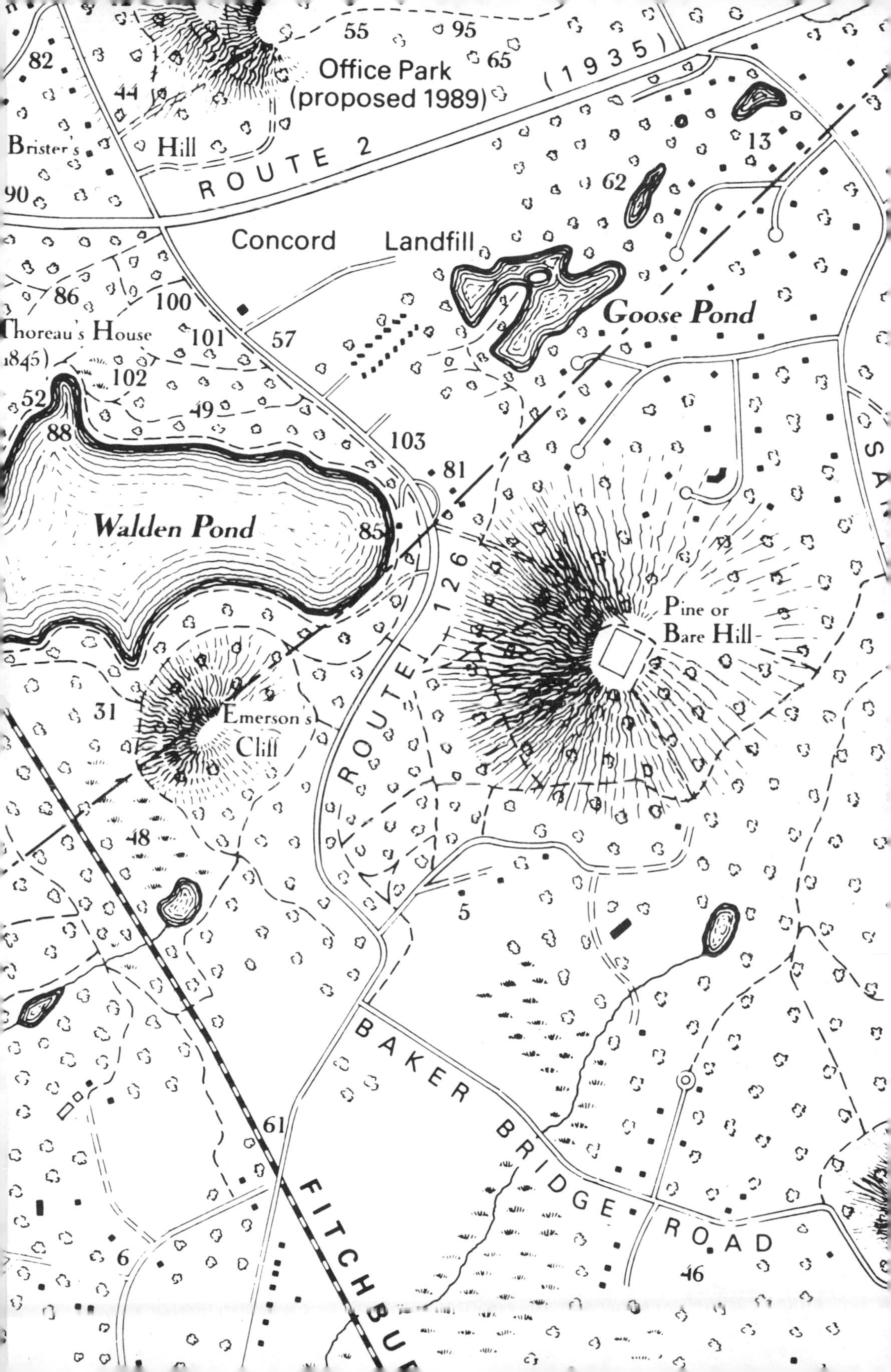

Office Park
(proposed 1989)

55   95
65

ROUTE 2 (1935)

82
44

Brister's   Hill

90

13

62

86
100

Concord   Landfill

Goose Pond

Thoreau's House
(1845)
101
57
102
52
49
103
88
81

Walden Pond
85

Pine or
Bare Hill

31
Emerson's
Cliff

ROUTE 126

48

5

61

BAKER   BRIDGE   ROAD

FITCHBU

6
46

I think that each town should have a park, or rather a primitive forest, of five hundred or a thousand acres, either in one body or several—where a stick should never be cut for fuel—nor for the navy, nor to make wagons, but stand and decay for higher uses—a common possession forever, for instruction and recreation.

"HUCKLEBERRIES"
HENRY DAVID THOREAU

CONTENTS

CONTENTS ▲ 4

ACKNOWLEDGMENTS

This book is the fruit of many labors. We gratefully acknowledge Pam Altschul, Barbara Cohen Aronica, John Aurin, Nina Avramides, Elizabeth Ayer, Irving Azoff, Joyce Harrington Bahle, Linda Balahoutis, Alison Balian, Bennett H. Beach, Tom Blanding, Julia Blatt, Jim Brasher, Barbara Carr, Jean Casella, Steve Cobble, Charles Cumello, Blythe Danner, Pat Demkowich, Diane Drummond, Robert Edgcomb, Cindy Faccone, Jean Fleischman, Peter Forbes, Carole Frankel, Sharon Fratello, Mike Frazier, Joan Fucillo, Jennifer Gendler, Theresa Greene, Lee Anne Haigney, Hale and Dorr (Counsellors At Law), Jennie Halsall, John D. Hamilton, Jr., P.C., Harry Hoffman, Pam Hughes, Adrienne Ingrum, Mary Jeka, Donna Kail, Lester Kaufman, Michael Kellett, Betsy Kenny, John Kings, Steve Klein, Owen Laster, May Louie, Sukey Love, Sampson Low, Pat Ludwig, Ed Macaulay, Patricia MacDonald, Daniel Madero, Laray Mayfield, Jane Malmo, Annie Marshall, Regan McLemore, Robbie Miller, Sasha Natapoff, Pat Newlin, Jim Ed Norman, Diana Ossinger, Sharon Palma, Mary Paris, Carey Parker, Ruth Poczik, Jeff Pollack, William Poole, Theresa Potter, May Quigley, Cindy Rogers, Bonnie Robbins, Ruth Salinger, Jan Halper Scaglia, Susan

Schader, Ed Schofield, Jenny Sciglimpaglia, Cynthia Shelton, David Simon, Mark Slavinsky, Frank Smith, Selina Smith, Andy Spahn, Sheldon Sroloff, Mary Lou Stock, Margery Tabankin, Janey Tannenbaum, Barry W. Tyerman, Dorothy Wachtenheim, Nick Wechsler, David A. Westenberg, Esq., Jonathan Winer, Michael Wisner, Daniel Woolf, Sarah Woodhouse, Wendy Worth, . . . and all the people whose literary contributions made this book possible.

PRESIDENT JIMMY CARTER

Henry David Thoreau's life and literature revolved around his experiences and observations in the forests and fields of New England—particularly the area around Walden Pond, known as Walden Woods. It was here that Thoreau contemplated the natural world and formulated his now-famous theories on conservation, so evident in many of his works, including his literary masterpiece *Walden*. The environmental problems which plagued this microcosmic universe in which he lived and wrote were strikingly similar to those which besieged the larger world of the mid–nineteenth century, and which have, to a great extent, persisted throughout this century as well. His literature, therefore, conveyed and continues to convey a universal message, with Walden Woods as the key symbol of his environment and our own.

As the pioneer of the American environmental movement, Thoreau brought the concept of conservation into the public consciousness. Cautioning mankind to be a vigilant custodian of the earth, he called for humanity to embrace nature for spiritual renewal and urged his contemporaries to find fulfillment in the simplicity of the natural world, saying, "A man is rich in proportion to the number of things he can afford to let alone."

The environmental challenges evident in Thoreau's era pale in comparison with the magnitude of global crises that confront us today. Perhaps the most sinister aspect of these crises is that they do not evolve "globally." Often they germinate as singular and sometimes "localized" environmental concerns—the death of a lake in the Adirondacks, the burning of an acre of tropical rain forest in Brazil, the contamination of a drinking water supply in Eastern Europe, an oil spill off the coast of Alaska, the extinction of an endangered species in Africa, or the leveling of an historic woodland near Walden Pond. The destructive impact of such disregard for the welfare of our planet cannot be overstated; environmental issues cannot be divided into "global" and "local" sectors. As in Thoreau's day, ecological crisis does not occur in several different worlds, but in the only one that all of us inhabit.

So we have come to a juncture in humanity's evolution, where we must call a halt to our uncontrolled assault on the environment. And what better place to make a courageous stand than where "environmentalism" had its humble beginning! The forest surrounding Walden Pond, a symbol of the American environmental movement, is in danger of being destroyed by the pressures of development. The future of Walden Woods rests with those of us who share a respect for its symbolic value as the unique landscape which inspired one of our country's greatest philosophers and conservationists.

This book is dedicated to that purpose. Although the topics covered in its pages are diverse, they embrace a common theme. Each is a deeply personal account and a unique representation of its author's commitment to the preservation of the environment, and each carries a message which is unalterably linked to the philosophical ideals of Henry David Thoreau. It is our fervent hope that the message this book imparts will inspire others to direct their attention and their energies toward the noble pursuit of conservation, which traces its modest origin back to a simple cabin on the shores of Walden Pond and to the solitary lover of nature who lived within it.

DON HENLEY

grew up outside. Outdoors and outside. I liked my home and my little town, but, in the company of other humans, I often felt like an alien—as if I had been dropped there in that place by space travelers that I couldn't remember. It wasn't a bad place, really. It was quite beautiful in the spring and fall, but pretty bleak in winter because it rarely snowed, which left the frozen earth in a dreary state of gray brown nakedness. I have learned, over the years, that this flies in the face of the general climatic impression of Texas that most people carry. Many seem to think of the Lone Star State as a perpetually blazing desert with cowpokes, armadillos, and cactus all around. That is true for a healthy portion of the state, but it's a big place and the climate, flora, and fauna vary wildly. Just as surely as a July sunburn will take all the skin off the unwary bather, livestock are commonly found standing up, frozen solid, in February. Cowsicles, we used to call them. Still, I found comfort and wonder outdoors in all seasons. In spring I would don my raincoat and go walking in thundershowers. This little custom scared the living daylights out of my mother, who was certain I would be struck by lightning or swept away by the malignant elements. We lived in tornado country and my grandmother, guided by some ancient wisdom, had spent a lifetime herding her family into the storm cellar every time a dark cloud appeared in the sky. But I loved weather. Still do. Storms heighten the senses. You know you're alive.

In summer I roamed the woods with my dog. There were streams and ponds, tadpoles and frogs and chameleons to catch—typical Mark Twain, Norman Rockwell, boyhood stuff. There was not much else to do. Fortunately, the advent of the video arcade was still over two decades away, though there was the occasional pinball game. The local "picture show" had gone the way of most small town cinemas, but the roller rink endured and, only a quarter of a mile from our house, the county rodeo grounds were bathed in a dusty, acrid halo every summer weekend. One steamy Saturday night, an escaped Brahma bull came tearing through my father's cornfield with three ropers in hot pursuit. The terrified animal somehow ended up on our front porch with his nose pressed up against the screen door, panting and snorting. In my young mind, it was as if he were asking us to let him in—to give him sanctuary from his tormentors. My parents, of course, didn't see it quite that way. The cowboys finally got a rope or two on him and dragged him back to his pen. Next morning, my dad cursed over his trampled corn. I felt sorry for the bull.

When I got a little older and learned how to use a rod and reel, Dad began to take me on fishing trips to Caddo Lake, a large, elongated body of water that lies half in Texas and half in Louisiana. Named for the Caddo Indians, it is one of those atmospheric, Southern places populated by cypress trees dripping with Spanish moss. It is also home to a good many alligators, pelicans, catfish, perch, and bass. According to local lore, this rich ecosystem was created by a major geological upheaval some two hundred years ago. This was my Walden. I caught my first fish there. Now, already half-choked by upstream reservoirs, this beautiful lake is, once again, under siege from two different development interests. A double pork barrel load, as it were. One proposal is to build a dam across Little Cypress Bayou (which feeds Caddo) thereby creating a reservoir which, according to all sane projections, is not needed. The locals, knowing a gouge when they see one, have twice voted down this scheme, but its perpetrators, hell-bent on turning a profit regardless of the will of the people or the detriment to the environment, are now seeking "private" funding.

The second threat calls for the construction of a canal or "navigation channel" with accompanying locks, which would begin at the Red River and be routed northwestward through Twelve Mile Bayou, Caddo Lake, Big Cypress Bayou and Lake o' the Pines. This project was authorized by Congress in 1968 and its merit at that time was dubious. It is now absolutely pointless. The sagging economy of the region has all but closed down the Lone Star Steel mill and there is now nothing to ship down or up this proposed canal. Nevertheless, the corpse has been resurrected and a study is underway in order to "re-evaluate the feasibility of a navigation channel for barge transportation." The study will supposedly give "equal weight to developmental and environmental concerns." There is doubt about this in many quarters because it is being carried out by that ultimate gang of tamperers, the U.S. Army Corps of Engineers. These are the people who never outgrew the sand pail and the spade. They're still moving dirt and water around, but it is no longer harmless child's play. It is now, on a grand scale, an attempt to "improve" upon nature in the name of "progress," and there are far-reaching consequences that are either unforeseen or ignored. We are just beginning to discover the extent of the damage, especially in the West. This has prompted me to come up with a new acronym for the Army Corps of Engineers (I always thought ACE was too bullishly complimentary, but upon checking the dictionary for alternate definitions— "3. to defeat, displace, or dispose of; gain a decisive advantage over"—perhaps it is appropriate after all.) Anyway, I like to think of them as BE NOT—Big Enemies of the Natural Order of Things. If the Corps had its way, every majestic, free-flowing river on this continent would be dammed and harnessed to a trickle and, conversely, every creek, bayou, marsh, and wetland would be dredged into something it is not and was never meant to be—another example of the Federal myopia.

A long with his love of lake fishing, my father was an avid gardener—a result of his Depression-era upbringing on a farm. He was meticulous and exacting about it, and on many a summer morning he rousted me out of bed well before sunup and handed me a hoe. We had over an acre to tend and the objective was to get as much as possible done before the sun got too high in the sky and the temperature rose above one hundred. The humidity in that region, while good for the skin and for growing vegetables, is oppressive, and heat exhaustion is always a possibility in summer. On several occasions, my thoughts turned patricidal. It was bad enough, getting up at such an ungodly hour, but to have to work all day in the sweltering heat and roiling dust was too much, especially, as I imagined, when everybody else was off somewhere having a great time. When he detected signs of rebellion, my dad would remind me that, although I might not like the toil involved in growing the vegetables, I certainly did like to eat them. I found this line of reasoning difficult to argue with, but it usually didn't improve my mood. Still, once in a while on a Saturday, the old man would lighten up and grant me clemency for the afternoon while he finished up the work by himself. There was a certain amount of guilt that went with me, which, I'm sure, was his intent. But, as the years have passed, I have grown to appreciate, more and more, what he taught me, not only about growing things in the earth, but also about responsibility and the value of hard, physical work. I now derive physical and spiritual pleasure from gardening and there is tremendous satisfaction in knowing that I could survive almost anywhere if I had to. All this galls me a little because he always said it would turn out this way.

I began to read when I was five. My dad sometimes read the "funny papers" to me on Sundays and my mother, a college graduate and former schoolteacher, read to me almost every day from books. As I grew, she made sure that there was always reading material in the house that was suited to my age and ability. The Great Depression had halted my father's schooling at the eighth grade, but he had a native intelligence, was very good at math and quite competent at reading and spelling. He and my mother were determined that I would go to college. It wasn't even a question in our home—it was just understood. They didn't necessarily care what I became, so long as I *went*—a good, college education—that was the thing. To that end, my father saved from the day I was born, bought savings bonds, and by the time I graduated from high school, there was enough (in 1965 dollars) for my college tuition.

I honestly don't remember when I was first introduced to the works of Henry David Thoreau or by whom. It may have been my venerable high school English teacher, Margaret Lovelace, or it may have been one of my university professors. I was lucky enough to have a few exceptional ones and that is sometimes all a kid needs—just one or two really good teachers can make all the difference in the world. It can inspire and change a life (but alas, all the money and attention nowadays is going to athletes, actors, musicians, C.E.O.'s, doctors, lawyers and the military industrial complex).

Thoreau's writing struck me like a thunderbolt. Like all great literature, it articulated something that I knew intuitively, but could not quite bring into focus for myself. I loved Emerson, too, and his essay, "Self-Reliance," was instrumental in giving me the courage to become a songwriter. The works of both men were part of a spiritual awakening in which I rediscovered my hometown and the beauty of the surrounding landscape, and, through that, some evidence of a "Higher Power," or God, if you like. This epiphany brought great comfort and relief because the Southern Baptist Church just wasn't working for me.

I have volunteered all this because, as Thoreau declared in the beginning of *Walden,* "I should not talk so much about myself if there were anybody else whom I knew as well . . . Moreover, I, on my side, require of every writer, first or last, a simple and sincere account of his own life, and not merely what he has heard of other men's lives . . ." Also, there has been a great deal of curiosity, speculation and, in some quarters, skepticism bordering on cynicism, as to how and why I came to be involved in the movement to preserve the stomping grounds of Henry David Thoreau and his friend and mentor, Ralph Waldo Emerson. What, in other words, is California rock & roll trash doing meddling around in something as seemingly esoteric and high-minded as literature (pronounced "LIT-tra-chure"), philosophy and history—the American Transcendentalist Movement and all its ascetic practitioners. Seems perfectly natural to me. American Literature, like the air we breathe, belongs—or should belong—to everybody. I'm an "Everyman" kind of guy. I studied the big "E" in college and subsequently, with a little hard work and some stroke of fortune, have had a respectable degree of success communicating with him for the past twenty years.

In short, there is a job that needs doing; needs some "plain speaking," and I think I can help—even from here in Gomorrah-by-the-Sea. Indeed, living and working in Los Angeles has taught me a great deal about the stormy confluence of art and commerce—about how the "real world" operates. And, though I often disagree with some of the principles (or lack thereof) involved, the preservation of historic Walden Woods is going to require a healthy dose of "operating" in the real world. The great halls of learning may keep Thoreau's literature and principles alive, but they will be of little help in fortifying the well whence they sprang.

Recently, an American writer whom I have long admired and who, like Thoreau, is something of an iconoclast and independent thinker, stated in a rather surly letter that he would not participate in this book because he doesn't believe in shrines. He has sadly (and surprisingly) missed the point. Walden Woods is not meant to be a shrine to Henry David Thoreau nor, I think, would he have wanted it to be one.

In Thoreau's time, although Walden was not heavily inhabited, it was home to a number of ne'er–do–wells, transients, freed slaves, and shanty Irish. Thoreau, a Harvard graduate, apparently had no qualms about sharing the woods with such company. The townspeople, however, looked upon Walden Woods as a dark and forbidding place. Over the years, the woods have been ravaged by fire (Thoreau accidentally burned down about a hundred acres in April of 1844), uncontrolled woodcutting, and political neglect. Unfortunately, the focus of preservation efforts has come to rest on the pond and its immediate surroundings. That is all well and good, except that there remain approximately two thousand six hundred acres that are inside the historic boundaries of Walden Woods and deserve protection as well. Thoreau did not live *in* Walden Pond, he lived beside it. The man did not walk on water, he walked several miles a day through the woods and his musings and writings therein figure at least as prominently in his literature as Walden Pond does. In other words, the width and breadth of his inspiration, the scope of his legacy is not limited to one sixty two-acre pond and it is absurd to think so. Walden Woods is not a pristine, grand tract of wilderness, but it is still, for the most part, exceedingly beautiful and inspiring. It is, for all intents and purposes, the cradle of the American environmental movement and should be preserved for its intrinsic, symbolic value or, as Ed Schofield, Thoreau Society president, so succinctly put it, "When Walden goes, all the issues radiating out from Walden go, too. If the prime place can be disposed of, how much easier to dispose of the issues it represents." Otherwise, we might just as well turn all our national parks, our monuments to freedom and independence, into theme parks and shopping malls. Hell, why do we need Yosemite? We've still got the big, glossy coffee table book that we can remember it by!

People seem to be very attached to their symbols although they can sometimes not articulate why (witness the recent brouhaha over flag burning). In the

United States, we revere the flag, the Cross, the Star of David, the Mississippi River, the Grand Canyon. These things tell us who we are as a people; they tell us where we stand in the world, in the universe, and, more importantly, they show us that there is ultimately something larger and more important than ourselves. Being the proud nation that we are, that's a hard one for us to swallow. Symbols, therefore, get perverted and their meanings twisted because we fail to see the connectedness of things. We, the thinking, reasoning animal—the "highest" form of life on the planet—tend to view ourselves as outside of, or *above* the natural order. Historically, we have often been diametrically opposed to it. The formidable Wallace Stegner, Pulitzer Prize–winning novelist, historian, and biographer, in his book *The American West as Living Space,* reminds us:

> Behind the pragmatic, manifest-destinarian purpose of pushing western settlement was another motive: the hard determination to dominate nature that historian Lynn White, in the essay "Historical Roots of Our Ecologic Crisis," identified as part of our Judeo-Christian heritage. Nobody implemented that impulse more uncomplicatedly than the Mormons, a chosen people who believed the Lord when He told them to make the desert bloom as the rose. Nobody expressed it more bluntly than a Mormon hierarch, John Widtsoe, in the middle of the irrigation campaigns: "The destiny of man is to possess the whole earth; the destiny of the earth is to be subject to man. There can be no full conquest of the earth, and no real satisfaction to humanity, if large portions of the earth remain beyond his highest control." . . . That doctrine offends me to the bottom of my not-very-Christian soul.
>
> Our very virtues as a pioneering people, the very genius of our industrial civilization, drove us to act as we did. God and Manifest Destiny spoke with one voice urging us to "conquer" or "win" the West; and there was no voice of comparable authority to remind us of Mary Austin's quiet but profound truth, that the manner of the country makes the usage of life there, and that the land will not be lived in except in its own fashion.

I have always had some difficulty with the Christian concepts of Armageddon and The Rapture because the supposed inevitability of these events absolves believers of any long-term responsibility regarding the future of life on this plane. Since this world is temporal, there is an inherent hopelessness for what God has created here; for what humankind in particular is capable of. When I look around the battered landscape, I sometimes almost accede and yet I cannot see the difference between this kind of apocalyptic vision and nihilism. Exactly where does the responsibility lie? It seems to me that this, at least for the time being, is a pretty nice place to live. It nurtures us both physically and spiritually. It provides us with the very foundation of our existence. It seems to me that believers and nonbelievers alike have an obligation as tenants here to act responsibly toward the Landlord; that if one insults the Creation, one insults the Creator (even if you're a full-out atheist, you could at least try not to be a lousy roommate). Unfortunately, most of us tend to think only in terms of our own lifetime, or, if we have offspring, one or two generations beyond. It seems to me that we should proceed in good faith, with our best efforts, as if life here were a possibility until the sun dies.

> And God said, "Let us make man in our image, after our likeness: and let them have dominion over the fish of the sea, and over the fowl of the air, and over the cattle, and over all the earth, and over every creeping thing that creepeth upon the earth." (Genesis 1:26, King James Bible.)

If the Lord did, in fact, utter these words sans any kind of cautionary caveat, then they must have lost something in the translation because we have just about "dominioned" ourselves to death.

God, the Divinity, the Over-Soul, (or whatever term you wish to use) is manifest nowhere as surely and as magnificently as in untrammeled nature, and I think that a great deal of the spiritual groping and confusion now inherent in our society stems from the fact that we have strayed so far from our roots which are in the land. One hundred years ago, approximately 95 percent of the people in this country lived on farms or in rural areas. Now it is exactly the opposite. An overwhelming majority of the population now lives in urban areas (in fact, between two and three million acres of farmland are gobbled up each year by urban sprawl and we have hacked down all but five percent of our forests). We have distanced ourselves from contact that we once had on a regular basis with the natural cycle of birth, death, decay and rebirth. To be sure, there is birth, death and decay in the city. There is even rebirth, but it does not spring naturally from the decay. A new building, for instance, does not spring up nourished by the rotting carcass of the old one that it has replaced. The debris of demolished edifices is generally hauled away and dumped somewhere upon the landscape or into the sea.

I'm not saying that everybody should pack up and move back to the country. The country couldn't take the onslaught. What I am saying is that we should make an effort to rekindle respect for the values that come from life lived in harmony with the land. Though it seems almost like a cliche now, we would do well to take a lesson from the Red Man as he existed before the coming of the frontier, before we beat him into submission and packed him off to the arid wastelands—out of sight and out of mind.

What we lack is humility, and underlying that is a dearth of self-esteem.

From the endless stream of macabre, self-congratulatory, pep rallies for returning soldiers, to the heedless destruction of our ancient redwoods (the oldest living things on the planet), to the building of more powerful weapons of war, to the fevered paving over of precious farmland, the construction of impersonal malls and ever-higher skyscrapers, and the slaughter of defenseless animals for the manufacture of vanity items such as make-up and fur coats, it appears that we, as a people, must go to greater and greater lengths to feel good about ourselves. "What we call man's power over nature turns out to be a power exercised by some men over other men with nature as its instrument." (C.S. Lewis, *The Abolition of Man*, p. 35.)

President Calvin Coolidge once said that the business of America is business. This, I fear, will finally be our undoing unless we change our current direction and thought. In the ongoing battle between commerce and the natural environment, nature is almost invariably the loser.

> Habits persist. The hard, aggressive, single-minded energy that according to politicians made America great is demonstrated every day in resource raids and leveraged takeovers by entrepreneurs; and along with that competitive individualism and ruthlessness goes a rejection of any controlling past or tradition. What matters is here, now, the seizable opportunity. 'We don't need any history,' said one Silicon Valley executive when the Santa Clara County Historical Society tried to bring the electronics industry together with the few remaining farmers to discuss what was happening to the valley that only a decade or two ago was the fruit bowl of the world. 'What we need is more attention to our computers and the moves of the competition.'
>
> A high degree of mobility, a degree of ruthlessness, a large component of both self-sufficiency and self-righteousness mark the historical pioneer, the lone-riding folk hero, and the modern businessman intent on opening new industrial frontiers and getting his own in the process. (Wallace Stegner, *The American West as Living Space*, pp. 75, 76.)

Stegner goes on to lament the disappearance of the true culture hero—"the individual who transcends his culture without abandoning it, who leaves for a while in search of opportunity but never forgets where he left his heart."

Yet another problem, and perhaps the most insidious of all is *denial*. One hears that word quite often of late. In my vicinity, it is generally used in connection with alcoholism and drug abuse and the myriad programs designed for the cure of these maladies. However, it is now more than appropriate to describe the state of American, or in most cases, global consciousness concerning the crisis facing the ecosystem. Where the environment is concerned, according to reams of scientific data (any sane person can see it with his own eyes), there is definitely an elephant in the room. Unfortunately, there are still an alarming number of people, including a great many officials in our Federal Government, who insist there isn't. "Further studies . . ." I believe is the popular talismanic phrase.

A sign of the times: both left and right, with equal vehemence, repudiate the charge of "pessimism." Neither side has any use for "doomsayers." Neither wants to admit that our society has taken a wrong turn, lost its way, and needs to recover a sense of purpose and direction. Neither addresses the overriding issue of limits, so threatening to those who wish to appear optimistic at all times. The fact remains: the earth's finite resources will not support an indefinite expansion of industrial civilization. The right proposes, in effect, to maintain our riotous standard of living, as it has been maintained in the past, at the expense of the rest of the world (increasingly at the expense of our own minorities as well). This program is self-defeating, not only because it will produce environmental effects from which even the rich cannot escape but because it will widen the gap between rich and poor nations, generate more and more violent movements of insurrection and terrorism against the West, and bring about a deterioration of the world's political climate as threatening as the deterioration of its physical climate.

But the historical program of the left has become equally self-defeating. The attempt to extend Western standards of living to the rest of the world will lead even more quickly to the exhaustion of nonrenewable resources, the irreversible pollution of the earth's atmosphere, and the destruction of the ecological system on which human life depends. "Let us imagine," writes Rudolf Bahro, a leading spokesman for the West German Greens, "what it would mean if the raw material and energy consumption of our society were extended to the 4.5 billion people living today, or to the ten to fifteen billion there will probably be tomorrow. It is readily apparent that the planet can only support such volumes of production . . . for a short time to come."

These considerations refute conventional optimism (though the real despair lies in a refusal to confront them at all), and both the right and left therefore prefer to talk about something else—for example, to exchange accusations of fascism and socialism. But the ritual deployment and rhetorical inflation of these familiar slogans provide further evidence of the emptiness of recent political debate. (Christopher Lasch, *The True and Only Heaven* pp. 23, 24.)

This book, then, is written by those who realize that ultimately our best hope for salvation is ourselves and that we must communicate with one another in whatever forum is open to us—or, as James Hillman put it, we are born, first and foremost, citizens and we abandon citizenship when we stop talking. Guided by the wisdom of history, we will hopefully be able to regain a sense of our inextricable linkage to the natural world and a recognition for the value of the symbols and signposts that point the way.

To that end, Longmeadow Press has been kind enough to donate a portion of the proceeds from the sale of this book to the Walden Woods Project, a nonprofit organization dedicated to the preservation of historic Walden Woods. These funds will be used to purchase land currently under threat of development, but it is also our hope that these chapters will inform and motivate the reader.

The people who contributed to this book are respected, prominent members of their particular professions and if it is true that the cream always rises to the top, it also follows that the cream rises to the occasion. Because of their busy schedules—commitments and obligations of all kinds—a majority of the contributors had little or no time to spare, but they all found a way to get the job done because they realized the importance of this endeavor. The officers and staff of the Walden Woods Project would like to take this opportunity to express their gratitude for the overwhelming show of support for this cause. In *Life Without Principle* (1863), Thoreau writes, "Men will lie on their backs, talking about the fall of man, and never make an effort to get up." The people who contributed to this book have at least gotten to their knees.

▲ ▲ ▲

Don Henley, founder and co-chairman of the Walden Woods Project, was born and raised in Texas. He attended public school in his hometown of Linden, and furthered his education with two years at Stephen F. Austin University and two years at the University of North Texas. He moved to California in 1970. He is a recording artist, songwriter and record producer. He currently resides in Los Angeles with his dog, Bud.

"The problem of restoring to the world original and eternal beauty is solved by the redemption of the soul. The ruin or the blank that we see when we look at nature, is in our own eye. . . . The reason why the world lacks unity, and lies broken and in heaps, is because man is disunited with himself. He cannot be a naturalist until he satisfies all the demands of the spirit."

NATURE
RALPH WALDO EMERSON

INTRODUCTION:

A BRIEF HISTORY OF
THE WALDEN WOODS PROJECT

n July 1845, America's great philosopher, author, and conservationist, Henry David Thoreau, moved to Walden Woods on the shores of Walden Pond. He lived there for two years and two months, during which he chronicled his co-existence with nature in what would become one of his greatest literary achievements, a book called *Walden.*

In April 1990, the Walden Woods Project, a national nonprofit organization, was founded by recording artist Don Henley. Since then, the Walden Woods Project has worked toward acquiring and preserving historic and environmentally significant sites in Walden Woods, which is located in the towns of Concord and Lincoln, Massachusetts. The Trust for Public Land, a nationally acclaimed nonprofit land preservation organization, has assisted the Walden Woods Project, as has the Thoreau Country Conservation Alliance, a Concord-based preservation group.

Not far from the site of Thoreau's house at Walden Pond are two parcels of land that figured prominently in his life and literature, as well as in the lives of other famous Concord authors, including Ralph Waldo Emerson, Nathaniel Hawthorne, and Louisa May Alcott. Known as Brister's

Hill and Bear Garden Hill, the two sites are part of Walden Woods, a 2,680-acre area surrounding Walden Pond.

There are more than two hundred historic and scenic locales within Walden Woods. Although a large portion of the woodland is protected by the Commonwealth of Massachusetts, by the towns of Concord and Lincoln, and by local land conservation trusts, over 40 percent of Walden Woods, including Brister's Hill and Bear Garden Hill, remains unprotected and vulnerable to development.

Since 1984, a three-story office building with parking for more than five hundred cars has been proposed for the Brister's Hill site by Boston Properties, a firm owned by New York developer Mort Zuckerman. Brister's Hill and its vicinity are widely recognized as the cradle of the American environmental movement. It was here, in particular, that Henry David Thoreau studied forest succession and set in motion the theories of conservation that continue to guide the environmental movement today.

Should it be built, this commercial development will permanently destroy the historic integrity of Brister's Hill and open the door for further development in the area. The Walden Woods Project and The Trust for Public Land hope to acquire this site from Mr. Zuckerman so that it may be preserved for public enjoyment and as a symbol for future generations.

Another equally important site, Bear Garden Hill, is also endangered. A condominium development planned for this area would have destroyed one of the most pristine locales in Walden Woods. Fortunately, the developer of the condominium project agreed to sell the Bear Garden Hill site to The Trust for Public Land. The Trust will hold the property out of the market until the Walden Woods Project raises sufficient funds for its acquisition. Since the 139-unit condominium project included forty-two units of low- and moderate-income housing, the Walden Woods Project is also buying a site outside Walden Woods on which to relocate the affordable units. It is anticipated that the cost of acquiring the Brister's Hill and Bear Garden Hill sites will exceed $8 million.

The essays in *Heaven Is Under Our Feet* were written as contributions to the Walden Woods Project. All of the royalties and a portion of the proceeds, donated by Longmeadow Press, will assist the Walden Woods Project in raising the necessary funds to permanently protect these historic and beautiful sites in Walden Woods—living symbols of the American conservation movement.

If you would like to do more to help the Walden Woods Project, please send your tax-deductible contribution to: The Walden Woods Project, 18 Tremont Street, Suite 630, Boston, MA 02108. For further information, call 1-800-543-9911.

Kathi Anderson
Executive Director
The Walden Woods Project

SAND AND WATER, FIRE AND ICE: WALDEN POND AND WALDEN WOODS, GIFTS OF THE GLACIER

I was seated by the shore of a small pond, about a mile and a half south of the village of Concord and somewhat higher than it, in the midst of an extensive wood between that town and Lincoln, and about two miles south of that our only field known to fame, Concord Battle Ground . . .

Thoreau, *Walden*

Walden Woods has always been a frontier of sorts, a tenacious no-man's land suspended precariously between the wild and the cultivated. In more than three and a half centuries, it has never fully succumbed to the Europeans' will, though at the height of agricultural activity in the 1850s—especially after the railroad cut a swath through its heart in 1844, opening up new markets for its wood—it nearly did so. But as agriculture ebbed in New England after the Civil War, and as coal and petroleum supplanted wood as fuel, Walden Woods made a slow resurgence, reoccupying most of the ground it had lost, much as a lake tops up after a long drought. Today, however, under the relentless pressures of suburbanization, commercialization, and even urbanization, Walden Woods is again in danger of succumbing.

By the mid–eighteenth century—125 years after the English settled here—Walden Woods was still quite wild, though most of the surrounding land had long since been tamed for farming. For some reason, Walden Woods proved far too dry to be farmed. When the new town of Lincoln was established on April 19, 1754, the line between Concord and Lincoln was drawn diagonally through the middle of Walden Woods, from one far corner to the opposite far corner. Walden Woods was perceived at that time, and would continue to be perceived, as a sort of never-never land lying far on the periphery of human concerns and therefore conveniently consigned to oblivion. From Fair Haven Bay on the Sudbury River in the southwest, the new town line trended northeastward through the heart of the thick woods, just nicking the southeastern tip of Walden Pond, where it jogged a bit more north and proceeded from there to the northeasternmost tip of the woods and then, a few feet beyond, shifted sharply eastward along the road to Lexington. Though it was only a line drawn on a map, this division of Walden Woods would prove to be the first in a long series of divisions and dismemberments, most of them not as abstract or subtle or benign. The railroad, which blundered in exactly ninety years after Lincoln was established, would be the second such division. Picture, if you will, the town line and the railroad as forming an X on the map, with Walden Pond cradled between the crossbars.

In one of Amos Doolittle's famous etchings of the first battles of the American Revolution at Lexington and Concord—that depicting the British regulars reconnoitering for the impending fight at Concord's Old North Bridge on April 19, 1775, when the "shot heard round the world" was fired—you can just discern Walden Woods looming boldly on the horizon, a kind of palisade or outpost of the wild, holding fort against the legions of plowed fields, a Masada of wildness in a desert of cultivation. During their ignominious retreat to Lexington and Boston that day, the bedraggled British regulars passed within a few feet of the northeasternmost tip of Walden Woods, along the very town line that had been drawn between Concord and Lincoln twenty-one years before, to the day. Perhaps an American farmer or two fired at them from behind one of the trees deep in Walden Woods.

Though until recently few maps actually bore the name "Walden Woods," all maps of the Walden area drawn since that time (and later, all photographs) attest to the predominance of woodland in the area we now designate as "Historic Walden Woods." While bits and pieces of it may have disappeared from time to time as individual landowners cut down their respective woodlots, Walden Woods has harbored an irreducible core of woodland from earliest settlement to our day. In due time, the cut-over woodlots always reverted to forest.

Why wasn't the forest in what we call Walden Woods obliterated early on, along with all (or nearly all) of the surrounding primeval forest? Surely, the settlers could have made very short work of the remaining woodland.

The explanation lies in the ecology of Walden Woods, which in turn reflects the area's geology, especially its glacial geology. Most of what we call Walden Woods sits on a kind of low plateau consisting of clean, very porous, layered sands and gravels that were laid down ten to twenty thousand years ago at the northern end of a glacial lake called Glacial Lake Sudbury.

Ecologists used to call these and similar landforms "pitch pine plains." Not all pitch pine plains were formed in glacial lakes, and fewer still at the northern ends of glacial lakes. (Few rivers in New England flow northward, and thus few could have been dammed by retreating glaciers.) But most, if not all of them do form on dry, well-drained sands and gravels laid down by retreating glaciers, or on coastal dunes. Today we call the living communities that developed on such dry terrain "northern pine-oak forests." Closely associated with the pines and oaks are plants and animals adapted to the heat and dryness of sand plains. On this basis, Walden Woods is far more similar to the northern pine-oak forests of Cape Cod, Long Island, and New Jersey than it is to most of the woods nearby in Concord and Lincoln.

Unless human beings interfere, not many decades go by before a pine-oak forest is swept by fire—whether from lightning or human agency, deliberate or accidental. (The Indians regularly burned such stands of pines and oaks on purpose, to catch game; Henry Thoreau accidentally set fire to Walden Woods on April 30, 1844, during a long period of extreme drought.) Pitch pines, being resistant to fire and in some cases even adapted to it, are among the first species to revegetate a burned-over sand plain. Hence the term "pitch pine plain." Because fire has been suppressed for so long on the Walden sand plain, pitch pines now are rare in the Walden ecosystem; white pines are much more abundant.

Glacial Lake Sudbury, which lasted for tens of thousands of years, stretched as long as fifteen or twenty miles from north to south, was created when the slowly retreating (and melting) Pleistocene glacier dammed the north-flowing Sudbury River. The abundant meltwater and suspended sand and gravel pouring copiously southward from the mile-thick glacier formed an eighty- or ninety-foot-thick delta at its base. Scattered over the surface of the delta were small knobby mounds or hillocks called kames, as well as chunks of glacier ice—some of them small, some of them exceedingly large—that broke off and were left stranded in the sands and gravels as the glacier itself melted. When these chunks melted, the surface was pocked with numerous depressions of various sizes called kettles. Fair Haven Bay, an embayment in the Sudbury River that forms the extreme southwestern corner of Walden Woods, is an enormous kettle. Walden Pond, which is 1.7 miles in circumference and well over 150 feet deep if measured from the level of the delta surface to the pond's deepest point, is another. It lies very near the center of Walden Woods.

When the glacier had retreated to a certain point just beyond the northern-most extension of the Lincoln hills, which for thousands of years had formed the eastern shore of Glacial Lake Sudbury, the dam was breached and the lake quickly drained away, its waters flowing into the Charles River valley to the east. Glacial Lake Sudbury was no more, but the kame-delta plateau, left high and dry, remained. It was on this unusual landform that the pine-oak forest we now call Walden Woods eventually developed. Because the woodland soils that developed on the sand plain were very porous and drained very quickly, they were exceedingly dry, unfit for farming, of use (in the early days of settlement) only for raising fuelwood.

Thus it was that, a full two hundred years after settlement, the sand plain was still heavily wooded. And thus it was, too, that Henry Thoreau had a beautiful woodland lake named Walden (the name in fact means "wooded") beside which he could construct a little house, ten-by-fifteen feet, in which to compose some of the best prose in the language, only a mile or so from his home in Concord and only two miles south of that Concord's "only field known to fame," Concord Battle Ground. If Walden Pond "was made deep and pure for a symbol," as Thoreau said it was, and if it still lay "in the midst of an extensive wood" over two hundred years after settlement, then it is to the great Pleistocene glacier that all the credit must go. Appropriately enough, Thoreau moved into his Walden house on Independence Day, July 4, 1845.

The name Walden Woods is well documented in hundreds of manuscripts, legal documents, diaries, and publications, but its boundaries were always ill-defined. Perhaps no one saw any need to determine precise borders for what had always been an area of expanding and contracting woodland anyway. When the railroad was built in the 1840s, the area lying to the west of the tracks gradually lost its association in people's minds with Walden Pond, which lay to their east. But the bulk of Walden Woods had already been "lost" ninety years before, when Lincoln was established. Recall that by definition all of Walden *Pond* lay in Concord; thus, many people tended to believe, all of Walden *Woods* must lie in Concord as well. Unfortunately, because no one thought very hard about it, this erroneous impression colored people's thinking about Walden. In his book *Walden*, Thoreau reinforces this impression when he states that he "lived . . . on the shore of Walden Pond, in Concord, Massachusetts."

In 1922, the Commonwealth of Massachusetts established the Walden Pond State Reservation, comprised of eighty-odd acres of land lying immediately around the pond—land donated by the Emerson, Forbes, and Heywood families. Since then, the Reservation has grown to about 295 acres, primarily through purchase. Suddenly, it seems, the idea of Walden Woods—imprecise as it was—imploded as people began to interpret the reservation as the full and proper extent of Walden Woods, everything lying within its borders being confidently referred to as Walden Woods, and most of the woodland lying outside its borders being of dubious status. Then, in the mid-1930s, the commonwealth built Route 2, lopping off the northernmost tier of woods from Walden Woods. At this point, the exact extent and boundaries of Walden Woods were anybody's guess. The world became all too willing to settle upon Walden Pond State Reservation as synonymous with what had once been a far more extensive tract. In fact, the term Walden Woods fell into almost total disuse for half a century or more; in people's minds, all that was left was Walden Pond. What had originally been more than 2,600 acres of woods had been reduced to a mere sixty-plus acres (the pond) surrounded by a beleaguered buffer zone of another 235 acres (the rest of the reservation).

In the meantime, however, the sciences of ecology and geology were developing apace. After World War II, ecologists began to think more and more in terms of ecosystems (the term had been coined in the mid-1930s) rather than in terms of individual species or environmental factors, or even biological communities. Geologists had solved most of the remaining questions about New England's post-glacial geology and had begun producing very detailed and meaningful maps of the region's surficial geology.

When pressed, preservationists were now able to marshal convincing scientific arguments that Walden Woods was an ecosystem in every sense of the term, that it was, in fact, an unusually well-defined and highly integrated example of a terrestrial ecosystem, and that the boundaries of the ecosystem coincided exactly with certain geological features. All of the kettle ponds in the ecosystem are connected by the deep-seated groundwater, which rises and falls over a period of decades. The springs and streams issuing from the edges of the sand plain are other expressions of the groundwater's unifying influence. With the realization that exact boundaries could be assigned to this highly integrated ecosystem, in concert with the growing national and international resolve to protect Walden as a symbol, the fortunes of pond and woods took a dramatic turn for the better. We are beginning to see the results of that felicitous reversal of fortune.

Edmund A. Schofield
President
The Thoreau Society

We had a remarkable sunset one day last November. I was walking in a meadow, the source of a small brook, when the sun at last, just before setting, after a cold, gray day, reached a clear stratum in the horizon, and the softest, brightest morning sunlight fell on the dry grass and on the stems of the trees in the opposite horizon and on the leaves of the shrub oaks on the hillside, while our shadows stretched long over the meadow eastward, as if we were the only motes in its beams. It was such a light as we could not have imagined a moment before, and the air also was so warm and serene that nothing was wanting to make a paradise of that meadow. When we reflected that this was not a solitary phenomenon, never to happen again, but that it would happen forever and ever, an infinite number of evenings, and cheer and reassure the latest child that walked there, it was more glorious still.

The sun sets on some retired meadow, where no house is visible, with all the glory and splendor that it lavishes on cities, and perchance as it has never set before,—where there is but a solitary marsh hawk to have his wings gilded by it, or only a musquash looks out from his cabin, and there is some little black-veined brook in the midst of the marsh, just beginning to meander, winding slowly round a decaying stump. We walked in so pure and bright a light, gilding the withered grass and leaves, so softly and serenely bright, I thought I had never bathed in such a golden flood, without a ripple or a murmur to it. The west side of every wood and rising ground gleamed like the boundary of Elysium, and the sun on our backs seemed like a gentle herdsman driving us home at evening.

So we saunter toward the Holy Land, till one day the sun shall shine more brightly than ever he has done, shall perchance shine into our minds and hearts, and light up our whole lives with a great awakening light, as warm and serene and golden as on a bankside in autumn.

"WALKING"
HENRY DAVID THOREAU

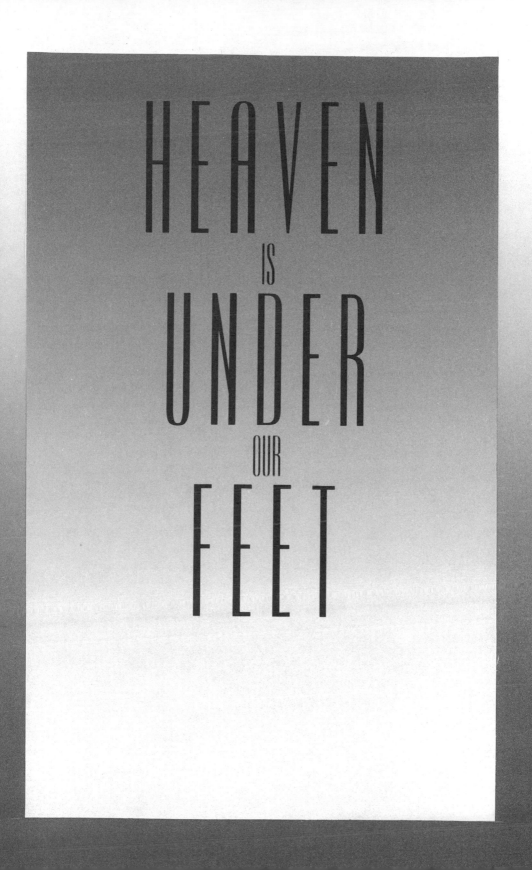

As surely as the sunset in my latest November shall translate me to the ethereal world, and remind me of the ruddy morning of youth; as surely as the last strain of music which falls on my decaying ear shall make age to be forgotten, or, in short, the manifold influences of nature survive during the term of our natural life, so surely my Friend shall forever be my Friend, and reflect a ray of God to me, and time shall foster and adorn and consecrate our Friendship, no less than the ruins of temples. As I love nature, as I love singing birds, and gleaming stubble, and flowing rivers, and morning and evening, and summer and winter, I love thee my Friend.

A WEEK ON THE CONCORD AND MERRIMACK RIVERS
HENRY DAVID THOREAU

EDMUND A. SCHOFIELD

WALDEN, SYMBOL OF HOPE

When I first visited Walden as an adolescent more than thirty-five years ago—it was in 1955, or perhaps 1956—I was dismayed by what I saw. The place seemed forlorn, distinctly down at the heels, and not half as wild as I'd hoped it would be. Yet I did not complain or share my misgivings with anyone. Instead, I took private delight in knowing that there was still a Walden Pond to gaze upon and that, if it was no longer quite wild, it had survived in something like a natural state, a perennial symbol of hope nestled deep among the scraggly pines and oaks of Walden Woods. After all, I reminded myself, it was publicly owned and, theoretically at least, forever protected. Someone—"the authorities," no doubt—would see to that. In spite of all the abuse heaped upon this humble lake-of-the-woods during three centuries of occupation by Europeans, Walden remained the same woodland vision that had formed the drapery of Thoreau's dreams. I was deeply grateful that Thoreau's own Walden was there for me to experience a century after he had known it. I could forgive the authorities some temporary or partial lapse in carrying out their legal mandate to "preserve the Walden of Emerson and Thoreau." They had not failed entirely.

Today, three and a half decades later, Walden's shores bear signs of further neglect and abuse, yet for me and for millions of others it remains a precious symbol. It is not well cared for, but endures nonetheless as a visible source of hope for this world, a tangible expression of our deepest yearnings. If, in this world-gone-mad of ours, a little lake like this can prevail against all the odds, then surely there are grounds for universal hope. The spirit-nurturing thought that Thoreau perceived welling upward from Walden's cool, pure depths continues to wash over and around this miraculous planet, drawing home to its battered shores a constant stream of pilgrims from all over the globe. They have been coming here since 1863 in ever-increasing numbers, from India, Japan, Europe, China, the Soviet Union, Canada, every state of the Union, and countless other places besides—a silent, respectful, reverential, and healing wave of perennial devotion coming to rest at last on Walden's pebbled shores. In certain lights and at certain seasons or times of day, Walden still can be sublimely beautiful: "God's Drop," as Emerson called it.

Like me, these pilgrims cannot be entirely disappointed with what they see. Like me, they must find solid ground for hope in the fact that the very Walden of Emerson and Thoreau endures, still veiled amid the living, protective mantle of Walden Woods. Their sincere devotion attests to the symbol's abiding power and holds out hope that its power will endure for ages.

"Our village life would stagnate," Thoreau wrote in *Walden*, "if it were not for the unexplored forests and meadows which surround it. We need the tonic of wildness. . . . At the same time that we are earnest to explore and learn all things, we require that all things be mysterious and wild, unsurveyed and unfathomed by us because unfathomable. We can never have enough of nature. We must be refreshed by the sight of inexhaustible vigor, vast and titanic features, the sea-coast with its wrecks, the wilderness with its living and its decaying trees, the thunder-cloud, and the rain which lasts three weeks and produces freshets. We need to witness our own limits transgressed, and some life pasturing freely where we never wander."

I would first ponder these words as a seaman in the U.S. Navy, not long after that first visit to Walden, in my new copy of *Walden,* which I'd smuggled aboard ship in a subversive scheme to protect my sanity, my sense of self and personal integrity. Eventually, I would take them to heart as covert sailing orders, as my eyes-only commission to go forth into all the world, scouring the planet for Nature's hiding places, probing her deepest and most intimate secrets. Almost certainly, I realize now, these and other words of Thoreau awoke in me a potent wanderlust that would last two and one half decades.

I also took to heart Thoreau's pointed injunction to explore my own "higher latitudes," my "private sea, the Atlantic and Pacific Ocean" of my being. There are, he said, "continents and seas in the moral world to which every man is an isthmus or an inlet, yet unexplored by him. . . . England and France, Spain and

Portugal, Gold Coast and Slave Coast, all front on this private sea; but no bark from them has ventured out of sight of land, though it is without doubt the direct way to India." I launched, therefore, an intensive program of inner explorations in close tandem to the outer. Poetry was my prime vehicle.

When I began to wander this wild and mysterious planet in the mid-1950s, Nature did indeed seem "vast and titanic," did seem "unfathomable"—certainly, well beyond humanity's power to harm in any permanent or measurable way (short, perhaps, of sustained nuclear war). But before my personal odyssey was half over I realized with a sense of profound shock and anger that Nature was subtly vulnerable to myriad human depredations, that in fact all of wild Nature might be doomed. The realization eventually set me on a homeward tack—home to New England, home to Walden, home to the sources of whatever hope and inspiration I had set forth with. For surely at Walden one could always find grounds for hope and abundant ammunition for defending wild Nature against human folly and greed and aggression.

The 1950s were a strange period in our history, I recall—a watershed decade in many ways, a period of jolting transition from the soon-stifled optimism of the early postwar years to the despair and rage of the sixties. Yet for people like me who valued wildness and other expressions of Nature's benevolence, these had been halcyon days, days of hope and a carefree confidence in Nature's infinite resilience. We were naive. We never dreamed that our energy-crazed civilization was fast becoming a planet-altering force fully on a par with the great and vital cycles of Nature, only death-dealing and sinister. Few of us dreamed that our way of life, however materialistic and relentlessly aggressive it might grow, could ever threaten the biosphere. A species or two might be extinguished, we granted with due regret, an ecosystem obliterated here or there—but surely not the entire arena of life, not life itself!

The Cold War was another matter, easily perceived. We saw it clearly as a lethal threat. But if and when humanity came to its senses we whispered, the threat would vanish. And besides, humanity would never commit suicide It would turn back in time Nuclear war might stalk and radioactivity threaten the face of the planet, but at least for now we could breathe easily and confidently enough. The atmosphere was secure. Air was air. Our race could by then fly and had begun to lay waste the sky, as Thoreau had feared it might, but it had not yet cut down the clouds, had not yet blotted out the sun or stolen the rainbow.

Earth's ocean of air was vast, seemingly endless, well beyond our power to harm or permanently alter. It might be polluted during rush hour in L.A. or New York or London, or downwind of the smokestacks of Pittsburgh or Cleveland, or during some persistent temperature inversion in the Ohio Valley, or—in the wake of a nuclear test blast in the Nevada desert, on the steppes of some Soviet republic, or over the South Seas—it might even become radioactive for a while. But it seemed otherwise and elsewhere to be forever pristine.

If the air and the rain and the sunshine were essentially secure for all time, or at least salvageable as such, we acknowledged that at any moment the planet itself might be blown to bits beneath us, or our food supply laced with radioisotopes washing out of tainted rain. But we could change our ways whenever we wanted to. It was simply a matter of coming to our senses, of ending the Cold War, and—presto!—we would have our destiny firmly under control. End the Cold War, we agreed, and the earth would still be firm, the air again pure, the sea gloriously strong and mysterious, the sun still brilliant, and the cope of heaven sweet once again. Peace was the way, and we knew it, and peace was achievable. Dylan's hard rain had not begun to fall or even cloud our daydreams. Eliot's filthy air still waited to pounce.

For me, as for nearly everyone else in those days, Nature was vast, titanic, eternal, invincible. In Nature we could confidently live and move and have our being. I took great comfort in this fact. Let man do all he might, Nature's sun would continue to shine impartially on the evil as well as on the good. As yet it did not scorch. Her rain would continue to fall on the just and on the unjust alike. As yet it did not bite. And when her wandering air touched us it would always impart health, was sure to give us something of its pureness and beauty. For as yet the air around us did not sting.

This parcel of assurances tucked snugly in my backpack, as it were, and Thoreau's Great Commission stowed away securely in my duffel, I had set forth from home in my late teens, spending a full quarter-century wandering this globe as a none-too-adept sailor before the mast, as polar explorer and writer of slight consequence, as earnest student, teacher, and scientist, always in hot pursuit of, as Thoreau put it, "the indescribable innocence and beneficence of Nature,—of sun and wind and rain, of summer and winter," inquiring of shipmates and passersby where she might have her seat, where her dwelling place, whether they might have spoken her as she passed them on some high sea, though few presumed to know and fewer still would deign to tell or guide me. Yet I insisted upon having intelligence with this earth. I wanted to see Nature for myself, wanted to interact with her one-on-one, close-up, on her own terms. Henry Thoreau had told me to do so. I was insisting, I realize, upon knowing myself.

Hoping to ensure a life lived in Nature, I eventually became a botanist and ecologist. I hoped thereby to see Nature as she was, as she ought always to be: primal, wild, untrammeled—on the sea, in the mountains, in the tropics, in the Arctic, in the Antarctic, in the setting of countless wilderness suns. I wanted to confront her in all her essentials and guises, to understand and apprehend her, nourish her if necessary, and above all defend her if called upon to do so. For her sake I became a gypsy in all but name. Yet I was never able to track her to her furthest lair. Her wildness forever recedes. She eludes me to this day, though I seek her still. In the final analysis, I realize, she is like all of us, simply unknowable and unfathomable. An irreducible wildness or reticence lurks deep within her core.

Lucky wanderers eventually find their way home, even receive forgiveness and absolution should they have sinned greatly. For me, home was New England; Concord was the heart of New England, and Walden New England's heart of hearts. Why, here was Walden still, I would exclaim with delight upon my return, the same woodland lake I visited so many years before. But Walden, this planet's only Walden Pond, the selfsame Walden of Emerson and Thoreau—*the* Walden Pond, no less—was even more forlorn than I had remembered her, still a victim of neglect and abuse.

During the quarter century I was away, Concord's people had moved their dump within a few hundred feet of the pond, and then vastly enlarged it: A gross, ugly, rubbish-strewn abyss now gawked at pilgrims approaching these sacred precincts—a malevolent, malodorous, troll-like presence forever haunting and fouling the gateway to Walden Woods. Even as I was embarking in the mid-1950s, the pond's alleged guardians—the faithless "authorities" in whom I once had naively placed my trust—were clearcutting an entire slope and bulldozing it into the pond, ostensibly to create a beach where the Red Cross might teach children to swim. And now, in the 1980s, there were rumblings about motels and helipads and office parks and condominiums and an eight-lane highway with cloverleafs to be built in the woods nearby. Each winter, the state's highway department hauled away truckfuls of Walden Woods' pure, underlying sands, apparently to spread on the existing four-lane highway so that commuters in the tens of thousands could rush safely to and from Boston in their automobiles, rather than take the train.

All of Walden Woods seemed now under siege. The enchanted landscape that gave birth to and nurtured both pond and woods and that ultimately gave birth to the symbol was being bulldozed out of existence, stripped away piecemeal, in ever more significant pieces. Not-insignificant bits of its thousand hectares had already been carted away, and the pace of dismemberment was about to accelerate greatly. The landscape that had yielded for Thoreau key insights into the inner workings of natural phenomena—not to mention into the subtle workings of his own soul—and that had inspired his seminal ideas on conservation of the natural and wild was being obliterated bit by bit. We were attacking the actual Walden, the sign and symbol of hope, forcing her to recede from this material world and take refuge once and for all in the realm of the ideal, there to make her last stand, there to judge us from on high. Clearly, we occupied different planes of existence. We seemed to be sinking even as she was rising.

In that same quarter century the entire face of the earth—all of earth's air and waters, soils and wildlife, forests, mountains and tundras—had been under relentless assault by modern man, too. Earth—the current and only abode of wild

Nature—was no longer invulnerable. If Walden, too, was at risk, where were the grounds for hope? It was at this point, and upon this grim realization, that I privately vowed to help keep that source and symbol of hope alive, help keep Walden here within the mundane, upon this fleeting plane of existence, as a witness to that other, ineffable plane.

During the late 1960s in Antarctica, I had measured sunlight in my own ecological studies, little realizing that the sunlight-softening layer of ozone hovering high above—the very vault of heaven itself—was dissolving even as I labored, that the stark Antarctic sunlight was growing harsher and more dangerous by the year—and all so that people could refrigerate their food, or cool their fancy cars, or spray their hair. In northern Alaska, I had studied reindeer lichens. Arctic haze (acidic, laden with heavy metals, a kind of frozen smog moving in from as far away as central Russia and Japan) and ice fog (caused by polluted fumes from tailpipes and chimneys during cold snaps in Alaska's frigid winters) were threatening them, and threatening therefore the reindeer and caribou that would starve in midwinter without lichens as their food of last resort.

"God's ozone sparkles in every eye," wrote John Muir, describing the delight of Sierra Club members during their first excursion into the Sierra Nevada in 1901. No more! If anything, as God's ozone disappears from the stratosphere, the sunlight striking Earth will burn out those sparkling eyes, singe vegetation, and pock fair skins with myriad melanomas. In the summer of 1989, air hellishly thick with ozone invaded the heart of Thoreau Country for week after week, lethal brown waves rushing in from the Midwest, submerging and suffocating everything and everyone here—all the ponds, woods, meadows, streams, hills, islands, capes, and mountains that Thoreau knew and loved, stinging our skins and nostrils and burning our runny eyes. For the rest of that stultifying summer the large conspicuous leaves of every horse-chestnut tree that I saw had been singed brown and brittle by the filthy air. I later heard of terror-stricken children who cried out many a night during that summer that they could scarcely breathe. Frightened parents resolved to flee to Alaska with them at once, while there was still time, as though that could be the solution. Tender leaves, tender lungs—with no escape in sight.

In the 1960s, Rachel Carson wrote about silent springs, and others sounded equally grave alarms. Pesticides had begun turning up everywhere—even in the tissues of Antarctic penguins! The amount of carbon dioxide in the air was rising significantly and inexorably, and had been doing so for over a century. By the 1970s, acid rain was bombarding lakes and forests in Scandinavia, New England, Canada, and Germany, and was fouling the Sierra Nevada. More and more oil was pouring into the world's oceans in larger and more devastating spills. And for the past fifteen years, from Pennsylvania to Chernobyl, nuclear power plants have been seriously malfunctioning. What once were local, temporary events were becoming chronic, global phenomena.

Nothing seemed beyond the clutches of our collective economic greed; nothing and no place seemed safe. The tropical rain forests, I knew, had come under savage assault. Entire habitats were being destroyed and species driven to extinction everywhere. All of these threats I had known about, some of them as soon as they were discovered or announced. A few I had even studied during the 1970s as part of my own modest research projects. But they seemed to be multiplying—increasingly deadly genies released from bottle after bottle with no possibility of recapture, and no end to them in sight.

For me, this relentless proliferation of ecological folly was more than a person could cope with. When would the ecological equivalent of critical mass be achieved, I wondered, and a chain reaction of destruction commence? What would be the first regional ecosystem to collapse? When would it end, this insidious war with the earth? If nothing was sacred, then nothing could be taken for granted—not the air, not the rain, not the sunlight, not the rainbow, perhaps not even the planet itself. We had lost all sense of the sacred. The entire globe had been profaned.

It occurred to me that if I could not "save the world," as cynics often sneeringly put it, I at least might do something to help save one special part of it: modest little Walden, whose promise had set me wandering the planet so many years before, Walden, that enduring symbol of peace and sanity which had sparked and sanctioned my love affair with the earth. By saving the very source and symbol of this earth-love, I reasoned, I might indirectly help save the world after all. It occurred to me that this beleaguered woodland lake, which had so haunted Thoreau's dreams and fired his genius, might just hold some key to the entire planet's salvation: Save Walden and you may save the world! Save Walden, the Pond, for a sign and symbol, like the rainbow. Save Walden, the Woods, for instruction and recreation, as a leafy guidepost to the sublime, as wild Nature's final refuge, out of which one day her sanative influences will again go forth, permeating and revivifying a fallen world. Save Walden the symbol. Save this last refuge of hope, this rainbow's retreat, though it be in the shadow of a thousand Kuwaits. Make yourself personally a part of the Walden ecosystem: By your efforts, insinuate yourself into it, like the rain, like the secret waters moving deep within its clean glacial sands. Forget making Mars or some other planet Nature's next home. This is not a throwaway planet! Take your stand here, on *this* planet, at the portal to Walden Woods! Save this solid earth! Most important of all, save your own soul!

Walden was made significant for us by a book written by a man of extraordinary genius. We would have neither symbol nor book apart from him, perhaps not even the shadow of hope itself. If Walden Pond is deep and pure for a symbol, if the book's prose gleams like thought and poetry crystallized, it is because the poet himself was profound and prophetic and inspired. To understand fully the power of Walden—Walden the Pond and the Woods, Walden the book and the symbol—we need to confront Thoreau himself: his genius, his vision, his words. It is not always easy to do so. We need—some of us, at least—to forge our way bravely past his assaults on our house-bred and man-centered sensibilities, to relinquish some of our most cherished prejudices. Only then will we be able to meet him on his own terms and thereby understand him. If we should see his finger pointing us-ward, why, then, we should take heed.

Thoreau saw clearly, and never minced words, however subtle his prose might become. He had no choice; for him it was an inescapable imperative, his cup. To communicate his vision and pour out his insights he could not be content with soft words. The raw edge to his prose merely reflects the clarity and starkness of his vision: hard words for hard realities clearly seen. He saw that the usages and received wisdom of his day were deeply flawed, ultimately even deadly. From birth, the individual is coerced by institutions and custom into false relationships with mankind ("society"), Nature, and God ("the divinity"), he felt, and for him, the sham in each case derived from the same source: the individual's false relation with his or her own soul. Liberate yourself from illusion, he admonishes, abolish the shams. Explore your own higher latitudes! Get right with yourself and all these things will be added unto you; get right with yourself and perforce you will develop at last the proper relationship with others, with Nature, and so with the divinity. For this, he himself went to Walden.

Saving this world's Waldens at this aggressively materialistic hour—the actual Pond and the actual Woods and all of the Waldens beyond—will not be easy. But save them we must if we are to save Walden the sign and symbol of hope. It will be more than a matter of money, however, though that is important. It will be more than a matter of public relations, though that, too, is important. Ultimately, I think, saving all of this world's Waldens will mean confronting and changing ourselves. Each Walden saved clears the way to our own salvation, and, through ours, to that of the world.

▲ ▲ ▲

Edmund Schofield is president of the Thoreau Society, which celebrated its fiftieth anniversary in 1991. A botanist, he has traveled three times to Antarctica and twice to Barrow and Prudhoe Bay in northern Alaska to study their ecology. He has been an advisor to the Sierra Club for many years, and to Walden Forever Wild since 1981, and has been editor of *Horticulture* magazine. He is a founder of the Thoreau Country Conservation Alliance and a member of the Walden Woods Project Advisory Board.

E.L. DOCTOROW

Thoreau's *Walden; or, Life in the Woods*, like Twain's *Huckleberry Finn* or Melville's *Moby Dick*, is a book that could only have been written by an American. You can't imagine this odd, visionary but very tough work coming out of Europe. It is peculiarly of us; it is indelibly made from our woods and water and new world ethos. But more than that, it is one of the handful of works that make us who we are. *Walden* is crucial to the identity of Americans who have never read it and have barely heard of Thoreau. Its profound complaint endures to our century— for example, it was the text of choice in the 1960s, when the desire to own nothing and live poor swept through an entire generation.

It is a sometimes prickly book about independence, and a practical how-to book on the way to live close to the earth in a self-sufficient manner; it is a sometimes philosophical book about values—what we need to live in self-realization and what we don't need, what is true and important, what is false and disabling; and it is a religious book about being truly awake and alive in freedom in the natural world and living in a powerful transcendent state of reverence toward it. *Walden* is all of these together. Presented as the story of Thoreau's life at the pond over a period of two years, it fuses his political, economic, social, and spiritual ideas in a vision of supreme common sense.

All right, that begins to describe the book. What about the place? We have the book, why do we need the place?

Literature, like history, endows places with meaning, and in that sense it composes places, locates them in the moral universe, gives them a charged name. So in effect literature connects the visible and the invisible. It finds the meaning, or the hidden life, in the observable life. It discovers the significant secrets of places and things. That is what makes it so necessary to us; that is why we practice it; that is why it is such an essential human function. Uncharged with invisible meaning, the visible is nothing, mere clay; and without a visible circumstance, a territory, to connect to, our spirit is shapeless, nameless, and undefined.

"Near the end of March, 1845," Thoreau writes, "I borrowed an axe and went down to the woods by Walden Pond nearest to where I intended to build my house, and began to cut down some tall arrowy white pines. . . . " Walden is the material out of which Thoreau made his book—as surely as he made his house from the trees he cut there, he made his book from the life he lived there. The pond and woods are the visible, actual, real source of Thoreau's discovered, invisible truths, the material from which he made not only his house, but his revelation.

That Walden is a humble place—an ordinary pond, a plain New England wood—is exactly the point. Thoreau made himself an Everyman, and chose Walden for his Everywhere.

Clearly there is an historical luminosity to these woods. They stand transformed by Thoreau's attention into a kind of chapel in which this stubborn Yankee holy man came to his and, as it turns out, our redemptive vision. So there is a crucial connection of American clay and spirit here: If we neglect or deface or degrade Walden, the place, we sever a connection to ourselves, we tear it asunder. Destroy the place and we defame the author, mock his vision and therefore tear up by the root the spiritual secret he found for us.

We need both Waldens, the book and the place. We're not all spirit any more than we are all clay; we are both and so we need both—as in: You've read the book, now see the place.

You have to be able to take the children there, and to say "This is it, this is the wood Henry wrote about. You see?" You give them what is rightfully theirs, just as you give them Gettysburg because it is theirs.

But in fact you don't even have to see the place as long as you know it's there and it looks much as it looked when he was cutting the young white pines for his house. Then it is truly meaningful in spirit and in clay—like us, and like the world invisibly charged with our idea of it.

And so for these reasons, to defend a masterwork from desecration and ourselves from self-mutilation, I stand with this group of citizens today and declare that Walden Woods must be returned to its natural state.

▲ ▲ ▲

E.L. Doctorow's novels include *The Book of Daniel, Loon Lake, Ragtime,* and *Billy Bathgate.* He is a member of the Walden Woods Project Advisory Board.

"Mr. Thoreau dedicated his genius with such entire love to the fields, hills and waters of his native town, that he made them known and interesting to all reading Americans, and to people over the sea."

"THOREAU"
RALPH WALDO EMERSON

JAMES EARL JONES

WINTER PONDS

[ven as he wrote *Walden*, Thoreau anticipated that one day it would be "profaned." That was his word. He found Walden Pond to be a "forever new, and unprofaned, part of the universe." He predicted that one day the "ornamented grounds of villas" would be built there. In Thoreau's time, woodchoppers stripped some of the shoreline, the railroad "infringed on its border." Concord citizens thought of piping water from the pond into the village. Thoreau feared that he himself "profaned" Walden. But he revered its purity, and explored his own nature in that cosmos.

I remember with pleasure walking in Walden Woods along the shores of Walden Pond. As a child I lived on a farm in Mississippi, and later, on a farm in Michigan. When I found my own country landscape in New York State, one thing that attracted me to the place was the presence of a winter pond. Thus I read with appreciation what Thoreau had to say about his pond in winter, where "a perennial waveless serenity reigns as in the amber twilight sky. . . . Heaven is under our feet as well as over our heads."

I have always thought it quite wonderful and necessary to keep connected to nature, to a place (Thoreau would say an unprofaned place) where one can rest and muse and listen. My winter pond was very important to me, and when I could afford it, I brought in some equipment to clear away some of the growth and discover if there was a spring feeding the pond. If so, I wanted to stimulate it. The area was pear-shaped, and I wanted to keep it that way, but to make a dam of the muck and debris we cleared from the pond.

My son Flynn and I populated the winter pond with fifty fish—all bottom-feeding fish, catfish, goldfish, carp, and Chinese goldfish, which are huge. We wanted creatures to inhabit our pond. We planted lilies around the edge, and we aerate it in the summer so the fish can thrive. It has been fascinating to see the pond take on a life of its own, and it has been a laboratory for my son.

When the pond is full, I can stand in water up to my chin. I was convinced that if the pond was deep enough, the fish could survive the winter. At certain depths the water is a barrier to the cold, and Flynn has watched fish swimming under the ice near the edges. Thoreau wrote of the quiet winter parlor of the fishes, "pervaded by a softened light as through a window of ground glass, with its bright sanded floor the same as in summer."

Modern civilization is so heavily oriented toward technology that we lose spirituality. To rupture the bond with nature is to risk destroying the spirit. It is dangerous to try to conquer nature—to kill rain forests or grizzly bears or even gentle winter ponds. We should not let our need to industrialize and modernize overcome our affinity for nature. We find a spiritual wisdom in the natural world which is hard to retrieve once it is lost. There are aspects of the universe far beyond our powers to observe or understand. We belong to them as they belong to us.

Walden Pond and Walden Woods are monuments. That is all the justification we need to protect them.

▲ ▲ ▲

James Earl Jones, voice of Darth Vader and CNN, starred in the ABC TV series, "Bird and Katt" (formerly "Gabriel's Fire"). He won a Tony Award and an Oscar nomination for his portrayal of Jack Johnson in *The Great White Hope.* He has also starred in *Field of Dreams* and *The Hunt for Red October,* and on Broadway in August Wilson's *Fences,* among many other films and stageplays.

Walden Wood was my forest walk.

JOURNAL, APRIL 12, 1852
HENRY DAVID THOREAU

SENATOR EDWARD M. KENNEDY

REMEMBERING THOREAU AND
PRESERVING WALDEN POND

My warm and vivid memories of Walden Pond and Walden Woods date back to early childhood. On occasional summer Sunday mornings in the 1930s, my mother would bundle as many young Kennedys and Fitzgeralds as she could find into the family station wagon for an excursion from Hyannis Port to the pond. Even today, when I hear of crowds from Boston descending on the pond on weekend afternoons, I cannot help but recall the crowds of Kennedy children erupting from the station wagon and racing toward the pond.

On our visits, we would enjoy a swim, then gather on the steep woodland bank by the shore for picnic sandwiches while Mother told us a little about Thoreau and his times. At day's end, we would regroup at the dinner table on the Cape and relive the outing. Mother is the best teacher that any of us ever had, and she would gently draw us out about the day. She would drive the lesson home by asking us to recall an event from Thoreau's life or a passage from his writing.

I still remember that Thoreau was once Ralph Waldo Emerson's gardener. I still see Mother in my mind's eye, sitting by the pond, telling us about Thoreau. We laughed over lines from *Walden,* like, "Beware of all enterprises that require new clothes," and, "The man who goes alone can start today; but he who travels with another must wait till that other is ready." Waiting for Teddy was not uncommon in our family in those days.

We sat more quietly and tried not to squirm while Mother attempted to plant her lesson of the day in our young minds by quoting some of Thoreau's most famous lines. She loved epigrams on life, and found a rich lode in Thoreau:

"Any man more right than his neighbors constitutes a majority of one."

"It is never too late to give up our prejudices."

"In the long run men hit only what they aim at."

"It is life near the bone where it is sweetest."

"There are a thousand hacking at the branches of evil to one who is striking at the root."

"Under a government which imprisons any unjustly, the true place for a just man is also a prison."

"If a man does not keep pace with his companions, perhaps it is because he hears a different drummer. Let him step to the music which he hears, however measured or far away."

Mother talked often of Thoreau's love of nature, explaining what he meant when he wrote that "heaven is under our feet as well as over our heads." She was the first environmentalist in our family. If my generation and my children's generation of Kennedys care deeply about environmental issues today, including the preservation of the pond, it is largely due to Mother's well-planted lessons nearly half a century ago.

As she wrote in her memoirs, *Times to Remember*, "the more experiences a child has and the more things he sees and hears the more interested in life he is likely to be, and the more interesting his own life is likely to be." Mother practiced what she preached. She was constantly organizing weekend outings while we were growing up, so that we could learn something of the beauty and history of Massachusetts and its importance to the past and future. A Rose Kennedy field trip had the right blend of education and enjoyment to leave a warm and lasting memory of the thousand lessons she instilled. Because she herself loved history so much, she made it come alive for all her children.

Mother's appreciation for Thoreau began in her own childhood at the turn of the century. Between the ages of seven and thirteen, she lived in West Concord, only a few miles from Walden Woods. Church picnics at Walden Pond were frequent, as were impromptu swimming lessons organized for Rose and her brothers and sisters by her father, John Fitzgerald, who was then serving in the House of Representatives and was preparing to run for mayor of Boston.

Among Mother's other favorite activities were her almost daily trips to the Concord Library during summer vacations from school, where she would read and reread the works of her favorite authors—including her first exposure to the books of Thoreau and the other famous local authors.

In the spring of 1936, my oldest sister Kathleen was studying in France; her Easter vacation lasted for several weeks, and mother decided to visit her and take her to the Soviet Union. While there, they were escorted through one of the country's largest and most impressive libraries. What mother wanted to know most was whether the works of Thoreau, Emerson, and Hawthorne had escaped the Soviet censors. Believing that differences between nations should be bridged by cultural ties, she was heartened to learn that the books of these famous Massachusetts champions of individual liberty were still on the Soviet shelves, available for local citizens to read.

President Kennedy shared this love of history and admiration for Thoreau. In my brother's 1960 Presidential race, one of his favorite campaign phrases was from Thoreau's essay "Walking": "Eastward I go only by force; but westward I go free. . . . I must walk toward Oregon, and not toward Europe. And that way the nation is moving."

My brother often quoted those words when he was campaigning in the West. One of my most cherished gifts is a page containing that quotation in Jack's handwriting from his address to the Nevada legislature on January 31, 1960. Jackie framed the page for me as a Christmas gift in 1966, and it's been hanging on my wall at home for a quarter-century.

To President Kennedy, Thoreau's nineteenth-century words about the building of the old frontier came to symbolize his twentieth-century "New Frontier"— the expanding role of America in the world, and the enduring pursuit of the nation's best ideals, not only for our own citizens but also for those in many other lands.

Robert Kennedy, too, found inspiration and solace in Thoreau. During the difficult and trying times of recent decades, Thoreau's eloquent essay on "Civil Disobedience"—written as a protest against the Mexican War and the expansion of slavery—became the philosophical underpinning of both the civil rights movement and the anti–Vietnam war movement. Millions of Americans, searching for more effective ways to change the policies of modern government, found help and justification in the century-old writings of Thoreau on peaceful protest and the power of individuals to make a difference in their communities, even if they are acting alone and against the odds. Robert Kennedy took those ideas to South Africa as well. As he told the students at Capetown in 1966: "Each time a man stands up for an ideal, or acts to improve the lot of others, or strikes out against injustice, he sends forth a tiny ripple of hope, and crossing each other from a million different centers of energy and daring, those ripples build a current which can sweep down the mightiest walls of oppression and resistance." In a sense, that day, the ripples from Walden Pond were washing ashore in South Africa, half a world away.

In addition to his eloquent defense of peaceful protest against unjust laws, the most enduring aspect of Thoreau's writings is his respect for the environment, especially his plea for the preservation of our priceless natural resources. One hundred fifty years ago, with breathtaking foresight, he saw the trend of the nation's increasingly industrialized society in his day, and spoke to it in terms that are equally relevant to our own age. He predicted the difficult choices that lay ahead, and understood that progress is not worthy of the name if it means ravaging the "heaven under our feet."

Today, as we face local, regional, national, and global environmental challenges of a magnitude imaginable only to Thoreau a few decades ago, we cannot help but marvel at the depth of his knowledge, the wisdom and eloquence of his words, the courage of his life, and the intensity and insight of his vision.

Thoreau belongs to our day and our generation too. In a sense, Walden Pond is where it all began. The pond is more than just an antiquated memory. It is a contemporary reality capable of inspiring future Americans, as it has inspired many in the past. The lessons of Thoreau will be passed more faithfully from generation to generation if the stewardship of Thoreau's beloved pond and woods is passed securely from one generation to the next. Walden Pond and Walden Woods must be preserved. If we fail, we have failed our heritage itself.

▲ ▲ ▲

Edward M. Kennedy was first elected to the United States Senate in 1962, to fulfill the unexpired term of his brother, President John F. Kennedy. He serves as chairman of the Senate Labor and Human Resources Committee, and is also a member of the Judiciary Committee, the Armed Services Committee, and the Joint Economic Committee. He is an honorary member of the Walden Woods Project Advisory Board.

All Walden Woods might have been preserved for our park forever, with Walden in its midst.

JOURNAL, OCTOBER 15, 1859
HENRY DAVID THOREAU

MARTIN J. ROSEN

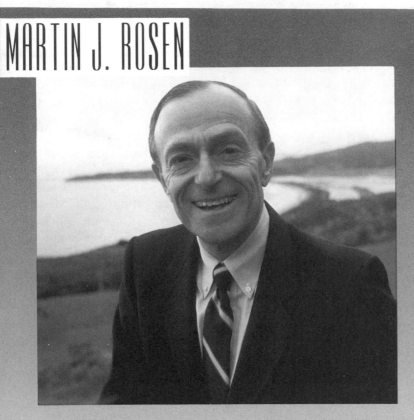

A WORLD OF WALDENS

mong the multitude of lessons in the life of Henry David Thoreau, I keep coming back to a single cautionary maxim: One should never underestimate either a person or a place. The person, of course, was Thoreau himself, whose quiet, quirky life revealed but a hint of the transfiguration it would ultimately visit on American thought. The place was, and is, Concord, Massachusetts, and especially the few hundred acres around Walden Pond—a lovely, leafy locale, but never on any top ten list of breathtaking American spots.

Thoreau was a "slight, quaint-looking person" by one contemporary description, and he was an authentic introvert, most at ease in his own company. By the time of his death, at forty-eight, he had acquired a modest literary reputation, and was also respected for a kind of practical knowledge about the natural history of Concord, his hometown.

All the same, many of his fellow townsmen never knew quite what to make of Thoreau: the Harvard graduate turned handyman, surveyor, schoolteacher, manufacturer of pencils. He bent to all these employments at various times, but never so thoroughly as to be long deflected from his reading and rambling, or from the passionate jotting of his introspective texts.

Even from his literary friends he received love tinged with disappointment. Why did Henry work so slowly, and seem in some matters so disorganized? There were times when his friends must have believed that it was not so much that Thoreau marched to the beat of "a different drummer" as that he didn't march at all. Before his death, Thoreau had published but a handful of magazine articles and two books, one of which sold so poorly that a large shipment was returned by the publisher. "I now have a library of nearly nine hundred volumes," Thoreau confided to his journal, "over seven hundred of which I wrote myself."

In contemporary terms, the bard of Walden would never have made the six o'clock news or the *New York Times* best-seller list—and in this is the first lesson for our celebrity-loving time. In life, as in art, such qualities as originality, patient craftsmanship, and attention to vision do not always walk away with the blue ribbon.

But while many writers of Thoreau's time are little studied now, *his* work has changed the world. Sales of *Walden,* disappointing at first, have been on an ascendent trajectory for nearly a hundred and fifty years. Thoreau's reasoned espousal of civil disobedience has influenced human rights activists from Mahatma Gandhi to Martin Luther King. His passionate quest for the right way to live has inspired unnumbered students and disciples worldwide.

Americans have come back to Thoreau again and again as we puzzle out who we are as a people. In his studied contemplation of the world we sense a counterweight to our own frantic lives of getting and spending, and his retreat to Walden remains a powerful symbol for us. "The mass of men lead lives of quiet desperation," he wrote famously, and as our own desperation grows noisier each passing year we cling to this Thoreau-inspired hope: that we can always go back to the woods and figure out who we are.

But what woods? Where should we look for our solace and self-knowledge? For Thoreau the answer lay adjacent to his own back door. For while he visited the forests of Maine, the White Mountains of New Hampshire, the gritty shores of Cape Cod, while he once voyaged as far west as Minnesota in search of health, he was at bottom a homebody and an explorer of internal realms.

He called himself a natural philosopher, and he sought out design in nature and what it could tell him about the best design for his own life. He did not need the canyon of the Yellowstone River or the cathedral ramparts of Yosemite to jump-start his imagination. He was moved as much by delicate motifs: the outline of an oak leaf in sunlight, the design of fox tracks in the snow. The sight of yellow birches in a swamp, he wrote, "affects me more than California gold."

He had decided, according to his journal, "to study and love this spot on earth," meaning Walden Pond, the surrounding woods and fields, the neighborhood rivers and marshes. "I have traveled widely in Concord," he proclaimed, as though bragging of an entire world.

Later, other naturalist-writers would become identified with specific chunks of American ground: Aldo Leopold with Sand County, Wisconsin, Mary Austin with the deserts of California, Joseph Wood Krutch with the Sonoran desert, John Muir with the thin-aired heights of the Sierra Nevada.

But it all started with Thoreau. He confronted Concord in all its seasons and moods. He went for aquatic strolls, naked and half submerged, up and down the local rivers. He hiked the moonlit fields until dawn. He studied the droop of a spruce bough, the deposition of mud at the bends in the rivers, the maturation of tadpoles, the progression of the seasons—and leaves, always leaves, of which he wrote, "their figures never weary my eye."

The result was *Walden,* and what other endorsement do we need for the value of close-to-home ground? Thoreau engaged nature in an ongoing dialogue, and he would not understand the way so many of us now relate to the natural world: as a place of escape for two weeks every summer, as a region "out there" rather than in our own backyards. Or perhaps he would understand too well, and he would fear for us—for what we do not know, for what we cannot learn.

Because we are a people attracted to celebrity, we have designated celebrity landscapes—Mount Everest, the Grand Canyon, the aforementioned Yosemite and Yellowstone. But landscapes need not make us gasp to teach us about ourselves, need not be the biggest, the highest, the deepest, the brightest, the steepest, the oldest or the most spectacular to enrich us, move us, reflect to us nature's intent for our own growth.

The key to our relationship with any landscape, Thoreau suggested, is patience—not a common coin in our own time. "To appreciate a single phenomenon," he wrote, "you must camp down beside it as for life."

So here is the lesson, part two. Each time some close-to-home field or woodlot is slated for the bulldozer—each time some swamp is to be drained, some hilltop leveled, some stream channeled, some meadow paved—we must weigh carefully not only the anticipated biological losses but the loss to our own soul as people. And we must let no one denigrate that loss by claiming that a piece of land is common, ordinary, average, unexceptional, garden-variety or run-of-the-mill.

For there once was a slight, quaint-looking person who taught us that to write off any natural place as "ordinary" is really to write off the power of our minds and imaginations in confronting that place. The world is full of Waldens waiting to be discovered, waiting for people both as ordinary and extraordinary as you and me.

▲ ▲ ▲

Martin J. Rosen has been president of The Trust for Public Land, a national nonprofit land conservation organization, since 1978. He is a commissioner of Bay Vision 2020, a project to help chart the future of the San Francisco Bay area. He is a member of the Walden Woods Project Advisory Board.

> ". . . a man is rich in proportion to the number of things which he can afford to let alone."
>
> *WALDEN*
> HENRY DAVID THOREAU

THOMAS McGUANE

WEST BOULDER SPRING

Warm wind comes in spring in Montana before anything else, before anything turns green, though not quite before some birds, owls, and juncos, for example, nest and even begin to hatch their young. The tiny ground-hugging phlox displays its chaste white flowers almost before grass; the harrier begins to lose his winter white and the red-tailed hawks haul all manner of junk, including the hot orange twine we use to bind hay bales, to build their messy nests in the black cottonwoods along the creek. The creek itself is some days pellucid, throwing the shadows of trout on its graveled bottom and on others milky with low country runoff. On the cliffs, the rock marmots aggressively pull up the bunch grass and take it under ledges and down holes to build nests. All the birds are particularly loud and indelicate just now; but the red-shafted flickers screeching from the tops of the tallest, barest cottonwoods seem the most brazen, the Brewer's blackbirds busiest in the bright sun that encourages their irridescence. In the summer pasture north of our house the teal pause in the water-filled buffalo wallows of ancient times; the magpies tumble and mob in the clumped junipers. The meadowlark stands on the stones of the Indian grave east of the Charlie Wild draw and sings his heart out.

When I hike, I frequently come upon groups of mule deer feeding, as though I were a great stalker; but the deer are so close to their physical limits at this edge between winter and spring that they are not very alert. When the shadow of a marsh hawk flickers through them, they don't jump as they would later on, and the ears of some hang down as they do on sick calves. When they flee, the inverted rowing motion of their synchronized legs doesn't send such a shudder of power through their trunks as it will in another month.

The sagebrush buttercup is the brightest thing in the landscape, a buttercup so early it follows the retreating snow in a yellow haze. It is the first flower the grizzly sees when he wakes up from his nap. Cousin to the cursed crowfoot, a poisonous, blistering, inflaming flower, sagebrush buttercup is an important spring food to the blue grouse. I stood in a field of this beautiful flower, feeling the strap of my binoculars cut into my neck and sensing in the vault of tremendous sky an uncertain skirmish between the winds of winter and the winds of spring. To the north, the Crazy Mountains looked starved for restoration; and it was good to remember that their slaggish forms would soon burst into something I always think I can imagine but never quite do.

In the cottonwoods below the house stands a crooked giant whose top is splayed into a garish, surrendering shape. At the crotch of these upper branches, a great horned owl has raised a single baby. And when the sun comes out, she encourages him to advance along the dead branch on the north side of his nest. Nearly her height, his downy looseness gives him away. He doesn't seem to know what is expected of him. He stares down at me amazed, while the wind takes bits of his down and sails them off toward the banks of wild roses. His mother, glaring down with her yellow eyes, looks like the wife of Satan, and as many times as I have seen her, I have never seen her first: She is always watching down from her tree as though she had a plan for me.

Over the sere landscape, the creatures are chasing each other just like the children at the local junior high. The kingfishers scream and the meadowlark sings as cascadingly and melodiously on the wing as she does standing on a strand of barbed wire. Some of our calves are buoyant; in some the rains have brought on scours: Their backs are humped, their ears are down and their legs are scalded with diarrhea. The cows have begun to "ride" each other, and our five bulls holler from their segregated pasture south of the county road. The long cold rains have given two calves pneumonia; one runs a high fever and stares at the ground, the other has compacted her lungs and will never do well. The vet said, "She'd be just as well off if she died." In the corral where the sick calves stand, mating barn swallows chase each other, fall to the ground, and breed.

I saddle a horse to tour the pastures looking for some spring grass. Everything is late this year. We're two weeks behind town, which is fifteen miles away. There's a yearling buck dead by the first spring, nearly devoured by coyotes who have seized intestines and backed several yards from the carcass. This is, of course, merely a boon to the coyotes, who have come by this meal as honestly as did the Pennsylvania wolves who devoured the bodies of Braddock's soldiers after the battle of Monongahela. The face of creation takes in everything with a level stare. When I was younger, these manifestations of life's fury were comfortably free of premonition. Now there is a gravity that dignifies the hatchlings, the one-day lives of insects, the terrible slaughterhouse journey of livestock, and, of course, ourselves and our double handful of borrowed minerals. The old man I see when I go to town who stares from his porch rocker is staring into tremendous distance. As surely as homeowners pride themselves on property that fronts the beach, the lake, the golf course, we all enjoy abyss frontage; and a few, like the old man on his porch, seem absorbed by the view.

The obsessive busyness Thoreau complained of is rooted in fear; fear of mortality, and then of pain and loss and separation. Only in the observation of nature can we recover that view of eternity that consoled our forebears. The remains of the young buck dead at the spring are sounded in the cliffs above our house in the calls of young coyotes, testing the future with their brand new voices, under the stars of outer space.

▲ ▲ ▲

Tom McGuane is the author of ten books, including *92 in the Shade, Nobody's Angel* and *Keep the Change*. He currently lives with his family in Montana.

He is the richest who has most use for nature as raw material of tropes and symbols with which to describe his life. If these gates of golden willows affect me, they correspond to the beauty and promise of some experience on which I am entering. If I am overflowing with life, am rich in experience for which I lack expression, then nature will be my language full of poetry,—all nature will *fable*, and every natural phenomenon be a myth. The man of science, who is not seeking for expression but for a fact to be expressed merely, studies nature as a dead language. I pray for such inward experience as will make nature significant.

JOURNAL, MAY 10, 1853
HENRY DAVID THOREAU

BETTE MIDLER

OUT OF ROT, ALL GOOD THINGS COMETH

t's a big world, full of problems so overwhelming that most people (the aware ones, that is) have difficulty coping. I am one of those. I usually sob all through the evening news, and have had to give up newspaper reading altogether. This doesn't mean that I am disinterested in the fate of the earth; far from it. I remember the day I lifted my tear-stained face to the sky and vowed to serve the planet in my own fashion. To paraphrase Ralph Waldo Emerson, it's hard to have an idea that is utterly and uniquely our own. What follows is not my own idea, I (reluctantly) have to admit, but the scale of the scheme, the sincerity with which I flog it, and the global impact that I envision could only belong to me.

I am talking about compost. I love compost and I believe in it with every fiber (so to speak) of my being. I believe that composting can save—not the entire world, but a good portion of it. It is cheap, easy to make, low-maintenance, and just what the land needs, not to mention everyone who calls himself a farmer or gardener. It is the oldest form of agricultural renewal, superseded only about forty-five years ago in the United States by man-made commercial fertilizers, the manufacture and use of which has polluted our streams, lakes, and seas.

What is it, you ask—a big, ugly pile of garbage in the middle of my lawn that's going to attract VERMIN? The vermin issue is the one that usually gets the nonbelievers sniping. People in general are terrified of rodents of any sort— and I don't blame them, although recently I have become infinitely more tolerant and interested in all God's creatures, rodents included. First let me define composting in my traditionally superficial way, and then try to tackle the vermin question.

Compost is the humus-rich result of the decomposition of plant material. This means to you, the manufacturer, grass clippings, leaves, and kitchen wastes such as potato peelings and eggshells. You start with green material, alternate with dried kitchen waste and thin layers of soil, and maybe add a little nitrogen. Pile this stuff up somewhere where the sight of it won't bother you, sprinkle again with soil, fluff it up to make sure there's air in it, water it a little so that it's moist, not dank, turn it a couple of times during its lifetime, and that's it. When the microbes and bacteria get at it, and the earthworms arrive and start working their magic on it, the whole thing breaks down into the most fabulous mush, that when you work it back into the soil provides tremendous and inestimable benefits to your plants and to the soil as well.

As to the vermin—the trick is no cooked food. Some chefs put all kitchen waste into their heaps—but these heaps are usually far away from the kitchens. These souls are truly fearless. My favorites, though, are the ones who go to the zoo for elephant dung, to ensure a *really* rich pile.

There are whole libraries of material written about composting. People get quite demented about the subject. Some of this material is quite technical, a good deal of it is quite emotional—but it all boils down to this: Let It Rot. Then put it back into the earth from which it came. It is so sensible; less garbage in the public dump, at least 50 percent of which is lawn clippings, hardly ANY LABOR required, and solid benefits in the form of healthier plants, which can withstand pests and disease, leading to less use of pesticides, which we must encourage if we are to survive.

Now, while it is hard to have an idea that is yours and yours alone, it is easy to have an experience that is utterly unique to you, especially if you live in California. My whole life had been spent waiting for an epiphany, a manifestation of God's presence in the world, the kind of transcendent, magical experience that lets you see your place in the big picture. And that is what I had with my first heap. I had come to gardening late and was learning by trial and error, slowly and expensively. This certain autumn I really had no idea what I was doing or why, but I felt compelled to do it. I had to build that heap! We set up a ring of stakes in our small vegetable garden, surrounded it with chicken wire, and proceeded to dump everything organic into it: leaves, small branches, fruit and vegetable peels (nothing cooked), some animal droppings from hither and thither . . . it grew and grew and grew. It wasn't long before it was huge, and it didn't seem to be doing much, just a-mouldering. Being a rank amateur in this business, I was terrified. Maybe all I had was a wet, stinking pile (although it didn't smell at all like everyone I talked to said would happen). I decided I needed help. I was too chicken to dig into it AND DISCOVER THE TRUTH. I called Jack, a farmer from down San Diego way, whom I heard had tremendous knowledge of composting. He came to my rescue, bearing his "Biodynamic Compost Starter." Pulling the pitchfork from my trembling hands, he dug into the pile and began to turn it. What do you know! It was steaming! Amateur though I was, I recognized this as a good sign! It meant that the bacteria were going at it and causing breakdown, which released heat! And the earthworms—not one, but hundreds, all carrying on with tremendous abandon—well, to say I was thrilled doesn't really capture it. My knees began to knock, my eyes filled and I had to sit down. I was overwhelmed! So close to nature! I had actually done something! Something to benefit the earth; something private, not public; something teensy, but intensely meaningful for me and my family. Something that cost nothing.

After this experience, I was a convert, and now I am an evangelist. I can imagine the whole nation composting. But why be a piker? I imagine the whole world composting! I imagine an end to man-made fertilizers with their polluting production. I imagine an end to pesticides, because organically grown plants are strong enough to resist disease and pests. I imagine a tomato grown in the United States that actually has some flavor! I imagine homeowners turning their lawns into vegetable gardens! I imagine the worms attracting birds that citizens have never seen before and that they will come to know and love. I imagine people wanting to protect their wildlife and giving up hunting! I imagine people turning AWAY FROM guns! And after they stop killing wildlife, perhaps they'll stop killing each other! Hey! I think . . . I believe . . . I can even imagine . . . World Peace! Through Composting!

▲ ▲ ▲

Bette Midler is a confirmed organic gardener and loves all living things.

The earth I tread on is not a dead, inert mass. It is a body, has a spirit, is organic, and fluid to the influence of its spirit, and to whatever particle of that spirit is in me.

JOURNAL, DECEMBER 30, 1851
HENRY DAVID THOREAU

DON JOHNSON

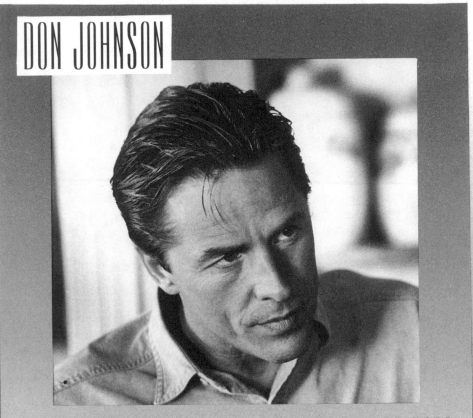

THE END OF MORE

When I first arrived in California, the year was 1968. Heading for San Francisco, I drove with three of my buddies from Wichita, Kansas. I was eighteen. It took us four solid days of driving to make the trip. Although we did a good deal of driving at night, it was during the day, over the long stretches of America's highways, that I was able to see the most profoundly beautiful landscapes any boy who'd never been further west than Garden City, Kansas could hope to see. The Great Plains unrolled before us, which beckoned my eyes to gaze into seeming infinity over rich hues of gold and brown, auburn, and multiple shades of green. The majestic mountains commanded awe-slung jaws and reverence. I fully understood the adjective in "breathtaking views." And the deserts blended into a mirage, a landscape that was so beguiling that at first glance it all looked like one stretch of monotonous sand. Only when we stopped to look closer did I realize the incredible diversity and abundance of plant and animal life in this mystical part of the world. Nature's profound beauty made a deep impression on this young heart of mine.

Ever since I could remember, even as a small boy growing up in the land-locked hills of Missouri and Kansas, I dreamed of going west—going all the way to *California*. The lure of California was so strong in me that, at times, I considered it high entertainment just to sit and think about it. If you've ever spent much time in Kansas, you'll understand. As I crossed the state border, the vision of California was no longer in my imagination. I had arrived.

Cruising through the natural splendor of this blessed state, I soon found myself in Los Angeles. Right there . . . on and off the Sunset Strip, up and down the Hollywood Hills, and being in, oh-my-God, Hollywood itself. It was pretty hard to be blasé, so fresh out of Kansas, but I tried nonetheless. My coolness was shattered when I found *The Pacific Ocean!!* I swear to God! It was right there! I could just walk right out on Santa Monica State Beach, (home to Frankie A, Annette F., et al), take my clothes off, (or not) and jump right into the Pacific Ocean! And I did. Many times. In fact, Santa Monica Beach became the place for this troubled, confused, and angry young man to sit, think, and chill. Back then, it was like a mild sedative for me; it made me feel a little calmer and a little more fortified to face the universal quest of young people . . . Who am I?

Now, as the years have passed, sometimes at breakneck speed, sometimes taking eons, (usually the former), I find myself on the brink (dare I say it?) of middle age. I've realized that the quest for "Who am I" is a lifelong endeavor and is accompanied by a cute, little side preponderance—"What have I become?" This last little item brings with it the responsibility to take inventory, and is (in my case at least) usually followed by, "What am I going to do about it?"

I'm not going to get into that in this writing (far too revealing and painful), but in terms of the environment, I would like to use the same approach. Who are we? What have we become? And, what are we going to do about it?

Clearly, we are people who want more. This is not intrinsically a negative, given the primordial instinct to achieve, to improve, to realize a need for personal betterment; i.e., to find a cave that didn't leak, to develop a more efficient way to slay a saber-toothed tiger, and then, in later civilization, to expand our minds through philosophy, literature, music, and the arts. These days, however, that instinct for achieving has mutated our value system, twisting our strive-for-more consciousness to the excess, regardless of any cost. We go for *more*, not because it's good for us or because it expands our experience or minds, but because it's what we think we "need" to be satisfied. More condos, more vehicles, more entertainment, more developments, more spending, more things, *more waste*.

So, who are we? I guess we're accumulators of more and more of the same. "What have we become?" This is far too deep and painful to address on a sociological level in one chapter, so let's change it to, "What has our *world*, our environment, become?"

You'll recall at the beginning of this narrative, I mentioned my first gander at the Great Plains, the Rocky Mountains, and the deserts of the Southwest some twenty-odd years ago. Recently, I've had the occasion to revisit some of these locales, some of which I haven't seen since that first trip across our land, and I wonder if they too will suffer a "before/after" shocking discrepancy. More times than not, it is like stepping into a bad dream or an episode of "The Twilight Zone" as I gaze out at landscapes that have so drastically been changed by man. The Great Plains have become what appears to be a giant mall, dotted sporadically with condos and "total environment neighborhoods" for that civilized effect. Strip malls and fast food clusters agonizingly jar the eye. The mountains have smog. The healthy and trout-filled river beds of yesterday are dry, and those beds that haven't been reduced to sandy gravel are polluted. Thousands of acres of lush forest have vanished, and those "breathtaking" views are only displeasingly breathtaking because of the overwhelming development that is now prevalent. The deserts are colonized as if they were the moon, with little regard for the delicate ecosystem at work there. Furthermore, I wouldn't advise a therapeutic dip in the Pacific Ocean off Santa Monica Beach, unless you have a yen for a potent dose of hepatitis! Am I exaggerating? Sadly, very, very little. All of this natural devastation and *more* has happened, and I promise, without our conscious attention, it will continue to happen at an accelerating speed, lest we look to the final, soul-searching question, which we must answer, individually and collectively.

What are we going to do about it? The first necessary step is to unite; to get everyone involved with the solution. Family and community awareness must begin with personal vigilance—from the youngest member of each family to the eldest. The idea that the earth is a never-ending supply source of natural resources needs to be banished from our minds. We must stop the ongoing rape and ravaging of our planet in the euphemistic names of "development" and "progress." It is terrifying and mind-boggling to think what our children will endure if it continues. The human race seems to be the only living organism with no instinct for nature's balance of give-and-take. Our waste from having "more" is unique to our species. Every other specimen in the animal and plant kingdom has recyclable waste. Everything is fully used and returned to nature. Through intense education, powerful examples, dedicated recycling and heightened awareness, the human race may be able to break this runaway train of natural disaster. If we still can find a place to sit and ponder, maybe we can all give some serious thought to our values and our responsibilities as visitors on this precious planet. Together we'd surely find that there is more to life than having more. If we have turned our backs on our future, we have denied our children and our planet the ability to sustain life itself.

Daily solutions, attention to planning and zoning policies, reevaluation of our needs and goals, and conservation of our natural glory: to this list I only add that we should pray.

▲ ▲ ▲

Don Johnson's "overnight" success in "Miami Vice" was really the result of sixteen years as a developing actor. He also starred in the films *Sweethearts Dance, The Hot Spot,* and *Paradise.*

Nowadays almost all man's improvements, so called, as the building of houses and the cutting down of the forest and of all large trees, simply deform the landscape, and make it more and more tame and cheap.

"WALKING"
HENRY DAVID THOREAU

ANNE LaBASTILLE

WALDEN WOODS

One of Thoreau's finest lines in *Walden* describes wild geese flying above the pond to settle in and rest for the night. He heard them "lumbering in the dark with a clangor and a whistling of wings." Every fall since these memorable lines were written, Thoreau and thousands of others have stood on these shores awaiting this event.

But imagine, if you will, what it would be like if wild geese no longer flew our skies. If Walden and other ponds lay silent all autumn. If no one ever heard geese honk again.

Impossible, you say? Not so. Let me tell you what happened to another species of waterbird on another body of water. In my short life span and career as a wildlife ecologist, I watched the giant grebes of Lake Atitlán, Guatemala disappear. From a longtime, stable population of two hundred to three hundred birds, they dwindled to eighty, rallied back to 232, then plummeted down to fifty—thirty—four—and then extinction.

Naturally, the giant grebes were different from Canadian geese. For one thing, they didn't fly, could barely walk, and lived only on this one huge lake in all the world. Geese, on the other hand, fly and walk quite well, and are found over much of our nation and Canada. Being such an evolutionary oddity and being so isolated meant that grebes were far more vulnerable to calamity than geese. Yet, as far as I can surmise, they had managed to survive at Lake Atitlán, and perhaps originally in other Central American lakes and ponds, for perhaps ten thousand years or more. You might even call them an Ice Age relic.

Nevertheless, over a span of twenty-four years I watched them plunge into oblivion, nudged by a terrifying combination of biological, geological, social, and political factors. As far as is known, I'm the first ecologist to have observed and recorded *in detail* a living animal's actual extinction.

When I saw my first giant grebe in 1960, there was no mention in any field guide, no photograph, and no popular description to identify this species. After checking into the scientific literature, I found that two ornithologists had discovered, named, described, and censused the bird (*Podilymbus gigas*) in 1929 and 1936. That was all.

How great it would be, I thought, to study, photograph, and write about such a rare and virtually unknown waterbird. In addition, Atitlán is one of the loveliest lakes on earth, with its aquamarine water, towering volcanoes, springlike climate, and gaily dressed Indian inhabitants. What an article this would make.

My chance came in 1965. I returned for four to eight weeks to write, living in Panajachel, one of twelve small Mayan villages along the lake shore. Atitlán means "big water," and it is. I came to respect the 1,200-foot-deep lake and dread the strong winds which daily whipped its waters into wild waves. For the first month, I cruised cautiously around the entire seventy-five-mile shoreline, counting *every* giant grebe, as well as other types of grebes, ducks, coots, and gallinules. I also measured all the reed and cattail beds since this was the principle—and only—habitat in the lake for aquatic birds, small fishes, freshwater crabs, and insects. I tried to get pictures, but was outfoxed by the wary, wily grebes every time.

At the end of that month, I knew something was wrong. Only eighty giant grebes—two-thirds less than counted on previous censuses—existed! I decided to stay longer and find out why.

First, I thought that hunting by the Indians was the reason for the sudden decline, but I learned that the Maya rarely ate grebes and had only slingshots and machetes for weapons. Then I reasoned that reed cutting—for woven sleeping mats and little seats—might be to blame. But the Maya had harvested these plants for centuries to make their simple furniture.

Then I discovered that the local offices of Pan American Airlines and Panajachel tourist board had brought in two thousand largemouth bass fingerlings in 1960 and released them in Lake Atitlán to encourage foreign sport fishing and tourism. In those days, no one made environmental impact statements or even *thought* ecologically. These fish are highly carnivorous. Some specimens grow to twenty-five pounds. They could easily capture grebe chicks, frogs, small fishes, and crabs—and they did, upsetting the aquatic ecosystem of Atitlán. Local Mayan fishermen confirmed this by the dramatic drop in their catches of crabs and little fish.

Realizing there was no way to eliminate this exotic fish introduction from such an enormous lake, I became very worried for the grebes. I lengthened my stay to six months. And I increased my observations of these jaunty, charcoal gray birds, with their broad white bills, for I'd come to love them.

I spent hours alone in my boat, recording grebe calls, watching grebe chicks, photographing their floating nests (which weighed close to one hundred pounds each), and noting grebe food habits. Gradually, I hatched a plan to try and save them. It would be called "Operation Protection Poc" (*poc* being the Mayan word for giant grebes). There would be four parts: enforcement, conservation education, habitat management, and creation of a bass-free refuge. Although there existed two laws—one protecting all waterbirds at Lake Atitlán, and the other declaring it a National Park—these laws were entirely unpublicized, and there were no game wardens or rangers to enforce them.

In 1966, I returned to Guatemala and met with Guatemala's minister of agriculture. Fortunately, I'd gotten a small grant, so now I asked him to match it. He did by appointing and paying for a part-time game warden, Edgar Bauer, plus providing gas and oil for his boat. World Wildlife Fund International generously gave two patrol boats to Operation Protection Poc over the fourteen years that Edgar was involved.

We campaigned around the lake to save the grebes. Posters were put in the twelve villages and lectures were given in the schools. Meetings were held with Indian reed cutters and a compromise reached not to cut and to protect half the reed beds every year. Eventually, this agreement became a presidential decree.

The Guatemalan Postal Service printed stamps of the grebes and a handsome first-day cover. Local painters and weavers began using the grebe motif in their arts and crafts. Lastly, we worked feverishly to build the refuge and a small visitors' center, and to remove the bass. I reasoned that if the wild population of *pocs* vanished, we'd still have a small nucleus of captive birds.

The hardest part of all, though, was catching two pairs and transferring them to the sanctuary. Because the birds are so wary, the waters so deep and rough and the reeds so thick, I had to develop special snares, on the advice of the Bronx Zoo.

Yet in 1968, the habitat was declared Guatemala's first national wildlife refuge. Staying on in Guatemala for much of the year, in 1966, 1967 and 1968, I watched the *pocs'* numbers increase—to a high of 232 in 1975.

Meanwhile, a series of completely unpredictable tragedies occurred. In 1969, creation of a hydroelectric project at Lake Atitlán threatened to lower its level by twenty to thirty feet. That would undoubtedly kill most of the reed and cattail habitat and all its resident fish and wildlife. A strong letter-writing campaign by top-level conservationists led the Guatemalan government to stop the project and seek alternative sites.

Next, in 1976, came the massive earthquake that killed 25,000 people and opened up cracks in Lake Atitlán's floor. The level began dropping and the fragile, yet vital reed beds started drying and dying. When our refuge had only two feet of water in it, Edgar and I released the captive grebes and their chicks. Eventually, the lake dropped twenty-three feet in fifteen years, and is still dropping.

In the late 1970s, well-to-do people swarmed to Atitlán to build luxurious vacation homes. In 1965, I had counted twenty-eight such "chalets"; in 1991, there were 501.

Quaint little Panajachel now boasted several tourist hotels, restaurants, and a three-tower, sixteen-story condominium. No one knew where the sewage went. People were pulling out what reeds remained to make beaches, docks, terraces, and walls. Every morning, hundreds of Indian women laundered dirty clothes in the lake, adding to the pollution and phosphorus loading of the water. By 1989, almost 80 percent of the habitat was destroyed.

Worse was yet to come. The news was full of political unrest in Central America. Edgar Bauer stopped writing, although he'd been a faithful correspondent for years. I was afraid to make my annual visit (taken since 1969). At last a letter came, advising me Edgar had been murdered on May 7, 1982, by unknown assailants on his coffee farm at the lake. Also, the refuge had been used as a military outpost during the civil war.

In one blow, I had lost my best friend and colleague in Guatemala and Operation Protection Poc, and I was about to lose my *pocs*. Their numbers had plummeted to fifty.

From 1984 to 1987, many biologists, both American and Guatemalan, made last-ditch attempts to save the grebes. Captive breeding was attempted, a new visitors' center was built, fresh censuses were made. But the numbers kept dropping. When fewer than twenty individual *pocs* remained, the species (as a whole) was declared extinct, because it was now all but inconceivable that they could continue to mate successfully. That was June 1987. In March 1989, I encountered four (two pairs) on the entire lake, in 1991, zero. The reed beds were silent. Raw sewage entered the lake at Panajachel. Real estate still boomed. The *pocs* had been the biological indicators for the environmental sensitivity and demise of this beautiful lake. But more than that, those *pocs* offer us all a generic warning of what can go wrong in this world—even at Walden Pond.

▲ ▲ ▲

Anne LaBastille, ecologist and author, has written several books including *Woodswoman, Beyond Black Bear Lake, Women and Wilderness* and, most recently, *Mama Poc: An Ecologist's Account of the Extinction of a Species.* She is a member of the Walden Woods Project Advisory Board.

JIM HARRISON

A REVISIONIST'S WALDEN

Someone made the nearly absurd statement that the human race may be divided between those who wish to live in cabins, and those who would prefer castles—absurd because 90 percent of the human race is involved in a daily struggle for enough to eat. But in any case, I would have to add "farm" to this schizoid dichotomy. As a boy I hoped some day to live on a farm and to also own a cabin way back in the woods on a creek or river.

The farm and cabin dream came true by dint of reasonably hard work and a measure of luck, though "answered prayers" seem always to own a questionable freight of irony, the "nothing is what I thought it would be" school of bumpkin surprise (a week spent in a friend's castle proved vertiginous, though the fishing in the moat was reasonably good).

The farm has evolved, over a number of years, into a rather dreary model of modern agriculture for the usual reasons of efficient land use and tax advantages. This was all accomplished somewhat unconsciously, as my father was a county agent and a soil conservationist and I had worked my way through college on a horticulture farm.

I have undergone a recent sea change, and if funds present themselves in the near future, I am turning the whole sorry mess—the manicured cherry orchards and alfalfa, the canola and corn—into a hundred-acre thicket. I have already planned the menu and wines for a party when I unleash a bulldozer on the orchard, also a list of the trees, shrubs, and native grasses to be planted. I have written enough books. It's time to create a big thicket. If not myself as the years wane, the creature world will find salvation in this wildness.

The cabin is quite another matter. It was built of logs by a team of traveling Swedes in the 1930s and sits on forty acres dissected by a small river in Michigan's Upper Peninsula. The cabin is several miles from the nearest neighbor, and an equal distance from Lake Superior, whose often-stormy nature can be heard above the wind. The weather is unimaginably charmless, as is the landscape, long shorn of its virgin white pine, of which there are only left a few melancholy acres in the entire state. The land is hilly, sandy, ragged, pulped over, but basically empty compared to all but a few places in the U.S., in northern Maine and west of the Mississippi. Summer is frequently referred to as "three months of bad sledding," and even that period can be made quite unpleasant by the density of biting insects.

This all sounds rather grim, and there is the question of why I have spent half of each of the last dozen years there. The answer, quite simply, is that much of the area retains an essential wildness. The euphemism "gentrification" has not been heard lately. There are rumors of development of various sorts, but the evidence is sparse. My breath remains bated, however, as I am old enough, at fifty-three to have seen a number of wonderful areas of our country become sadly and permanently compromised. And I will never take a shrill position against any and all development which denies a population its livelihood, but will always stand against the brutal, rapacious, and random greed that totally denatures the inherent beauty of an area—say, as in the deliquescence of the Florida Keys in the past twenty-five years, surely a possible scenario for a future hell.

Back to wildness. The most prevalent misquote of Thoreau is that in "wilderness is the salvation of the world." The man said "wildness," a concept of quite a different order. There is a question, in any event, if wilderness truly exists if it is only by our permission and protection. The National Park Service has certainly confused all of us on this issue. It is fair to say that there are thickets within Iowa woodlots that have a greater essential wildness than the fabled Yosemite.

Over the years, on my scruffy U.P. forty, I have seen bear, deer, coyote, a single timber wolf, otter, beaver, mink, porcupine, perhaps a hundred species of birds. I have been fortunate enough to attend a raven funeral, and felt a tremor when a Cooper's hawk swept through the unmowed yard, taking a red squirrel off the bird feeder. Of course this creature world is somewhat protected by any number of game laws, but its basic survival is in the fact that it lives in a state of rarely intervened wildness. John Muir, surely a holy man, once said, "Bears are made of the same dust as we and breathe the same winds and drink the same waters, his life not long, not short, knows no beginning, no ending, to him life, unstinted, unplanned, is above the accident of time, and his years, markless, boundless, equal eternity."

Frankly, I have come to the perhaps errant conclusion that this creature world and its landscape have as much right to thrive and prosper as George Bush, the Pope, Madonna, and certainly Jim Harrison. Perhaps paradoxically, I have no objection to the local shooting and eating of deer because men have always done so, and such hunting is laughably far down the list of primary threats to wildlife.

When you spend a great deal of time alone you realize that much of the toughness with which you have addressed your public life is merely an accumulation of scar tissue. The brain and psyche are layered with this scar tissue that appears to be a vital component in surviving the world. To truly perceive and live within wildness you must shed the scar tissue and relearn idleness, vulnerability, a capacity to store the clocks in the dresser drawer. It takes a great deal of thought for the scar tissue to maintain its balance, and when you learn to drop this effort you can walk for hours in the wildness without thinking about yourself. It doesn't hurt to imitate your dog or cat, who alternate periods of the most intense attentiveness with naps. I have wakened from back-country naps to discover a warbler perched on my knee, a bobcat curious about my snores, a bear cub and sandhill crane regarding each other with curiosity and suspicion, a coyote pup stalking me from stump to stump.

It is difficult not to think of these sometimes lunar experiences as an unearned payoff. There is a natural and residual guilt that comes after lolling around on a hummock in the middle of a cedar swamp in mindless ease. Shouldn't I be trying to save other, less fortunate cedar swamps? Of course I should. You must defend what you love or you will lose your soul. Simple as that. It is well past the time on earth when we may safely delegate our passions to the voting booth.

The most cursory look out the window on a transcontinental flight reveals how we have peeled the land, scalped it thoroughly, even placing the original wild peoples on reservations, and the remaining wild land in the hands of a government that is a great deal less reliable than our collective interests. The actual power apparently rests in pressure groups and their lobbyists. Rather than bemoan the failure of representative government we must become a more agile and effective pressure group than the rest, surpassing their propaganda, which is not the less powerful for being so dimwitted. As an instance, to continue cutting the remaining first growth forest to "save jobs" is the moral equivalent of sending a hundred Italians into the Sistine Chapel with sledgehammers to keep them from idleness.

There was a recent local newspaper photo of two mating cormorants with grotesquely malformed beaks, the result of the industrial toxins dumped into the Great Lakes. The state government has a "thirty year plan" to stop the dumping of these toxins. Currently the future of the industrial Midwest is the present tense of Eastern Europe. I have never met an industrialist or politician who wishes to spit in the face of his and our grandchildren, but there, they are liable to do so freely if so permitted. Timber companies "respect" the first growth forest and replant lavishly, which is fine if you can hang around for three hundred years.

Unfortunately, wildness is everywhere imperiled. Nothing is safe—not a single humble thicket, swamp, or gully, or the creatures who live within them. How grand it would be if the exhausted and diminished Left would revive itself in the defense of the earth, if the legions of joggers and therapy addicts would turn some of their energies to preserving what remains, would turn from making shrines of their bodies and wounds back to the planet before she is mortally wounded. As the great Jungian James Hillman said, "If the fish turn belly up, that is far more important to what is happening to my soul than what my mother did to me when I was four."

In the early sixties, as a young poet with an onerous traveling salesman's job, I used to sit beside Walden Pond and think about Thoreau, then think about nothing but the woods and water. My father, who had directed me to Thoreau when I was fourteen, had recently died and I ached to be back in northern Michigan, where I thought I belonged. Then late one cold March afternoon at the pond, with only a single crow for company, it occurred to me I was "at home" anywhere there was water, woods, a thicket.

▲ ▲ ▲

Jim Harrison lives on a farm in northern Michigan with his wife. His last book of fiction was *The Woman Lit By Fireflies.* His most recent nonfiction book is *Just Before Dark.*

I am no more lonely than the loon in the pond that laughs so loud, or than Walden Pond itself. I am no more lonely than a single mullein or dandelion in a pasture, or a bean leaf, or sorrel, or a horsefly, or a humblebee. I am no more lonely than the Mill Brook, or a weathercock, or the north star, or the south wind, or an April shower, or a January thaw, or the first spider in a new house.

WALDEN
HENRY DAVID THOREAU

ROBERT REDFORD

TAKING IT PERSONALLY

My involvement with the environment began before I even knew it, when I was growing up in Los Angeles at the end of the Depression and during and after World War II. I remember the excitement when the country began to open up after the war and rebuild itself. We were the most powerful nation on earth, no doubt about it. We had won the war and kept the world free. Our idea of progress was to build with no limit. We were taught that this was our Manifest Destiny. I watched as the green, open spaces turned into concrete malls and freeways, and the clean, pure air turned into smog alerts. I watched as unbridled development became the order of the day. Oil drills appeared off the beaches, along with oil spills in the water and hunks of tar on the sand. The smell of orange blossoms turned into exhaust fumes.

I felt my home being taken away from me. I felt my roots being pulled out from under me. And I took it personally. I had to go further and further away to find places where the natural environment still existed.

Like most people of my generation, I was brought up to believe in progress. I still do. But we are now at a point where we have to ask ourselves if we are the beneficiaries of our progress—or the victims. Manifest Destiny doesn't work any more. Progress from now on has to mean something different. We're finding that we can't keep using up one place and moving on to the next. We're creating a world that is tipping dangerously out of balance. We are running out of places, we're running out of resources, and we're running out of time.

Scientists tell us the struggle to sustain life in this earth's environment could be won in the next decade—or lost. As we approach the year 2000, we've now heard the hard facts:

- Over one hundred million people—half our population—already breathe air that is unhealthy.
- Health experts tell us not to eat the fish from our own rivers, lakes, and oceans.
- We have chemical and nuclear wastes piling up at dump sites and leaching into our land and water.
- Our oceans are warming, our ozone layer's got a hole that is getting bigger, and according to Carl Sagan, a whole football field of rain forests is vanishing—not every hour, not every minute, but every second! With each tick, a field of trees gone.

It's a pretty lousy legacy we've left for our children. We should be apologizing. Native Americans try to live with seven generations in mind, but recently we have been plunging blindly ahead without thought for even one generation.

The environmental movement has been growing for over twenty years, and in the seventies, the government seemed responsive for a while, passing regulations and supporting research for things like alternative fuels. Some corporations came up with energy plans, and some companies even discovered that conservationism is good business. But today, when people in every community put more and more concern into the environment, the government in Washington seems to treat it as just one more special interest to be appeased.

What happened? Where did we go off track? In the eighties, we had an executive branch whose major policy seemed to be to set loose selfishness. The idea was to open up all our institutions—banking, housing, real estate, energy— to fast-buck kings with a minimum of regulation. What a step backwards!

The results have been catastrophic. I think, for the environment, there has never been such a time of naked greed and exploitation as we have seen in the last decade. The damage that's been done will be felt for a long time.

But I am not a prophet of doom and gloom. I have always assumed that love of land and love of country go together. I think I'm like a lot of other people who are tired of being humored and handled.

When George Bush was campaigning and was pressed on global warming and the greenhouse effect, he said, "Wait till you see the White House effect!" We've seen it—it's a call for more study. Well, that's an old stall.

Of course, scientists disagree on some things. But what they agree on in this matter is more than enough to justify taking action. America has played a big role in causing these problems, and the world looks to us to take the lead in solving them. But you don't solve such problems just by labeling yourself an environmentalist. You solve them with planning and commitment.

It used to be that, in the minds of some, environmentalism meant camping out, eating granola, and hugging a tree. I remember Senator Jake Garn of Utah once called environmentalists "backpacking kooks." It later became clear that it was the Senator who was out in space.

Today, three of every four Americans call themselves environmentalists. More people see that the claim that saving the environment is a trade-off for losing jobs is just an old political dodge. In fact, environmentalism is good business. Advances in environmentally safe products can open new economic horizons. Whole industries will be created through energy conservation, and retooling existing industries will create more jobs than it takes away—jobs with a sense of accomplishment and connection to others. This will build a more human side to economics.

There is some good news. Almost every major city in the United States now has a recycling program; citizens are beginning to question the need when developers come into their neighborhoods. All over the country, there are other wonderful examples of people and communities taking things into their own hands. But individual action alone cannot solve our environmental problems. Pollution has no boundaries. Solutions require leadership.

In the last two years, we have seen people rising all over the world asking more from their leaders and beginning to get it. Poll after poll indicates that the people are way ahead of the politicians. We can't wait around any more for solutions to come from the top. It isn't going to happen. And as for Congress, the action there is too late, too slow, and too full of compromise.

American democracy has a long history of change won by popular movements—women's suffrage, labor laws, the civil rights movement, the end of the Vietnam war. It seems to me the grassroots activism we see around the country is evidence that there is a movement underway that wants action on behalf of the environment.

What we're living with is the result of human choices. And it can be changed by making better, wiser choices.

▲ ▲ ▲

Robert Redford, an actor, director and producer, is president of the Institute for Resource Management, which sponsored a conference on global warming with the Soviet Academy of Sciences in Sundance, Utah in 1989. He is a board member of the Environmental Defense Fund and the Natural Resources Defense Council. He received the 1989 Audubon Medal and the 1987 United Nations Global 500 award.

The authority of government, even such as I am willing to submit to,—for I will cheerfully obey those who know and can do better than I, and in many things even those who neither know nor can do so well,—is still an impure one: to be strictly just, it must have the sanction and consent of the governed. It can have no pure right over my person and property but what I concede to it. The progress from an absolute to a limited monarchy, from a limited monarchy to a democracy, is a progress toward a true respect for the individual. Is a democracy, such as we know it, the last improvement possible in government? Is it not possible to take a step further towards recognizing and organizing the rights of man? There will never be a really free and enlightened State, until the State comes to recognize the individual as a higher and independent power from which all its own power and authority are derived, and treats him accordingly. I please myself with imagining a State at last which can afford to be just to all men, and to treat the individual with respect as a neighbor; which even would not think it inconsistent with its own repose, if a few were to live aloof from it, not meddling with it, nor embraced by it, who fulfilled all the duties of neighbors and fellow-men. A State which bore this kind of fruit, and suffered it to drop off as fast as it ripened, would prepare the way for a still more perfect and glorious State, which also I have imagined, but not yet anywhere seen.

"CIVIL DISOBEDIENCE"
HENRY DAVID THOREAU

CONGRESSMAN CHESTER G. ATKINS

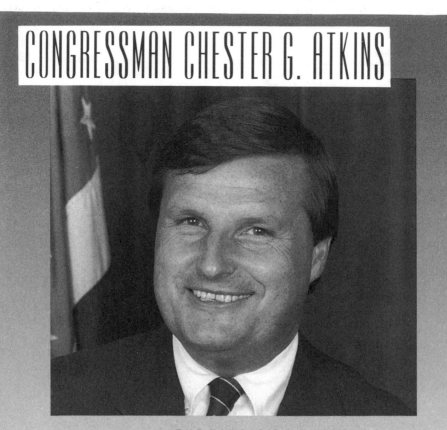

THE FABRIC OF THOREAU COUNTRY

I t is well known that Henry David Thoreau had little use for politicians, and held those residing in his hometown of Concord, Massachusetts in particularly low esteem. As an elected official from Concord, I confess I am guilty of both charges. However, I thought it might be useful to say a few words about the rivers running through Walden Woods—rivers much appreciated by Thoreau in his time for their scenery and wildlife, and still valued for those same attributes today.

Late in the summer of 1839, Henry Thoreau and his older brother, John, set off on a seven-day trip, in a boat packed with home-grown melons and potatoes, a bed made of buffalo skin, and a cotton tent. The outing was to become the subject of Thoreau's *A Week on the Concord and Merrimack Rivers*. The brothers' boat, which Thoreau likened to "a fisherman's dory, fifteen feet long by three and a half in breadth at the widest part," was equipped with oars, wheels, two masts, and a pair of poles "for shoving off in shallow places."

The two brothers began their journey in their hometown of Concord, paddling and poling until they reached the White Mountains of New Hampshire. Along the way, Henry and John observed farmers and fishermen, schooners, skiffs, canal boats, and all manner of fish, fowl, and plant life. Voyaging north, the Thoreaus floated past the quiet farming villages of Billerica, Chelmsford, and Tyngsborough, the bustling brick factory town of Lowell, and the emerging mill town of Manchester, New Hampshire. The two did not turn back until they arrived within view of Mount Washington.

One hundred and fifty years later, the scenery along Thoreau's beloved riparian passageway has changed. Farming villages have given way to suburbs, and condominiums stand along the shore where once stood meadows and woods. The rough dirt roads have been replaced with paved highways. The Concord River itself, so quiet in Thoreau's time, now swarms in summertime with weekend canoeists, motorboat enthusiasts, sport fishermen, and jet-skiers.

Human activity has changed other aspects of the river as well. Sediment beneath the picturesque, slow-moving Sudbury River, which feeds into the Concord, has been contaminated by an upstream industrial polluter. The Assabet and the Sudbury have long been receptacles for waste products dumped by the textile industries, as well as human waste. State agencies advise fishermen not to eat the fish caught in the rivers.

Yet Thoreau's rivers continue to attract and inspire. Artists, writers, naturalists, sportsmen and historians all visit the rivers and offer up their various tributes. A local artist has created a photographic exhibit of the Sudbury River. A journalist recently published a canoeist's guide to the Sudbury, Concord, and Assabet, and historians point out the role the rivers played in the lives of Native Americans, the American War of Independence, and, of course, the writings of Henry David Thoreau. An annual kayak race attracts world-class paddlers to the Concord's whitewater stretches in Lowell. My family and I can occasionally be found amongst weekend canoeists navigating calmer stretches of the Concord.

I am encouraged by signs that in recent years our attitude toward rivers has changed. Where waterways once were taken for granted, we are beginning to realize that rivers and streams in urban and suburban areas require care to survive. Residents in my district have taken an active interest in nursing Thoreau's rivers back to health, and preserving them for the use and enjoyment of future generations. Local river advocacy groups for the Sudbury, the Assabet, and the Concord organize clean-ups, sponsor education forums, lead river trips, and work with their legislators to protect rivers permanently from some of the more damaging effects of human activity. Local and state governments have passed laws and ordinances limiting and regulating what may be discharged into rivers, and a concerned public has begun to see to it that these rules are vigorously enforced.

There are signs that these efforts are bearing fruit. The Assabet, Concord, and Sudbury are cleaner now than they were ten years ago. The industrial polluter responsible for contaminating the Sudbury is being sued under the federal Superfund laws, and plans for clean-up are underway. Communities are working with the National Park Service to create a management plan for the rivers, and portions of the rivers are being considered for permanent protection from diversion under the federal Wild and Scenic Rivers Act. The future holds promise that Thoreau's rivers will be alive, healthy, and flowing for decades to come.

Today, these rivers are the threads holding together the fabric of "Thoreau Country." As groups work to preserve Thoreau's haunts, so, too, are the rivers he enjoyed gaining appreciation as an endangered ecosystem. As I've said before, Henry Thoreau cared little for meetings or politicians, and would have sooner walked barefoot across hot coals than have chaired a river advocacy group's subcommittee. However, I think he just might have been cheered to learn that the good citizens of his old neighborhood—and even a few politicians—have chosen to work for this worthy cause.

▲ ▲ ▲

Chet Atkins is the U.S. Representative from the Fifth District of Massachusetts, which includes Concord, the home of Thoreau and Emerson. He spent fourteen years in the Massachusetts legislature before being elected to Congress in 1984. He is an honorary member of the Walden Woods Project Advisory Board.

In all my rambles I have seen no landscape which can make me forget Fair Haven. I still sit on its Cliff in a new spring day & look over the awakening woods & the river & hear the new birds sing with the same delight as ever— It is as sweet a mystery to me as ever what this world is—

JOURNAL, MAY 1850
HENRY DAVID THOREAU

WESLEY T. MOTT

THAT "DIRTY LITTLE ATHEIST" THOREAU:
CONFESSIONS OF AN EMERSONIAN

The composer John Cage tells the story of a proper Concord lady who each year would put flowers on the grave of Ralph Waldo Emerson. As she passed the nearby grave of Henry David Thoreau, she would mutter, "And none for you, you dirty little atheist!"

Thoreau's admirers like to depict their hero as misunderstood by the Establishment, with whom they associate Emerson (even though it was Emerson who coined the term "Establishment" in the pejorative sense). I teach both writers but spend more time writing about Emerson. My mixed allegiances make me something of an interloper among diehard Thoreauvians—a strange development considering where I began.

My first encounter with Thoreau taught me that he was a dangerous man. It was the spring of 1964, and I was one of three seniors at Foxboro, Massachusetts High School selected to deliver a graduation speech on the theme of "rights." I was filled with the exhilaration of senioritis, but I didn't want to talk on the safe, cliched "rights" that so often mark self-congratulatory occasions.

Emerging as it was from the era of Eisenhower innocence and Kennedy idealism, the Class of '64 faced a world of social injustice and uncertainty that spring. Medgar Evers had been murdered in Mississippi, and four black girls had been blown to bits in their Birmingham Sunday school the year before. Martin Luther King, Jr. had stirred us with his "I Have A Dream" speech the previous August, but only three months later, President Kennedy had been assassinated. Meanwhile, what would become the Civil Rights Act of 1964 had been mired in congressional debate. Racist senators filibustered for months.

The answer to both my anger and my topic dilemma came unexpectedly from our school librarian. Helen Henry was a real authority figure—a strict disciplinarian intolerant of bad manners and frivolous reading. And here she was recommending that I read Thoreau and talk on "The Right to Civil Disobedience." Thoreau's stance of resistance to unjust government had already inspired Tolstoy, Gandhi, and King, of course, but for me in 1964, his argument was a revelation. I took Miss Henry's suggestion. And though I bowed to the urging of advisors and toned down my title to "The Right to Civil Dissent," I traced this "inalienable" principle from Sophocles' tragedy *Antigone* through our own revolutionary heritage to the civil rights movement, arguing, with Thoreau, that the majority rules by numerical superiority, but not necessarily by right, and that while this might do in matters of "expediency," each individual is obliged to determine right from wrong. To forfeit conscience is to become morally and politically powerless, to oppose unjust law is a moral imperative; civil disobedience, moreover, is a very "civil" way of redressing great wrong.

This all seemed self-evident—and perfectly reasonable, too, given the century of unkept promises to "freed" blacks and the atrocities faced by civil rights workers. It came as a surprise, then, when, as is customary, my speech appeared in the town's weekly newspaper—but with a new conclusion silently supplied by someone who thought the sentiments too disturbing for home consumption without a humble apology. So my own townspeople were no better than Thoreau's fellow Concordians in "Civil Disobedience": "their friendship was for summer weather only; . . . they did not greatly purpose to do right."

Throughout the sixties and early seventies, Thoreau would be invoked in support of all manner of protests, his image adorning posters calling for resistance to the draft and nonpayment of taxes. He became a cult figure among angry youth, a phenomenon that teachers came either to lament or exploit, so much so that critical study of his works became nearly impossible. The image of Thoreau as voice of conscience was fixed most dramatically by Jerome Lawrence and Robert E. Lee in *The Night Thoreau Spent in Jail.* In the play's preface, the authors make explicit the relevance of Thoreau's protest of the Mexican War to the war in Vietnam. And to create dramatic tension, Emerson plays the intellectual, cold, friendless foil to passionate, engaged young Henry. I vividly recall from a Boston production (cruelly staged in the auditorium of the First and Second Church, descended from Emerson's own Second Church), a particularly dramatic scene in which an aloof Waldo pontificates from a balcony, going on abstractly about the "Intelligence" that "governs the universe," unhearing as a righteous young Henry (played by a young David Morse) rages at his obtuse townspeople, who failed to see "the sun rising above Concord this morning."

While it was powerful political drama, the play reinforced an almost comic-book stereotype in which the bold Thoreau practiced what Emerson only preached. This distorts one of the most important friendships in American literary history. Emerson was for Thoreau (who was fourteen years younger) a desperately needed example of the literary life; a "great man" to emulate; a patron, promoting Thoreau's career and publishing his early writings; a benefactor, providing the land on which Thoreau built his "house" at Walden Pond. Some Thoreauvians have never forgiven Emerson for charges—made by others—that Thoreau was merely imitating Emerson's philosophy, manner, and voice—in one account, that he was even brushing his hair and "getting up a nose like Emerson's."

The stereotype denies Emerson his own genius and enduring appeal. To those who know Emerson only as the saint of uplifting greeting card sayings, or as the butt of cartoons depicting him as an impractical egghead dreamer, he must seem cold and remote indeed. Far from a beaming optimist, Emerson continually wrestled with a sense of ambivalence. His central doctrine, "self-reliance," he knew, could be perverted into "laxity" and self-indulgence if one failed to acknowledge that it also applies to others, and that it derives *not* from self but from God, or the Over-Soul. He privately confessed that his vision of the nation and sense of his own power were in flux: "Most of my values are very variable. My estimate of America, which sometimes runs very low, sometimes to ideal prophetic proportions. My estimate of my own mental means and resources is all or nothing: in happy hours, life looking infinitely rich; and sterile at others." This honest, vulnerable Emerson seems remarkably contemporary.

What is more, Emerson himself must be credited with speaking out on moral and political issues of his day far earlier, more forcefully, and more consistently than we have been led to believe. One might even argue that, contrary to the stereotype, Emerson—lecturing across the land and attracting intellectuals and reformers to Concord like a magnet—exerted *greater* influence than Thoreau on the course of abolition and other reform movements.

Emerson by temperament and conviction was averse to contention ("Jesus simply affirmed, never argued," he wrote in his journal). But when the occasion demanded, his voice could be sharp, and it often nettled those in authority. In his notorious 1838 Address at the Harvard Divinity School, he challenged the young prospective ministers not to parrot doctrine but to preach from experience. With masterful irony, he recalled being subjected to a "formalist" minister: "A snow-storm was falling around us. The snow-storm was real; the preacher merely spectral. . . . He had lived in vain. . . . If he had ever lived and acted, we were none the wiser for it." Emerson's aim was to reinvigorate religion, but his performance stirred up a vicious pamphlet war and left Emerson *persona non grata* at Harvard for nearly three decades. His brand of Transcendentalism was no retreat into serene contemplation. Emerson's insistence on integrity is echoed by Thoreau when he announces that *Walden* will be told in the first person. "I, on my side," he declares, "require of every writer, first or last, a simple and sincere account of his own life, and not merely what he has heard of other men's lives."

As Emerson is far more than a straw man for Thoreau, so Thoreau's indispensable legacy to our time is far richer than the cliched counterculture figure of the sixties. Thoreau was not just an abolitionist and reformer; he was also a naturalist, mystic, conservationist, civil engineer, writer. Nor, despite his importance to conservationists, was he a mindless back-to-nature primitivist. Emerson, knowing that this was fashionable, cautioned his readers: "let us be men instead of woodchucks." Thoreau knew the difference. And his greatest legacy to the modern environmental movement is not simply the voice of angry protest, but an extraordinarily diverse response to nature.

Emerson wrote that "Nature always wears the colors of the spirit." Thoreau's experience—shaped by mood, setting, and literary purpose—embraced not just the humanized landscape of river and pond, but also the vastness and momentary terror of the impersonal Mount Katahdin in *The Maine Woods* (*"Contact! Contact! Who* are we? *Where* are we?"), and the cruel savagery of the shipwreck and Darwinian struggle for survival in *Cape Cod*.

Even in the tamer setting of *Walden*, nature is a complex presence. Thoreau—an engineer himself—does *not* lash out simplistically at technological progress. The locomotive that rumbles and screeches past the pond on the Fitchburg Railroad stirs ambivalent feelings of fascination as well as dread. There are moments of well-being as mystical as that described by Emerson in his *Nature*. For Thoreau, such moments when nature and self become virtually indistinguishable could occur while fishing at night.

Nature in *Walden* guards its own integrity and is not to be controlled or found out, as when the elusive loon mocks Thoreau's paddling pursuit. Thoreau is always "anxious to improve the nick of time." But he knows that often what most matters is an alert anticipation, a grateful participation: "It is true, I never assisted the sun materially in his rising, but, doubt not, it was of the last importance only to be present at it." In one of my favorite passages in *Walden*, Thoreau describes the experience of being lost in a snowstorm on a familiar road. Deliberately invoking the Bible (Matthew 10:39), he expresses one of the book's central truths, that "the vastness and strangeness of Nature" is a tangible and spiritual antidote to the rut of routine: "Every man has to learn the points of compass again as often as he awakes, whether from sleep or any abstraction. Not till we are lost, in other words, not till we have lost the world, do we begin to find ourselves, and realize where we are and the infinite extent of our relations."

Thoreau's abiding gift to us is his openness to the continually shifting play of nature on the imagination, the way he confronts and conveys the joy of life. *Walden*—like Walden Pond—reflects our own best natures, capable of diversity, change, surprise. Thoreau's "nature" is not plants, animals, and water alone: It is the very medium of his understanding of life. In this sense, Thoreau thought nature a symbol of freedom, of harmony, of wholeness. But he witnessed the disappearance of open land accessible to many people. Thus the urgency of his appeal, in his late, unpublished lecture "Huckleberries," for conservation. "Each town," he declares, "should have a park, or rather a primitive forest, of five hundred or a thousand acres . . . where a stick should never be cut for fuel—nor for the navy, nor to make wagons, but stand and decay for higher uses—a common possession forever, for instruction and recreation." "All Walden wood," he hoped, "might have been reserved, with Walden in the midst of it. . . . As some give to Harvard College or another Institution, so one might give a forest or a huckleberry field to Concord."

Thoreau desired neither a hermit's isolation in the wilderness nor sentimental nature-worship. The issue was balance. When we save nature, he thought, we save ourselves. "Nature," he reminds us, "is but another name for health." Just as Thoreau believed that our civilized lives need the "tonic of wildness" for our re-creation, so we need the tonic of Thoreau's voice. Emerson and Thoreau lived in an age that valued eloquence. In our day, when entertainment is pursued for distraction or reassurance, the voice of moral prophecy is too easily switched off. Thoreau is inspiring but he is not smooth. He calls us to be *awake*—to social injustice, to the wonder of nature and our lives, to environmental degradation. We ignore his voice at our peril.

▲ ▲ ▲

Wesley T. Mott is an associate professor of English at Worcester Polytechnic Institute, secretary of The Ralph Waldo Emerson Society, and chair of the executive committee of The Thoreau Society. He is the author of *"The Strains of Eloquence": Emerson and His Sermons* and edited Volume 4 of *The Complete Sermons of Ralph Waldo Emerson.* He is a member of the Walden Woods Project Advisory Board.

> "It is easy in the world to live after the world's opinion; it is easy in solitude to live after our own; but the great man is he who in the midst of the crowd keeps with perfect sweetness the independence of solitude."
>
> "SELF-RELIANCE"
> RALPH WALDO EMERSON

TED DANSON

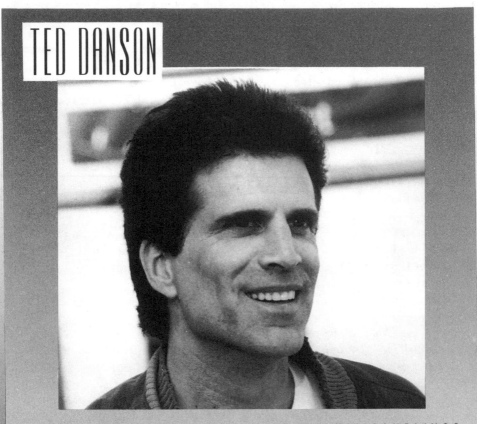

ENVIRONMENTAL RAMBLINGS

'm seven years old. For the last nine months I've been having fever dreams. When my temperature gets up to 102 degrees or so, I get up in the middle of the night and have a "walking nightmare."

To my parents I look awake and in great pain; the only thing that snaps me out of this state is water being splashed in my face. After the second or third time this happens my parents become bored with the routine, but it terrifies *me* to the point that I won't spend the night at friends' houses for fear of being struck by another "walking nightmare."

When asked to describe this nightmare, all I can say is that it isn't like other dreams. I'm not being chased by anyone, or being caught with a squirt gun in the middle of a real gun battle. There's nothing real about this dream. It's more of a *feeling,* an overwhelmingly terrifying feeling.

When asked to elaborate, I reply that it's *as if* I'm sitting on a beach and God, or a Godlike voice, says to me, "Ted, here's a spoon and a bucket. You have one hour to empty the ocean into this bucket or the whole world will disappear." As He is pointing to the ocean, I notice the spoon has holes in it and my heart sinks. The next thing I know, my mother is splashing water on my face and telling me everything is going to be all right.

Looking back, it seems like a silly little dream, your average guilt-ridden "I gotta save the world" dream with a bit of Messiah complex thrown in. But it is as good an explanation for my involvement with the environment as any.

I think I've matured a little since I was seven. I realize now that the world doesn't really *need* saving; it's our ability to enjoy the world that is in jeopardy. Or if I'm wrong and the world *does* need saving, I think it's okay if it's *your* spoon and not mine that empties the ocean.

On good days, I'm in touch with the thought that it's not whether or not you save the planet that really counts, it's the grace and integrity with which you engage the process that's important.

My father, among other things, is a professor of anthropology. My mother, although she hates to be pinned down, is a spiritual leader, at least in our house. My sister, a brilliant student, is the political scientist. And I'm the actor, so naturally I've stolen a little bit from all of them.

When I was five and six, my family joined my father in the White Mountains of Arizona where he ran an archaeological field camp for the university in Tucson. I wasn't allowed to do anything too important, but I did run into my share of skulls and bones belonging to people who used to walk around the same pine trees I was walking around, only two or three hundred years earlier.

Now I'm forty-three, and I have two daughters who are running around the same trees, and I'm becoming increasingly aware of my *own* bones, which ache a lot more than they used to. This makes me remember that life is not just about us, that there were people who came before us and there will be people who will come after us. Our job is to be good stewards of the world for the time we are here.

Unfortunately, we don't think that way in this country. We are more like the adolescent who feels only his power and does not yet see the arc of his life, thinking only of today.

Corporate America doesn't seem to think much beyond the next quarter's profits, or we would not have such a hard time competing with the Japanese, who plan five to fifteen years ahead. Our political leaders often seem not to think much beyond the next election, and so our national dreams are bound by political expediency.

How do we tell this adolescent with all this power that he must not consume energy so recklessly, that he must start conserving, which sounds horribly passive to his ears? How do we tell him that he needs to think about those around him and those yet to come?

I don't know, but the question leads me to my mother, our family's spiritual leader, because at its most exciting level, the environmental journey is a spiritual one.

The environment is not a political idea or a belief system. It is a brick wall and it will not let us forget that we are all in this together—that what each and every one of us does has a direct impact on all the rest of us. If Russia has a nuclear hiccup, the rest of the world suffers. If oil wells in Kuwait are set on fire, Pakistan has to live with black rain. If I overconsume in this country, I deprive others of energy and make them live with my waste. If every country in the world were to clean up its environment except one, we would all still have pollution.

We must *all* be responsible or it won't work, because we *are* all in this together. As the Zen philosopher Alan Watts said, in *The Book: On the Taboo of Knowing Who You Are:* "The root of the matter is the way in which we feel and conceive ourselves as human beings, our sensation of individual existence and identity. . . . We suffer from an hallucination that 'I, myself' is a separate center of feeling and action, living inside and bounded by the physical body. . . . But this feeling of being lonely and temporary visitors in the universe is in flat contradiction to everything known about man in the sciences. We do not 'come into' this world, we come *out* of it, as leaves from a tree. As the ocean 'waves,' the universe 'peoples.' Every individual is an expression of the whole realm of nature, a unique action of the total universe."

The root of the matter, then, is not political, legal, or economic. It is spiritual.

If the spiritual awareness expressed by Watts could be held by all of us, then even the adolescent with all his power and technology would assume a spirit of stewardship; we could clean the air and water, feed the hungry, and stop AIDS in the blink of an eye.

So the anthropology of my father and the spirituality of my mother lead me to believe I am on the right path, and that this has to be my life's work. It's the political science of my sister that gives me the most trouble. Knowing you're on the right path and becoming effective are two different things.

Now, granted, the world may not need me to save it. But don't I have to play as if it does? Don't we all have to play as if it does, because it might? And if it does, we'd better be effective because we're not just talking about saving one's self, or a corporation, or a country. We're talking about saving the whole thing, the planet itself.

So let's talk about being effective, about being political. This is where we separate the doers from the thinkers, the activists from the actors. This is the part that, when I'm being honest with myself, fills me with doubt about our future.

Let's use the oceans as an example, since everything that we do on land is reflected in the oceans. We start with a sketchy list of the things that need to change if we are to have vital oceans: Most sewage systems will have to be updated, storm drains built or rebuilt to handle runoff; industry will have to stop producing toxic waste; agriculture will have to stop using certain pesticides; manufacturers will have to stop making toxic cleaning compounds; offshore oil drilling will have to stop; developers will have to stop building on the coastlines; and fishing of all kinds will have to be managed on a global level to stop the depletion of fisheries and to protect marine mammals.

Most of the poison we put in our air ends up in our water, too, so car companies will have to make cars that run cleaner. In fact, since the capacity of the oceans to absorb waste gases is being overwhelmed, we'll have to greatly reduce the burning of all fossil fuels, so no more coal-burning power plants. Nuclear waste contaminates our water, too, so no more nuclear power either; alternative sources of energy will have to be developed and encouraged by tax breaks.

We could go on, but it is already obvious that protecting our oceans will take huge sums of money and massive commitment at the highest levels of government.

Most scientists give us more than the hour that God gave me in my dream, but many feel that we don't really have much more time than that—ten or fifteen years, perhaps, after which some things can never be restored. They don't say that the world will disappear forever, but they do say that if we don't change our ways and start cleaning up our mess we will never again enjoy life on this planet as we now know it. As our population grows, doubling in thirty to fifty years, we risk the acceleration of catastrophe.

A quick look at the Bush administration and the U.S. Congress as of April 1991 reveals a tremendous reluctance to change the status quo. Even after the Gulf war, our President's energy policy consists of drilling for more oil in environmentally sensitive areas, and when that's gone, switching to nuclear power—in short, continuing our addiction to the two most toxic sources of energy on the planet. The Congress, meanwhile, hesitates to even raise the minimum miles-per-gallon standard for our cars. So the country with 5 percent of the world's population goes on using 25 percent of the world's oil, year after year.

Now, if we truly have only ten to fifteen years to change things, and we aren't getting any help from our leaders, why aren't we all becoming revolutionaries?

"Daddy, what did you do while there was still time to save the planet?"

"I, uh . . . I, uh, uh . . ."

Right about now it's time for my mother to splash water on my face and tell me it's going to be all right.

Or we may all wake up in time. Maybe people with little powers will start to do little things, and people with huge powers will start to do huge things, and everyone, every single human being, will participate in saving the planet. *That* will be the revolution—a revolution in human behavior, a revolution of the human spirit.

Henry David Thoreau was a revolutionary of the human spirit, and he took action as well. When his beliefs once landed him in jail, he was visited by a shocked Ralph Waldo Emerson. "Henry," Ralph Waldo said, looking into the cell, "what in God's name are you doing in there?"

"Ralph," Thoreau answered, "what in God's name are *you* doing out there?"

My first act as a revolutionary will be to read (I confess, for the first time) *Walden*.

▲ ▲ ▲

Ted Danson is best known for his role as Sam Malone in "Cheers." He has also starred in several movies, including *Cousins, Three Men and a Baby* and *Three Men and a Little Lady*. He and his wife, Casey, founded American Oceans Campaign after a 1987 trip to the beach where they found the water so polluted they could not swim. He is a member of the Walden Woods Project Advisory Board.

I learned this, at least, by my experiment; that if one advances confidently in the direction of his dreams, and endeavors to live the life which he has imagined, he will meet with a success unexpected in common hours. He will put some things behind, will pass an invisible boundary; new, universal, and more liberal laws will begin to establish themselves around and within him; or the old laws be expanded, and interpreted in his favor in a more liberal sense, and he will live with the license of a higher order of beings. In proportion as he simplifies his life, the laws of the universe will appear less complex, and solitude will not be solitude, nor poverty poverty, nor weakness weakness. If you have built castles in the air, your work need not be lost; that is where they should be. Now put the foundations under them.

WALDEN
HENRY DAVID THOREAU

REVEREND JESSE L. JACKSON

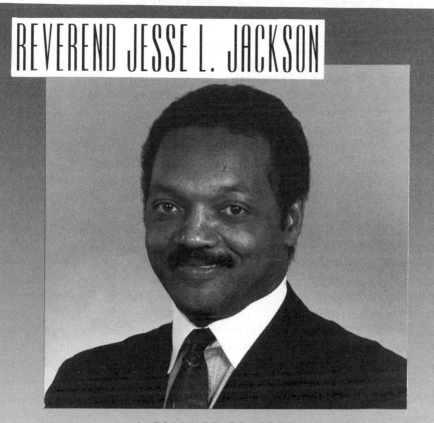

A TRIBUTE TO HENRY DAVID THOREAU

THE MORAL CENTER

Today, America is at a crossroads. The Cold War is over, only to be replaced with a set of new world disorders. Our military power spans the globe, yet our economic power has grown weaker under a decade of disinvestment in basic human needs. Our political power is great, yet our moral power is weak. As we seek to become a better nation in a better world, we do well to turn to Henry David Thoreau and the independence of thought that was his Walden.

Now, as then, there is a political center and a moral center. In Thoreau's day, slavery was the political center. Thoreau chose the moral center, and opposed slavery. In Thoreau's day, war against our neighbors in Mexico was the political center. Thoreau chose the moral center, and opposed the Mexican War as expansionist arrogance. In Thoreau's day, environmental exploitation was the political center. Thoreau chose the moral center, and struggled to preserve the Lord's earth.

Today we face the same challenge to choose the moral center over the political center, as we do battle for the soul of our nation. Civil disobedience must remain in the center of this struggle. In his retreat to Walden, in his renunciation of slavery and expansionism, in his refusal to pay his taxes to support immoral policies, Thoreau refused to let the politics of the day interfere with his moral commitment to justice.

Thoreau's words still ring as true today as they did in the midst of slavery and the war on Mexico: "Practically speaking, the opponents to a reform in Massachusetts are not a hundred thousand politicians in the South, but a hundred thousand merchants and farmers here, who are more interested in commerce and agriculture than they are in humanity, and are not prepared to do justice to the slave and to Mexico, cost what it may." ("Civil Disobedience," 1849)

Today, our nation's recent tradition of civil rights is under attack from the political center, from the White House itself. The chief lobbyists against the Civil Rights Bill of 1991 are not Klan members, but the National Association of Manufacturers and the Chamber of Commerce. The same people who want to put caps on suits for sex discrimination want to take the caps off to exploit cheap labor and lack of environmental laws in Mexico. There is bipartisan consensus for a fast track for trade negotiations with Mexico, instead of a fair track of mutual respect and deliberate discussion.

In a nation of conscience and democracy, these politics are intolerable. We must never surrender the moral center for the political center, and put winning and losing over questions of right and wrong. We need to find our own Waldens and our own strength to fight back. We need education, litigation, mass demonstration, and civil disobedience to bring the nation back to the moral center.

REMOVE NOT THE ANCIENT LANDMARKS

As we enter the twenty-first century, a century to be dominated by high technology, instant communications, and the threat of mass destruction, let us remember the Bible's injunction: "Remove not the ancient landmarks." The riches of the environment made possible the birth of humankind. Now children in cities cannot learn because of lead in the soil, and crops cannot grow because of poison in the water. Environmental destruction is an injustice visited upon the most vulnerable—the poor, the young and elderly, red, yellow, black, brown, and white. Most of all, it is an injustice to our children, who cannot defend themselves from today's forces of greed and waste.

Remove not the ancient landmarks. Let us respect the sacred places of our civilization, and preserve them so that we might become a better nation. Thoreau demanded two things: respect for the earth, and pursuit of the moral center. For us as well, these two principles must guide our steps. We have entered an era in which time and distance are of no matter, in which humankind has the power to destroy the world, in which the only constraint on human greed is human reason and morality. Let us preserve the principles of justice that lie in each of our hearts, and sacrifice neither the environment nor our morality on the altar of expediency.

The earth is the Lord's and the fullness thereof. It is not for us to destroy the Garden of Eden, be it in suburban Boston, in the cities where the people struggle to breathe clean air and drink clear water, or in rural areas where farmers struggle to feed the nation. It is not for us to pave over the sacred places of discovery and enlightenment in which generations of people have found inspiration. We must preserve Walden, and the spirit of Thoreau that has helped so many of us to do what we know to be right.

▲ ▲ ▲

Reverend Jesse L. Jackson, president of the National Rainbow Coalition, is an author, activist, orator, politician and spiritual leader. He has twice run for President, and was chosen "Statehood Senator" by Washington D.C. voters in 1990, in which post he lobbies for statehood for the nation's capital.

My profession is to be always on the alert to find God in nature, to know his lurking-places, to attend all the oratorios, the operas, in nature.

JOURNAL, SEPTEMBER 7, 1851
HENRY DAVID THOREAU

RICHARD F. FLECK

MOUNTAINEITY: THOUGHTS ABOVE TREELINE

Psychic awareness of mountains began for me, as it did for Thoreau, with an ascent of Mount Katahdin in northern Maine. If it is clear enough up there, high above the north woods, one can see both the Saint Lawrence River and the Atlantic Ocean. Mount Katahdin, rising above a dense wilderness of forest, is a breeding ground for mysticism, as much so as the Rockies or the Japan Alps where I would later explore. Perhaps it is the piercing voice of the white-throated sparrow or the cry of a distant loon. Or perhaps it is the pagodalike white pines reflected on waters of an unnamed pond. Or then again it might be the ghost of Henry Thoreau, seen faintly through the flickering flames of a campfire.

On my twenty-first birthday, and just prior to my senior year at Rutgers University, Jonny Boucher (an Englishman), Gordon Fader, Pete Barnhart, and I camped at Chimney Pond in the Maine woods before our first ascent of Mount Katahdin. It was late August, and the nighttime threads of Northern Lights pulsed throughout the sky. We had difficulty closing our eyes to get some sleep. And yet, seemingly only moments later, we rolled up our sleeping bags, covered with hoarfrost, and followed a trail through thick black spruce. We felt like those wandering French Jesuits of old to whom Thoreau often refers in *The Maine Woods*. The exposed granite of Baxter Peak loomed above us; if our eyes focused correctly, we thought we saw a skein of fresh snow on the summit. The black spruce and aspen all around stood utterly still and silent.

We worked our way through Katahdin's treeline of matted dwarf spruce; sometimes we'd sink up to our knees trying to get through it, soaking our boots in the rivulets of icy water underneath. With each ten or fifteen feet gained, we could see more of the lush forests below, which gave off an aroma like incense at a Buddhist temple in Kyoto or Nikko. As our feet touched naked granite, we began to see the distant waters of Moosehead Lake, and Mount Kineo, which the Penobscot Indians mythologized as a giant cow moose. We paused to take a few swallows of spring water; the sudden chill made our teeth hurt. Though the sky was bright and sunny, the wind chilled things considerably four thousand feet up the side of Maine's highest peak.

Finally, after a bit of rock scrambling, we stood on the summit of Katahdin, over five thousand feet above sea level, and peered down granite cliffs into the glacial cirque of Chimney Pond. I would not experience such sweeping alpine terrain again until I rambled through the Colorado Rockies one year later. As clouds poured over Katahdin's Knife Edge Ridge to the east, the temperature dropped twenty degrees, helping to preserve the tiny crests of fresh snow between the rocks. Dense clouds seemed to be born at our very feet. Henry Thoreau, a hundred years earlier, called this high rocky perch an unfinished part of the globe which robbed him of his "divine faculties." In a sense, all of us standing there could have agreed with him; the flood of sensations was too quick, too vast to be absorbed in a reasonable period of time. And yet, as Thoreau contends in *The Maine Woods,* Katahdin is a paradox. While it is vast and untamed and shocks man with its inhuman qualities, it nonetheless fosters and engenders metaphysical speculation: "But here [Katahdin's slopes] not even the surface has been scarred by man, but it was a specimen of what God saw fit to make this world. What is it to be admitted to a museum, to see a myriad of particular things, compared with being shown some star's surface, some hard matter in its home! I stand in awe of my body, this matter to which I am bound has become so strange to me. I fear not spirits, ghosts, of which I am one,—that my body might,—but I fear bodies, I tremble to meet them. What is this Titan that has possession of me? Talk of mysteries!—think of our life in nature,—daily to be shown matter, to come in contact with it,—rocks, trees, wind on our cheeks! the *solid* earth! the *actual* world! the *common sense! Contact! Contact! Who* are we? *Where* are we?" What God has used in the making of the surface of a star He has also used in the construction of a human body. For Thoreau and, indeed, for us, star matter and blood-and-bone matter had become irrevocably fused. Could not such speculation lead to the spiritual energies of Zen? Here is the beginning of mountaineity, or spontaneous psychic insight.

We elected to descend by way of the Knife Edge, sometimes straddling it between our knees with a thousand feet of space on either side. As clouds filled the cirque below us, we could readily imagine the glacier which once dominated the inner face of Katahdin with its icy blue fingers. By the time we reached the matted spruce shrubs of timberline under intensely blue skies, we realized that we had spent one of the most complete days in our material lives. The call of a loon that evening gave this impression even further emphasis. Like Thoreau, we had confronted mountains and stars with our very flesh and bones.

Mount Katahdin, more than any other place of my East Coast experience, readied me for the Rockies and points beyond. Not that the gentle mists of the Berkshires or the autumnal array of the Green Mountains of Vermont didn't stir my soul, but planetary alpine terrain is quite simply incomparable and awesome. To be caught in a thunderstorm above twelve thousand feet, where sheets of hail blur the snow-streaked tundra and where flashes of lightning crackle the air and make your hair stand on end, is to come face to face with cosmic energies. Electric air awakens the deepest recesses of the psyche to allow for a process of absorption, integration, and awareness. Clear stars over the tundra could do it as well; so, too, could the burning disc of white sun in pure blue air. Mount Katahdin, Longs Peak, and Fuji-San became for me a bedrock of existence, bedrock in Edward Abbey's sense of the word.

▲ ▲ ▲

Richard F. Fleck has written introductions to trade paperback editions of Thoreau, Burroughs and Muir, a novel, *Clearing of the Mist,* several volumes of nature poetry, and a scholarly study, *Henry Thoreau and John Muir Among the Indians.* He currently teaches at Teikyo Loretto Heights University in Denver.

If there is any central and commanding hilltop, it should be reserved for the public use. Think of a mountain top in the township—even to the Indians a sacred place—only accessible through private grounds. A temple as it were which you cannot enter without trespassing—nay the temple itself private property and standing in a man's cow yard—for such is commonly the case.

"HUCKLEBERRIES"
HENRY DAVID THOREAU

PAULA ABDUL

LITTLE GREEN: A PLACE TO GROW

Last month, warnings were posted on Santa Monica Beach. Swimming, they said, was hazardous, and the ocean was closed to bathers. All along the shores of Southern California, those signs sporadically dot the seaside. They're placed there because raw sewage has seeped into Santa Monica Bay, or an oil spill has poisoned the waters off Newport Beach, or the levels of assorted toxins have grown intolerably high for human health. For us, it's a terrible nuisance, a disgrace, and a disruption of our life-style. For the animals who inhabit those oceans, it's something more.

I grew up in Southern California and, as a little girl, I spent my summers in nature camps and at outings at the beaches and canyons that were a short ride from our San Fernando Valley home. The endless expanse of orange groves that once checkerboarded the valley was already mostly transformed into a patchwork of asphalt and buildings, and the air had long been spoiled by the fumes of cars and factories. Los Angeles was a boom town, but it wasn't so crowded back then that we couldn't find a stretch of beach where we could walk along and pick up seashells and rocks worn smooth by the ocean. And wandering through the canyons, I could easily imagine the beauty that had once graced the entire region. On those rare days when a westward breeze swept the brown haze off to the desert, I'd look north or east to mountain ranges that stretched endlessly into the distance. Not so very long ago, my home town must have been paradise.

It's impossible to live in Southern California and remain unaware of the changes in our environment. And during my high school years, the issue became a rallying point for our faculty and the students at Van Nuys High. I was class president during my senior year, and the local environment became the focus of our student council activities. We'd get kids together to clean up our neighborhood. We mounted expeditions to an imperiled wildlife preserve. We did what we could do.

It was apparent to me that the gradual ruin of our own country had to be stopped. Steps had to be taken to remedy some of the damage that had already been done and to prevent further catastrophe. I thought about it, from time to time, but as my life grew more cluttered with the demands of my work and day-to-day concerns, I'd put those thoughts aside for another time. One of these days, I told myself, I'd try to do something about it.

"One of these days" finally arrived for me when a friend, John Sebastian, helped make me more conscious that the same erosion I witnessed in my own environment was taking place on a far more frightening scale elsewhere in the world. Through some suggested reading, I learned of the importance of the world's rain forests to all life on our planet, and of the steady destruction of those lands. I became aware of the threat to thousands of species of animal and plant life posed by the devastating assault on that wilderness. I became aware of the consequences of the shrinking ozone layer and the deadly wash of acid rain, of the problems posed by overconsumption and our "throwaway" life-style. Awareness is the first step toward action. And as I became aware of the problem, I was obliged to do something about it.

John Sebastian's "Little Green" project provided me with a vehicle to express my concern and to make a difference, however modest, in what I've come to believe is one of the most alarming problems facing everyone on our planet. What I can do best, I believe, is to make other people, especially young people, aware of the severity of the problem.

Within the walls of the company John Sebastian founded, he's constructed a rain forest in miniature. Just as the rain forests of Brazil, Asia, and Central Africa magically recycle their rainfall and other resources, this glass-enclosed oasis, teeming with animal and plant life, represents nature reduced to pure poetry, the birth and re-birth of life in a never-ending chain. I love watching the young people of the Little Green project as they see it for the first time, as their minds begin to understand its significance. We can tell young people about the fifty million acres of rain forest that disappear each year, we can tell them about the million species of life that are threatened by that erosion. But that simple representation of the earth's mysteries and the wonderful, fragile chain of life touches them in a way that our words can never achieve.

When I look at those young people's faces, I see myself as a young girl, finding so much joy in just following a butterfly's flight through a canyon or wriggling my toes in the sand at the beach. Some day, I want my own little girl to share that experience. And it's my responsibility to see that it's there for her to have. The best way I can fulfill that responsibility is to help young people realize that, unless we all do our part, the hazardous condition signs at Santa Monica Beach will be permanently imbedded in the sand. The hills and canyons that surround us will be forever poisoned. There will be no place left to dream, to grow, or to dance.

▲ ▲ ▲

Paula Abdul is a singer, songwriter, dancer and choreographer. Her album, *Forever Your Girl,* sold more than ten million copies.

Why should not we, who have renounced the king's authority, have our national preserves, where no villages need be destroyed, in which the bear and panther, and some even of the hunter race, may still exist, and not be "civilized off the face of the earth"— our forests, not to hold the king's game merely, but to hold and preserve the king himself also, the lord of creation—not for idle sport or food, but for inspiration, and our own true recreation? Or shall we, like the villains, grub them all up, poaching on our national domains?

THE MAINE WOODS
HENRY DAVID THOREAU

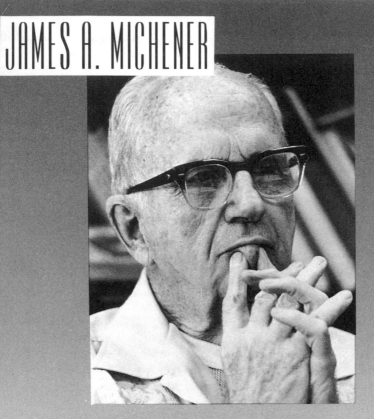

JAMES A. MICHENER

OF LIVING CREATURES

When I try to locate myself in the scheme of things, I discover that I am a rather puny member of the animal kingdom (weight 166, elephant two tons, gorilla 880 pounds) living in a small town (Doylestown 8,717 population, Shanghai 11 million, Calcutta 9 million), in a small state (Pennsylvania 45,333 square miles, Alaska 569,600, Texas 267,338), in a relatively small nation (United States 3,618,770 square miles, Russia, 8,649,490, Canada 4,014,263), in one of the smaller continents (North America 9.3 million square miles, Asia 17, Africa 11.7), on quite a small planet (if Earth is given the index 1, Jupiter is 1403, Saturn 832), attached to only an average star (millions of other stars are bigger and brighter), off to the edge of one of the smaller galaxies (it has only 400,000,000,000 stars, most of the other 100,000,000,000 galaxies appear to be larger, sometimes massively so).

I cannot, therefore, ever think of myself as highly unusual in any respect. Nor can I believe that the earth was created for my occupancy alone. My kind have lived here only a few million years; the dinosaurs thrived for a hundred million. And I am not homo-centric enough to think that man comprises all that is best in the animal kingdom of which he is a distinguished part. He cannot slither along on his belly like a snake or use his nose to feed himself the way an elephant can. He has not the incredible hearing system of a bat, the sense of smell of a bloodhound, or the capacity to survive underwater like a slug. He cannot cast off his aging skin covering like a crab nor stand motionless for hours on one foot like a blue heron. Man is quite a wonderful creature, majestic in his mental capabilities, but in many other respects he is limited or downright deficient. If he often assesses himself accurately when he compares himself with the other animals he can avoid getting a swelled head.

The transcending reward of such comparison is the discovery of a supervailing truth: Since man shares this earth with other creatures, he is obligated to treat them fairly. This is a moral debt which he is free to ignore, but only at his peril. He has constructed for himself agencies like guns and pesticides which can kill off entire families of animals the way we totally eliminated the American passenger pigeon.

It is a hideous act to terminate a natural species, made more so if one contemplates the millions of years it may have taken for that creature to evolve in meaningful ways from a prehistoric prototype. The overwhelming fact is that once a species has been killed off, there is no way in which it can be reinstituted. The primordial conditions which allowed, or even encouraged, it to evolve are now gone. There is no longer any seminal ooze in which creatures could experiment with various life forms; there are no vast, permanent swamps on whose shores they could climb to make their way to differing life forms. The temperatures of oceans may have cooled, their chemical components altered. It may be technologically impossible for a reptile to evolve into a bird the way the pterodactyl presumably did. The conditions are not right; the vast time required is not available.

There is, of course, a radical possibility. There is good reason to believe that the earth has about four billion years yet to exist and it is possible that some cataclysm of the kind that may have altered history in the past could recur to wipe out man and allow the quieter forces of genesis to repeat. (I do not believe or accept that theory, I believe genesis came about in an orderly, continuous way in obedience to the definable laws of nature.) Given three or four billion remaining years, anything could happen, but within the span of man's custodianship of natural treasures like water, forest, and clean air, we had best be extremely careful about eliminating any species, for it may not be replaceable in man's probable occupancy.

I therefore feel pain about my heart when I study the latest reports on species which are in danger of total extinction. Picture these magnificent animals, listen to them tramping through the bush or plodding their way over desert sands: the Bactrian camel, the tiger, the gorilla, the giant panda, the elephant to name only a few. That is a catalogue of majesty, a treasure of great images, an evocation of how diverse and powerful and noble nature can be when it is allowed eight or ten million years so that a mastodon can evolve into an elephant. Ten million years from now, our elephant could possibly become something even more wonderful, if we do not terminate the process now.

I think that an amusing symbol for those of us concerned with this problem might be a delectable cartoon that appeared some years ago, in what magazine I do not remember. It showed two hilariously drawn imaginary creatures climbing ashore out of the primordial ooze, one male, one female, obviously intent on something important,. But they are both distressed and frustrated, for planted on the sand dune they had hoped to use was a handsomely lettered sign such as one sees on military bases reading NO EVOLVING.

I am not an impartial witness in this matter. I love animals, have lived with them always, have tried to understand them, and have written about them with affection in an effort to remind others of what a significant addition to human life they can be.

I've had warm relationships with various kinds of animals. In Maryland two stately blue herons took residence in a swamp behind our house, standing silent hour after hour as they waited for fish to swim by. Victor and Victoria, my wife named them, and they became members of our family, communicating with us, waiting for fish scraps, guarding our house.

A family of bluebirds nested six inches from my study window and grew to ignore my typing. I lost a running battle with a squirrel who believed that the sunflower seeds I put out for the cardinals and evening grosbeaks were intended for him. Once, for several days in the Brazilian wilderness along the banks of the Amazon, I became familiar with a monstrous boa constrictor, tamed by others, who climbed about my arms and shoulders. But the wild animals I remember best among the buffalo, the Kodiak bears, the bald eagles, and the salmon I have studied so diligently were two hyenas, one in southern Spain, one on the Serengeti Plain in central Africa. The latter frequented a tourist camp—a kind of motel in the savannah—where he made himself the beloved pet. Lurching about, grinning in his hideous way at his friends, growling when necessary, he became passionately addicted to bottled beer, and we used to watch as he wandered from one bar table to the next, neatly reaching for half-filled bottles and chug-a-lugging their contents.

Toward sundown he would stagger off to find some place to sleep it off, and when the tourists, who'd been out on the veldt watching the hordes of animals, returned to their cottages, we always knew where our hyena was, for we would hear screams, especially from women, indicating that some traveler from London or Berlin or San Francisco had found the hyena asleep on his or her pillow. It could be, I was told, a rather frightening sight, especially when the hyena was so looped and comfortable that he ignored the screams.

It was on the Serengeti that I had my most extraordinary experience with animals. John Allen, the English protector of the great herds that passed through, and a man who cherished his relationship with animals, took me first on a low-flying plane trip over a large portion of the Serengeti to show me the elephants, the giraffes, and the water buffalo, but it was when he landed near a hillock and broke out an English wicker picnic basket packed with delectable treats that I saw Africa wildlife at its most awesome, for coming straight at us was a mixed herd of at least 500,000 wildebeests and zebras in the midst of their trek to new feeding grounds.

Leaving the food and the car, John, one of his assistants armed with a powerful rifle, my wife, and I walked out among the animals and in time found ourselves deep in the midst of this enormous migration. It was eerie. Slowly, relentlessly, the animals came directly at us, but when they reached a spot about ten yards from us they mysteriously parted, half to the left, half to the right, leaving us in a lozenge-shaped free zone, for as soon as they passed, they closed ranks again, heading purposefully for their seasonal feeding grounds. I tried several times to touch the passing animals, thousands of them, but they, without ever seeming to look at me, maintained that ten-yard distance and passed on. It was an experience few could have had, to be in the dead center of a herd so vast.

But the part I recall most often came as we returned to our car. Our path took us past the wooded hillock we had used as a guide point, and as we approached it, John Allen conspicuously moved me to the inside nearest the copse, while he and his armed assistant unlimbered their guns and walked well to my right, away from the scrub. When we were safely past I asked, "What was that all about?" and Allen explained, "Lions infest those woods, and sometimes they leap out to grab unwary travelers. Tom and I have to stand safely back if the lion leaps at you so that we have free range to shoot him dead before he gets you."

I asked: "Do you ever miss? Or does the gun ever fail to shoot?" and he said reassuringly: "It's our business to see it doesn't." Not many novelists in their seventies have been used as lion bait.

▲ ▲ ▲

James Michener won the Pulitzer Prize in 1947 for *Tales of the South Pacific*, which became Rodgers and Hammerstein's Broadway hit, *South Pacific*. Since then, he has published thirty-seven books, the most recent of which is *The Novel*. In 1977, he was given the Medal of Freedom, the highest civilian honor bestowed by the United States. He is a member of the Walden Woods Project Advisory Board.

The earth is the mother of all creatures.

JOURNAL, SEPTEMBER 9, 1854
HENRY DAVID THOREAU

GEORGE T. FRAMPTON, JR.

TOWARD A LAND ETHIC

W hile Odysseus was off fighting in Troy, Aldo Leopold once wrote, some of his slave girls reportedly misbehaved. So when he returned, he hanged them, all on one rope. No one questioned the propriety of this act. Those girls were his property, and nothing more.

As our species has evolved, so have our ethics. Originally, it was truly every man for himself. Eventually, family members were brought under the ethical umbrella. Slowly, so were other people, and we finally have come to the point where no one "owns" another person, with the freedom to treat that person as so much property.

Henry David Thoreau believed that nature, too, deserved a spot within our ethical framework. He certainly gave nature that status. "The earth I tread on is not a dead, inert mass," Thoreau wrote in his journal. "It is a body, has a spirit, is organic, and is fluid to the influence of its spirit, and to whatever particle of that spirit is in me . . ."

A century later, Aldo Leopold articulated the next evolutionary step in human ethics. He called it the land ethic. Best known as the author of the 1949 classic *A Sand County Almanac*, Leopold was a founder of

The Wilderness Society and the philosophical maven of the modern wilderness movement.

"The land ethic," Leopold wrote in *A Sand County Almanac*, "simply enlarges the boundaries of the community to include soils, waters, plants, and animals, or collectively the land." Accordingly, he said, "a thing is right when it tends to preserve the integrity, stability, and beauty of the biotic community. It is wrong when it tends otherwise."

As Leopold's list makes clear, this ethic is about much more than land. Leopold wrote of "the pyramid of life," explaining, "Land . . . is not merely soil; it is a fountain of energy flowing through a circuit of soils, plants, and animals. . . . Waters, like soil, are part of the energy circuit."

Is this a hopelessly old-fashioned idea? Doesn't it run counter to the history of our country? If adopted, wouldn't the land ethic mean economic stagnation? Must every undeveloped place be left as it is? These are legitimate questions.

Whatever the intellectual strengths of the land ethic, it is at war with our traditional notions of land and, to a certain extent, other species. Under our legal system, land is "real property," and it is "owned" by someone or some collection of people. The rights of the owner can be sold to another party without regard for the effects on the land and the species that depend on it.

In fact, a majority of modern societies have placed a positive value on the destruction of most of a given tract's life forms. We endorse such action with the term "development." Our low regard for original nature led Joseph Wood Krutch to say, "If people destroy something replaceable made by mankind, they are called vandals; if they destroy something irreplaceable made by God, they are called developers."

In many ways, this "conquest" of land has defined our nation as we have moved west on this vast continent. Our economic system has rewarded those who have conquered the most land and extracted the most from it.

Leopold strove mightily to steer future generations away from this distorted view of nature. "When we attempt to say that an animal is 'useful,' 'ugly,' or 'cruel,' we are failing to see it as part of the land," he used to tell his students at the University of Wisconsin. "We do not make the same error of calling a carburetor 'greedy.' We see it as part of a functioning motor."

Because Americans are economic creatures, our land management decisions tend to be based on economics. For instance, we may leave a particular forest intact because we have learned that the local economy depends more on the dollars of tourists who come to enjoy this increasingly rare resource than it does on the timber dollars produced by clearcutting the area.

In the Rockies and Alaska's southeastern panhandle, this is truer every day. In fact, companies are willing to pay so little for the timber that a federal taxpayer subsidy is required to keep them cutting, thus preserving the dwindling number of jobs in the local timber industry. In nearly two-thirds of our national forests, the timber programs lose money—but remain in operation due to entrenched political power. These losses regularly exceed $300 million a year.

At other times, the numbers might indicate that industrial use of a parcel would produce a bigger profit in the short run, but, in the long run, would produce a lower return than a gentler use. That ability to forgo short-term gain for long-term gain is a significant step forward, but it still bases the decision purely on economics.

This is not what Leopold advocated. For one thing, he doubted that it would result in much protection of the natural world. "[A] system of conservation based solely on economic self-interest is hopelessly lopsided," he wrote. "It tends to ignore, and thus eventually to eliminate, many elements in the land community that lack commercial value, but that are (as far as we know) essential to its healthy functioning. It assumes, falsely, I think, that the economic parts of the biotic clock will function without the uneconomic parts."

This is one reason why it is important to leave a few large areas as they are. The grizzly bears in Glacier National Park might not have survived an up-or-down, economics-based vote, but once the core of that ecosystem was protected, the bears were saved.

Another place that needs to be left alone is the coastal plain of the Arctic National Wildlife Refuge. Located in the northeastern corner of Alaska, the plain is bordered on the north by the Arctic Ocean and on the south, twenty-five miles inland, by the majestic Brooks Range. It is wilderness at its most spectacular, and is vital to polar bears, grizzlies, muskoxen, millions of waterfowl, and a fabled herd of caribou. But because there may be oil below the coastal plain, the oil industry wants to turn this area into a sprawling oil field. If there is oil—a one-in-five proposition, the Reagan administration concluded—the most likely output would satisfy just *2 percent* of U.S. demand over the thirty-year life of the field.

A decision to drill on the coastal plain would sicken Leopold. No doubt, it would sicken future generations, as well. In a sense, a land ethic is part of an intergenerational ethic. We understand that it is wrong to saddle our children and grandchildren with an enormous national debt. Politicians often campaign on this issue. But what about an environmental debt? By abusing the land, its waters, and its creatures, we are leaving future generations to hold a very big bag. Our land is their land, but we don't act that way.

Does the land ethic require us to retire all our bulldozers? No. "What I am trying to make clear is that if in a city we had six vacant lots available to the youngsters of a certain neighborhood for playing ball, it might be 'development' to build houses on the first, and the second, and the third, and the fourth, and even on the fifth, but when we build houses on the last one, we forget what houses are for," Leopold wrote. "The sixth house would not be development at all, but rather . . . stupidity." Thoreau, too, wrote about the desirability of a balance between nature and what he termed "civilization."

It is that sort of balance that conservationists believe should be struck at Thoreau's beloved Walden Woods. But will the works of man be allowed to push aside all that is natural? We have the power to protect Walden Woods, to keep this historic place from looking like every other piece of the developed world. For our generation, Walden Woods is a test.

Leopold took some comfort from the conservation movement in the first half of this century. He described it as "the embryo" of an affirmation of the land ethic. The wilderness preservation movement, in which Leopold played such a central role, was "a disclaimer of the biotic arrogance of *homo americanus*," he said. "It is one of the focal points of a new attitude—an intelligent humility toward man's place in nature."

Two encouraging signs were the Wilderness Act, passed by Congress in 1964, and the Endangered Species Act, which became law in 1973. Both recognized the vital importance of leaving portions of wild America in their natural state. "Wilderness is an anchor to the windward," wrote U.S. Senator Clinton P. Anderson in 1963. "Knowing it is there, we can also know that we are still a rich nation, tending our resources as we should—not a people in despair searching every last nook and cranny of our land for a board of lumber, a barrel of oil, a blade of grass, or a tank of water."

Leopold tried hard to be patient: "It required 19 centuries to define decent man-to-man conduct and the process is only half done; it may take as long to evolve a code of decency for man-to-land conduct." But Pulitzer Prize–winning author Wallace Stegner has written of our gobbling of resources as "a longer and longer stretching of a rubber band not indefinitely stretchable," and it is hard to believe that the rubber band could be stretched nineteen more centuries without snapping. Every day, another three animal species are believed to become extinct. Our ethical progress will have to be accelerated if we are to adopt a land ethic before it is too late.

▲ ▲ ▲

George T. Frampton Jr. has been president of The Wilderness Society for five years. He served on the Watergate special prosecution team, the Nuclear Regulatory Commission's special group on Three Mile Island, and in the investigation of former Attorney General Edwin Meese. Frampton is co-author with Richard Ben-Veniste of *Stonewall: The Real Story of the Watergate Prosecution*. He is a member of the Walden Woods Project Advisory Board.

TOM CRUISE

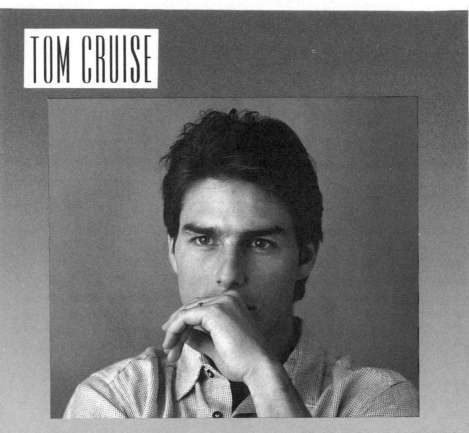

I CAN'T SEE THE FOREST IF THERE ARE NO TREES

Oh Wilderness were Paradise enow

The Rubáiyát of Omar Khayyám

THE AMAZON

We were in the heart of the Amazon jungle. We made our way on a path to "Camp 41." As we came through the jungle, I was struck by the incredible sounds. The whole place was teeming with life—birds, crickets, bats, bees—all in communication. This sharply contrasted with the mechanized, often discordant world we'd left behind.

After we unpacked at camp, Indy took us deeper into the jungle. "There's a snake in the jungle called the bushmaster," he said as we walked. "It's about fifteen feet long. It kills its prey with a venom that drops blood pressure to zero. Scientists studying this snake invented a medication that regulates high blood pressure for people. It saves millions of lives." The National Cancer Institute estimates that 70 percent of plants identified as effective in treating cancer are found only in rain forests.

We hiked further, as Indy explained, "The soil in the jungle is actually poor in nutrients. It supports such lush growth because of an incredible recycling system: Leaves fall to the jungle floor, moisture helps them decay quickly, nutrients are reabsorbed by the plant roots that grow close to or on the surface of the ground. That's why you are stepping over so many roots. The problem is when you take away the trees, the entire system fails. The soil is no longer nourished. Farming or cattle grazing won't last more than a few years because the soil dries up and dies. When the trees are cut and burned, the rainfall is less. The trees actually help create the rains."

We ate Brazil nuts off trees. For centuries native Amazonians have eaten this delicacy. When plantation owners tried to grow these trees on farms, the crop failed. It turns out that the tree only grows in the jungle because it's the only place where a special bee lives that pollinates the tree. It was fantastic. An entire world, each part different, yet symbiotic.

This forest had a utopian perfection to it. It worked together, and was self-sufficient. Had we lost something, missed a communication, forgotten a lesson, in the "civilized" world?

Later, we went to an area of the Amazon that had been destroyed for cattle grazing. As we drove up a long road, it was like death was suddenly all around us. There were no sounds. It was not moist. On both sides of the road we saw only miles of dried up fields. It was a wasteland. Indy told us how a large corporation had cleared this area for cattle grazing, but after a few years, the land would not support the cattle, so it was just left. In the distance, we saw more jungle burning. We were standing in a cemetery looking at a crematorium. It was astonishing how man could dwindle this far out of communication with nature. Communication had been reduced to only a torch.

The rain forests are burning at the rate of a football field a second. We are losing up to a hundred species a week from this destruction. Countries like Brazil have such large debts to world banks they cannot easily afford social or environmental programs. Ranchers, mining and logging concerns, and oil companies, exploit the Amazon without control. Small farmers are trying to eke out a better life for their families by cutting out small farms in the jungle rather than living in crowded city ghettos. What a debacle! How did it get so upside down, so backwards? Was this an overt failure to communicate with an environment, the absence of all ecology. Prospects seem only worse if we remain oblivious to the destruction.

NIGHT IN THE JUNGLE

It was very dark—black. The camp was dead calm at three in the morning. I asked Indy if we could go into the jungle to see and hear the animal life at night. Four of us trekked about a mile in. We came to a small clearing and stood very quietly. Indy whispered, "If you are very quiet you will hear birds fly under the jungle's canopy." We did. We saw glimpses of grey-dot blurs as they flew in the night through trees. "They have to have radar," I thought.

"Shhh," Indy said in a still lower whisper, "listen and you can hear the cries of the howler monkies." We did. The cries grew from a soft, background murmur, louder and louder until it seemed like we were surrounded by shrill screams. The howls somehow had an odd harmony to them. Just as suddenly as their volume would go up, the howls would pause—dead silence. It was fantastic. I had never seen or heard anything like this.

As we stood in this cathedral of nature, this forest, we could not help but understand it was dying. I looked through the tops of the trees at the stars, and felt life all around me. I knew that this had to survive, that I must do all I could to save this forest, these life forms, from destruction. This was a personal commitment that went beyond the color of my skin, my politics, my profession as an actor. It was the responsibility of a being who makes his home on planet Earth.

The most important lesson I learned in the Amazon was that care for this planet has to start in our own front yard. How can we ask the Brazilians to stop environmental genocide when we have been accessories to this crime in the United States for so many years?

Ironically, the teamwork and harmony between the diverse species in the jungle provide us the best lesson on how to clean up our own front yard—a lesson we'd never learn without taking a moment, walking in a forest, and observing life in full motion.

THE LEGACY

We've dumped millions of tons of waste into the ground, much of which threatens precious groundwater reserves. Certain U.S. companies export for profit pesticides that are banned as too toxic in the U.S. to unsuspecting third world countries. Only 5 percent of our ancient forests are left, and these are under siege. Parts of our national forests have been sold to the Japanese as wood pulp. Our coastal waters are polluted with toxins showing up in the tissues of the fish we eat. Some marine mammals are dying from immune diseases apparently caused by toxins in their bodies. The air in our cities is often too foul to breathe. In Los Angeles the air is rated "unhealthy" more than 250 days a year.

THE CHILDREN

Most insidious is the environmental attack on children. Some fifty-five pesticides are used that are known or suspected of causing cancer and which can leave residues on food. The deadly chemical dioxin has been found in bleached paper products like napkins, paper towels, milk cartons, and disposable diapers.

The Federal Environmental Protection Agency has shown pesticides and other toxins are present in the tissues of almost every person in the country. We don't know what this means to the future health of children. A University of Southern California study showed the likelihood of childhood leukemia increased three to seven times just from the use of household pesticides. Other reports indicated that the amount of lead in urban environments can significantly decrease a child's I.Q., and could retard mental and physical development. Children are our future. They face complex questions. Their education is essential. Many environmental words and terms are not even adequately defined for them. How can they sing a song if they don't know the words? If environmental pollution harms their health, impedes their education, reduces their capacity to learn, to understand, then we have all lost.

If we deplete resources and foul the environment, we are spending our children's environmental savings account without even asking them for a loan. We can no longer manage the environment like the national debt. Who would be against sensible care of the environment? The answer, which at first might be a little hard to confront, seems too simple, too obvious: those who profit from its destruction. But profits have no value on a dead planet.

The hole in the ozone is the same size on either side of the political aisle, even though they would probably debate it. The environment is not partisan. Economic development and the environment do not have to conflict. The idea that they do seems like a propaganda lie pumped out by those too lazy, too vested, too greedy, too blind to make new ideas into reality.

CLEANING UP THE FRONT YARD

It takes some confrontation. No one has a perfect record. It starts by getting back in communication with the environment and, step-by-step, beginning to do things that make a difference. At first, it might be as simple as planting a tree, or picking up litter, or recycling glass and paper. The key is action. This is not for an ivory tower. As care and responsibility grow, we see many more things to do:

• "Debt for Nature Swaps," pioneered by Doctor Lovejoy, exchange third world debt for rain forest preservation. We should support this initiative.

• Alternative energy vehicles can be made without sacrificing comfort or speed. Detroit should mass-produce these and make them affordable. If they won't, or can't, we should set government policies encouraging others who will.

• We must expand municipal waste treatment and put an end to the pollution of our coastal waters.

• We must demand foods free of pesticides. There are programs that produce increased crop yields without overdosing food with expensive pesticides.

(Nearly 30 percent of crops are lost to insects and weeds today, about the same amount as before "the chemical age.")

• We must preserve our ancient forests. It is unacceptable to negotiate them away anymore.

• Recycling should mature from a nice idea to second instinct in all American life.

• The ingenuity that produced a light bulb lasting ten times longer, using one-third the energy of a regular bulb, has to be exploited and nurtured.

• Alternative energy sources can no longer wait. We must provide incentives for the development of large, cost-effective sources of alternative energy now.

• We must stop the export of chemicals banned in this country.

• We must demand sensible environmental policies from government. If we get none, we must elect leaders with the courage to do the right thing.

• We have to clean up indoor pollution, EPA experts estimate that as many as 31,400 premature deaths occur annually as a result of indoor pollution. We need to develop and use less toxic alternatives to glues, paints, pesticides, and other building materials so families are no longer swimming in this swampy plethora of chemicals.

• First and foremost, we must protect the minds and bodies of children from the ravages of pollution. We must develop environmental youth education programs that teach the words, the concepts, the fundamentals of ecology. We need to tell them the truth. This is our future, and it's theirs.

Environmental change starts by caring. Go to a park, a forest, a vale, a lake, a stream. Listen. Look. Learn. Touch a tree, watch a bird nest, feel the grass, smell the scents. Do it. As care for the environment grows, so will the confrontation of those things that would destroy it.

ON WALDEN

We start in our own front yard. We must protect Walden Woods! Walden is not just a local squabble between developers and environmentalists over a sentimental icon. It is our environmental front yard. It's just nonsense that someone ever considered disturbing it. Walden is a place where man restores his communication with nature. Thoreau knew this. He saw the trees. He touched the plants. He cared for the wildlife. He lived there. He got his hands, feet, fingernails dirty with its life. He confronted his environment. He grew. So did his care and responsibility. So can ours. There is no better, more fitting place from which to send an environmental message to the entire world in the most powerful way by setting a good example. Preserve Walden Woods.

. . .

AUTHOR'S NOTE: I've learned that one of the major reasons a person is unable to grasp or understand a subject comes from a failure to define basic words. Last year for Earth Day we did a children's environmental booklet that contained a glossary of key environmental terms. I was amazed at how many parents told me they had never understood some of these basic terms themselves. The protection of our environment is so vital, it is important we define our words. There are estimates that over thirty million Americans are functionally illiterate today. Our planet's preservation needs the support and understanding of all people. Below, find a short, sequential glossary of terms used in this essay:

ENOW: an early British form of the word "enough."

CAMP 41: a Smithsonian Institute research camp in the middle of the Amazon where groups can go and learn about the area.

INDY: the nickname given to Doctor Thomas Lovejoy, who was the guide for my group. Doctor Lovejoy is the Under-Secretary for External Affairs for the Smithsonian Institution. He is a world-renowned expert on rain forests and species diversity.

SYMBIOTIC: the intimate living together of organisms, especially when this is useful to each.

CREMATORIUM: a place for burning.

DEBACLE: a total collapse or failure.

ECOLOGY: the relationship of living organisms to their environment and each other.

TREK: a journey, particularly one that is hard.

CANOPY: an overhanging covering; in the jungle this is formed by the tops of trees. Different animals live below and above the canopy.

GENOCIDE: deliberate and methodical annihilation of a nation or race.

LEGACY: anything received from an ancestor, predecessor, or previous era.

GROUNDWATER: water that has flowed or seeped beneath the surface of the earth. It is the source of water for underground springs. Wastes dumped in the ground can seep down and contaminate this water.

DIOXIN: a highly toxic compound found in the herbicide Agent Orange. It is produced in trace amounts when chlorine bleach and heat are applied to wood pulp. Controversy arose when the *Journal of Pesticide Reform*, Spring 1990, reported that Monsanto Chemical's medical director admitted, under cross-examination, that researchers had omitted deaths and data from a critical Monsanto study. This study was influential for years and apparently falsely minimized the perceived risk associated with this chemical.

PLETHORA: the state of being too full, overabundance.

ICON: an image, figure, representation.

▲ ▲ ▲

Tom Cruise's deep commitment to the environment was heightened in 1989 after witnessing the uncontrolled destruction of the Amazon rain forests firsthand. He served as master of ceremonies for Earth Day in Washington D.C., keynote speaker for the entertainment industry's environmental conference and as a contributor to "Cry Out," an environmental booklet for children. His twelve films include *Born on the Fourth of July*, for which he was nominated for an Oscar.

> At the same time that we are earnest to explore and learn all things, we require that all things be mysterious and unexplorable, that land and sea be infinitely wild, unsurveyed and unfathomed by us because unfathomable. We can never have enough of nature. We must be refreshed by the sight of inexhaustible vigor, vast and titanic features, the sea-coast with its wrecks, the wilderness with its living and its decaying trees, the thundercloud, and the rain which lasts three weeks and produces freshets. We need to witness our own limits transgressed, and some life pasturing freely where we never wander.
>
> *WALDEN*
> HENRY DAVID THOREAU

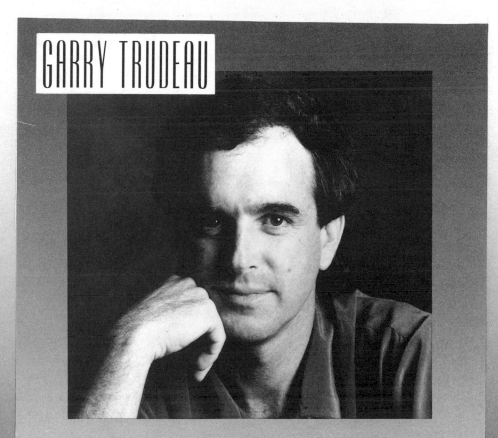

GARRY TRUDEAU

Garry Trudeau, the first comic strip artist to be awarded a Pulitzer Prize, created "Doonesbury," which currently appears in more than 1200 newspapers. He has contributed to *Harper's, Rolling Stone, New York, The New Republic* and the op-ed page of the *New York Times.* He has also written, produced and directed for television, and written for the stage.

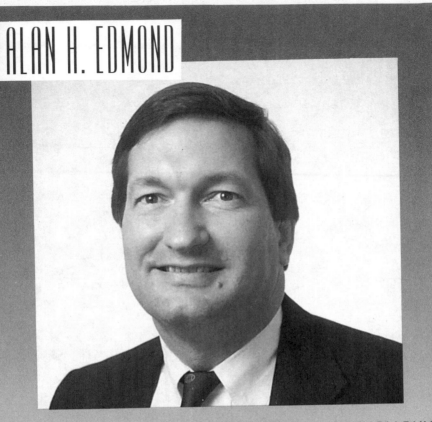

ALAN H. EDMOND

ON SPIRIT AND INITIATIVE

We now face what may be our last chance to save the undisturbed portions of Walden Woods from the intrusions of modern civilization. If this effort fails, boxlike condominiums and an uninspiring example of 1990s office building architecture will further blot a landscape already wounded by a landfill and an aging highway.

This may have been mankind's last hope for salvaging a buffer zone around Tranquility Base, otherwise known as the Walden Reservation. While removed from Walden Pond by hundreds of acres of forest, the long-established man-made intrusions, the condo complex and the office building, would stand for centuries as symbols of a victory of economic avarice over the gentler aspects of preservation; Walden Reservation itself would be hemmed in by the manifestations of the fast dollar.

But, upon reflection, wasn't the preservation effort inevitable, given the current attitudes and energy level of American social and political activists? Perhaps inevitable is too strong a word, but was it not at least highly probable that with the message that Thoreau Country Conservation Alliance president Tom Blanding was sending out about the impending surge toward development, someone with the motivation and resources of

Don Henley would pick up the gauntlet? We might attribute this to the power of television coverage or to the persuasiveness of Thoreau's teachings, but experience tells me that the environmental movement in the United States has progressed to the point where people like Tom Blanding and Don Henley can tap a vein of sentiment and, through hard work and diligence, bring enormous resources to bear upon a preservation effort in a relatively short period of time.

I have assayed this vein of sentiment many times since the Walden Woods Project began. Sitting in restaurants in various parts of the country, I have struck up conversations with a sampling of strangers who appeared to have no particular predisposition about conservation or preservation.

But when the conversation has come around to my place of residence, on most occasions the stranger has responded with "Concord—that's where Walden is!" Further on in this coffee shop discussion, when I've described the lay of the land and the distance of the proposed developments from the shores of Walden Pond itself, the retort quite often has been, "It doesn't matter—you have to stop the development!" This response is widespread, indeed, and must be attributable to more than just a media blitz.

To what, then, do I ascribe the mass movement that has arisen over saving Walden Woods? Does it stem from the craft and emotion through which Don Henley speaks to environmentalists, and music lovers, and philosophers, and teenagers, and you and me, and everyone else who cares at all about environmental symbols? Of course it does, in part. It has been said that all good singers are in love, and it's quite obvious that Don Henley is in love with the teachings of Thoreau and the forested manifestation of his linkage to the transcendental.

Another essential force, more than the power of love, enables Walden to capture imaginations, and it lies in the American spirit. It is elusive, but can be approached with words like "initiative," "self-reliance," "defiance," and "challenge." This spiritual drive and momentum cannot be described the way a tomato or a Chevrolet can be described, for example, but the essential force in the environmental movement in America must be felt in order to be adopted for life. A recent experience poignantly and forcefully brought this home to me.

Inspired by the eloquence and clarity of playwright-president Vaclav Havel, I struck up a working relationship with Czechoslovakia's Velvet Revolution. Invited to speak on the principles of American democracy, I traveled to Prague in January 1991, knowing that the economic, political, and ecological problems I would encounter would be immense and intractable.

On that journey, I learned that interrelated factors—economic and political, among others—had, over many years of socialist rule, created an ecological tragedy that, if somehow allowed to develop here, would cause a reactive mass movement beyond our power to comprehend. But the tragedy has been there for so long, and so extensively, that remediation is going to require not only a renewal in political and economic thought for Czechoslovakians, but is also a renewal of attitudes akin to what I have described above as an "American" phenomenon, roughly defined by initiative, self-reliance, defiance, and challenge. A Tom Blanding and a Don Henley could only offer symbolic leadership on an ephemeral level in a society which has been beaten and mugged by forty-five years of communistic rule following several years of Nazi occupation.

An illustration of this difference in cultural conditioning between democracy and autocracy came to me when I lectured in Pardubice, a city of military industry (where Semtex plastic explosives are produced) which has been ravaged environmentally. Planners in Prague nevertheless hope to transform Pardubice from an obsolescent producer of armaments to a model industrial city with a government fashioned along the lines of an American council/manager municipality system. Transition from making war matériel to peaceful uses of the industrial base will be a goal of this "model city."

I lectured an attentive audience of political science faculty and students, exploring the concepts of volunteerism and decentralized planning as we know them in the United States. The questions were extensive and thoughtful; I discerned an intense desire to know about democratic governance. But I sensed something sad and anxious in the audience, something that blocked a full dialogue between us. Their faces showed a fear of the unfamiliar concepts this American was so freely expounding.

Afterward I was approached by a professor of international affairs who told me in perfect English, "What you say about initiative and self-government is fine in principle, and the examples you give I know to be true. But you must understand that these people have far to go. They will not take on the tasks that government has managed, albeit poorly, all these years. The Communists have stolen their souls."

This brief but insightful description of the Czechoslovakian dilemma moved me. What I have internalized all my life I could not have imagined articulating without this Central European experience of a radically different approach to public affairs and collective action. In this respect, visiting Czechoslovakia put me in contact with the American spirit, as it is felt by individuals, and as it has developed over centuries of struggle and self-analysis, within a constitutional framework that is fiercely defended at all times, at all levels of society.

Perhaps the Walden Woods movement was not inevitable. But the preconditions for its success have developed over the years. In some ways, they are felt more than enunciated, and in many ways, they exist in forums and civic processes we are apt to take for granted. Even in our nation, the call to action inspires some but only heightens anxiety in others. The environmental movement, along with other calls for action and change, will face immense setbacks and the prospect of failure in those parts of the world where the human spirit has been held in bondage. Supporters of the Walden Woods Project know what challenges await us.

▲ ▲ ▲

Alan H. Edmond is Town Manager in Concord, Massachusetts. His government experience began in the Massachusetts Executive Office of Communities and Development.

I was seated by the shore of a small pond, about a mile and a half south of the village of Concord and somewhat higher than it, in the midst of an extensive wood between that town and Lincoln.

WALDEN
HENRY DAVID THOREAU

JOHN NICHOLS

YO, THOREAU!

Thoreau? Who he? I heard the dude had a nice move to the left and a pretty good jump shot from the paint, but *venerate* the old bloke? C'mon, get off it, cut me some slack, wake up and smell the coffee. This is America, land of Palo Verde, home of Stormin' Norman and yellow ribbon ecstasy. We bad, man, and you better believe it—ask Iraq. We dropped the bomb on Saddam, and we don't need no limp-wristed eco-geekos telling us what to do, 'specially not after they been a-mouldering in tomb city for almost a century and a half. Like, yo, Henry D., back off already, chill them jets. A leaf is a leaf is a leaf, and a tree is a tree is a tree. Plus, how the hell you gonna sleep at night with all those frogs honkin' until dawn? Sign up, get with the program! Cut off their legs and feed 'em to the French. Civil disobedience—? Where you been lately, anyway? That trend is history. Take a snort, but don't abort. We had our fill of you prancing aesthetes and nattering nabobs of negativism during Vietnam. Raise a stink nowadays, you get Grenadaed. Keep up the chatter, we send in the Contras. That don't do the trick, it's Panama City, bro. Get real, dweeb, this is *not* an amateur country anymore. We mean business. A new world order. The FBI sez broccoli is illegal. And no more freedom of the Fourth Estate, that was getting lame, said the generals. CIA is a code riff for Mom, Apple Pie, and Chevrolet. In Iacocca we trust, all others pay cash. Didn't you hear the news? It's sex, drugs, and rock 'n' roll, not butterflies and other bogus bugs. When the A-rabs got uppity, we nuked their cotton-pickin' fiefdom and capped a couple hundred thousand of the fang-toothed little fanatics like "shooting fish in a barrel." Moral—? Don't mess with Tio Sam. We mean to win—i.e., it ain't nice to fool with Mother Fascist. And you're liable to get a .357 snout in the snoot from Rambo to boot. Walden Pond—? What's that, a drive-in funeral parlor for widgeons and sticklebacks? Get outta my face, don't be a disgrace! Guns, guts, and glory is what made America great. Cats like you are livin' in a dream, Kareem. I say drain the swamp, kill *all* the alligators, let God sort 'em out. America, love it or leave it . . . and that means you too, Hank. Mellow out, kick back, get a driver's license, a pair of one-way Acapulco shades, a reliable sun-blocker, and a gram of toot. It's all happening, bro—why fight it? Don't forget: The road to Hell is paved with spotted owls and black-capped vireos. And anyway, you had your day. So close the door, batten down the outhouse, say goodbye to all the turtles, it's *our* turn now. Step right up, folks—Walden Estates, look at this nifty little split-level ranch, AC in every room, wall-to-wall Persian lambs from guggle to zatch, and five—count 'em, *five*—flush toilets. Ozone is a state of mind, not to worry; and we still walk a mile for a Camel. Not to mention my honey of a bass boat with a 429 twin-shafted Everglut and a Butterfield and Bascomb trolling motor. They got perch in that puddle you wrote about? Flip in a grenade. Chum it with squid. The suckers wouldn't have a chance. If you hadn't been so bored, Henry, you would of never got in trouble. Hey, we have MTV now, Cinemax, and satellite dishes that can pick up "I Love Lucy" reruns from Mars. You'll love it, buddy—civilization at last. We honk 'cause we love Jesus. And don't dump the Trump, okay? It ain't his fault he got caught short: The jugs will rise again. So bag it with the tweety birds and hoot owls, buster: Them days is dead, that's D-E-A-D, as in finito, kaput, sayonara, Eternity Junction. Progress is Our Most Important Product—like: Sic Semper Distemper!

And out.

P.S.: Earth Day—? Smurf day! Time for you to get a horse, Hank, and catch up to the rest of the West. Don't tell *me* growth for the sake of growth is the ideology of the cancer cell—Edward Abbey's dead.

Oops, I gotta go now, Amigo—smog alert. Too, I forgot my ration card, and they say the turnips arrive at ten.

▲ ▲ ▲

John Nichols is best-known for his *New Mexico Trilogy,* which includes *The Milagro Beanfield War, The Magic Journey* and *The Nirvana Blues.* His other novels include *The Sterile Cuckoo* and *The Wizard of Loneliness.* He has published five nonfiction books, four of which are photoessays using his own pictures. The most recent, *The Sky's the Limit,* is an environmental testament in defense of the earth.

> However mean your life is, meet it and live it; do not shun it and call it hard names. It is not so bad as you are. It looks poorest when you are richest. The fault-finder will find faults even in paradise.
>
> *WALDEN*
> HENRY DAVID THOREAU

MIKE FARRELL

AS POGO SAID...

t's curious. In the search for ways to bring people together to help solve the problems in our environment, I often find myself thinking about Henry David Thoreau, yet when I consider Thoreau I find myself thinking about integrity, commitment, and principle. Curious.

Or is it?

What if integrity, commitment and principle were common ingredients in the lives of all of us rather than the rare oddities they have become? What if political leaders, business leaders, and "opinion makers" were expected to be women and men of principle and were held to a standard consistent with that expectation? Would the social problems we face today be the same? Perhaps. Probably. But would the severity of those problems be the same? Would we likely be closer to or farther away from solutions?

If the answers to these questions are as obvious as I believe them to be, other questions arise. How then, for example, have the citizens of the greatest nation—certainly the greatest power—on the face of the earth allowed themselves to be led into such a situation?

Clearly, there is a great deal of frustration, even more confusion, a growing sense of fear, and a smoldering anger in this country, based upon the gnawing sense that something has gone terribly wrong with the American dream when the air in some of our major cities is polluted to the degree that it is "unhealthful" for children to play outside, when forests are decimated, pesticides and other toxics saturate the land, and many of our rivers, streams, and vast stretches of the oceans are contaminated by sewage, refuse, and industrial waste sufficient to pose a health hazard not only to wildlife but to bathers and to water supplies.

Who is to blame? Certainly technological advances, which offer so many fringe benefits while their environmental depredations are casually dismissed as "trade-offs," as "acceptable risks," deserve more scrutiny. But who sets the agenda for such technological advancement? Who basks in the luxuries afforded by these developments, apparently unaware of, or unconcerned by, any notion of cost?

Certainly the modern-day robber barons, who put the pursuit and attainment of profit above the health and welfare of both the consumer and the worker, deserve our criticism and more. But who buys these products without considering the hidden costs to themselves, the health of their families, loved ones, and communities? Who works in the plants, turning off their sense of personal responsibility as they turn out harmful products or spill-off disastrous by-products?

Local, state, and national leaders whose desire to remain in power overwhelms their ability to discern, much less do, their duty to "promote the general welfare," will be credited no more approvingly by future historians than those other "good Germans" who looked the other way rather than raising the alarm. But who is it that succumbs to the soporific notion, "They know better than I," returning the self-seekers to office time and time again, conveniently forgetting what the term "public servant" implies?

Advertisers and other promotion-specialists, along with their accomplices in the media, who promulgate the nineties equivalent of the notion that "What's good for General Motors is good for America" while failing to credit or report the moral, psychological, and human costs of such an ethos, bear a heavy burden of responsibility. But what of the unquestioning adherent who goes blithely along, assuming goodwill on the part of the proponent?

Integrity, commitment, and a willingness to stand on principle, those characteristics of Henry David Thoreau, are the qualities we find ourselves most often hungering for in our leaders. We continue to harbor the naive belief that individuals who embody these characteristics will come along to point the way out of the woods of pollution and despair, and put us back onto the road toward the realization of an American dream which includes a safe and healthful environment in which each individual can strive toward the fulfillment of his or her potential. And we are right. And we are wrong.

We are right because such people do exist and, given their commitment to principle, would surely be willing to be of service. We are wrong in believing that if we grope around hopefully for long enough they will simply appear magically, like some mythical savior, to do our unspoken bidding. And we are wrong in the hope that they will lead the way.

What is missing in this fantasy is an awareness that the direction must come from us. Integrity, commitment to a system of values, and a willingness to stand on principle can only come from within each of us. Only then will we be able to point the way for our leaders (as it must be done in a democracy), and only then will we have the right to demand such qualities from those whom we designate, temporarily, to lead the way.

The fundamental tenets of our democracy include certain "inalienable rights," most of which many of us can cite, should we choose to do so, by rote. But in our need to keep up with the madding rush of technological advancement, to maintain our sanity under the onslaught of misinformation that threatens to engulf us as it pours forth from the electronic media, to wade through the confusion that results from too many pressures in an over-accelerated society fraught with the unacceptability of being left behind, we lose touch.

Perhaps, like Thoreau, each of us needs to retreat to his or her own Walden Pond in order to get back in touch. Our Waldens don't have to be in Massachusetts; they can be inside us. There, like Thoreau, we can build a cabin of introspection in which to ponder, as he did, questions of personal identity and purpose, of our relationships with each other and the world around us. In doing so, perhaps we can reacquaint ourselves with the sense of joy available through living in harmony with nature. Perhaps we can come to know the power inherent in the recognition of the value and dignity of every living thing.

To approach life, each other, and the problems of our environment, our nation, and our world with a commitment to the principle that the value and dignity of every living being must be respected can provide a platform for the realization of the hopes of all humankind. To maintain the integrity of such a position would require that we demand the leadership we deserve, rather than accept that which is granted us.

In such an environment, the search for ways to bring people together to help solve the problems facing us would be both shorter and happier.

Thoreau would be proud.

▲ ▲ ▲

Mike Farrell, best-known for his role as B.J. Hunnicut in "M*A*S*H" and as host of "The Best of National Geographic Specials," is currently the American spokesperson for CONCERN, an international refugee aid and development organization.

BETTE WOODY

THE LESSONS OF WALDEN

LEAVES FROM A SCRAPBOOK

I start my lesson from Walden with three ideas from Thoreau: simplicity, economy, and government. Simplicity means nature; economy, the law of scarcity; and government, the ways we choose to balance what Thoreau calls the weakness of the majority against the strength of the minority and individual conscience. Countless encounters with Thoreau and Walden teach us the lessons of nature and natural law: how to ration our resources and build our institutions well to keep our treasures safe. There are separate roots to these lessons in my memories of childhood and in my experiences as an adult.

SIMPLICITY AND THE LAW OF NATURE

I do not have to cast too far back to remember the beginning of my awe of nature. My childhood memories are many and clear. They include planting sweet potatoes in the mud and rain when I was three or four, growing a garden a year or two later, nursing an injured owlet back to full flight, and exploring the end of our branch through the pasture to where it widened into Massey's Creek.

I grew up in Ohio, where springs had a special smell of fruit tree blossoms, and in freshly plowed topsoil. Agriculture and the make-believe I invented intertwined to dominate my childhood. The farm lay between small villages; it was composed of bare slopes where corn had scraped away topsoil and my father had replanted with alfalfa and clover. In a low pasture of swampy wetlands, jack-in-the-pulpits and buttercups grew in the spring. The house was an ancient saltbox with a gigantic, timbered, wood barn, three stories high with wooden pegs.

My father was the messenger of the family patriarch, his grandfather, Grandpa Peter—an ex-slave but the richest man in the county, known for his orchards and his secret still and brandy sales. Peter Woody was the prophet of land and trust. My father also brought the new religion from college: conservation. We were mobilized to plant the tiny spruce and pine in the gullies to stop the rain, and the honey locusts on the fencelines to stop the wind from blowing the soil away.

At age four, I probably learned my first lesson: On a rainy spring day, our family planted sweet potatoes; we pulled the tiny plants' stringy roots apart, then pressed each of them into the reddish mud. It was my first memory of the working of land, wind, and water—one to build on forever. Later, I learned another lesson by planting my own garden on a steep, dry slope near a magnificent black walnut tree. Water washed the soil away; the carrots sat on top of the ground and turned greenish in the sun. But the magic of the soil and water made the plants sprout and grow, day by day.

Each summer, it was a wonder for myself and my brothers to trace our branch to its end. It ran clear, sparkling over grey rocks and fresh-water crayfish we caught in buckets and tied on strings. We crossed the wooden bridge that carried the road that divided the farm. The branch ran through the swamp, the pasture and finally on to its end, where it joined the wide Massey's Creek near Cedarville, and then ran further on into the Scioto River and eventually the Ohio River, or so my father said. That was near Portsmouth, where our grandparents lived. We knew the great river and its mysterious flooding; every spring it came and deposited black silt.

Our tiny branch was the base of the explorer's tale. We relived the Indian lore, tracing the pow-wows of the Iroquois Nation of Ononda, Cayuga, and Seneca, and our great Midwestern chief, Tecumseh. James Fenimore Cooper helped us play out Natty Bumppo and Chingachook on the slippery clay that lined the branch until, one day, my father announced that we could no longer wade in the stream; it was dirty and polluted. White scum now sat on the water, the residue of washing tanks that emptied into the stream from a nearby dairy. The stream was dead, and its death marked the end of our wilderness.

ECONOMY

I learned the lesson of economy in cities, when I became a student of urban structure and settlement. But before I discovered the ideal in Michelangelo's Campidolio, that extraordinary *piazza* for the magnificent palace of the Rome Senate, or the Baron Haussmann's Paris, I discovered New York, where the street life creates a dance of life in theater, industry, movement, and art.

At pedestrian level, New York, like all nineteenth-century cities (Paris, San Francisco, London, Copenhagen, Shanghai) is meant to be connected, one part with the other, by walking. The nineteenth-century city is efficient because it can be walked easily, and because the technology—vertical technology, the elevator, the stair—makes it more efficient to move and communicate. But by the 1960s, suddenly, cities were invaded by the automobile and ceased to work. While the automobile destroyed the fabric of the pedestrian and vertical city, greed and profit fed the marketplace, building a stratified society composed of islands and pockets of people: isolated rich, isolated impoverished; multiple small and alienated groups.

The heterogenous mix that defined cosmopolitan and energetic New York rapidly declined. I left New York for Paris and eventually Rome and then North Africa, the new world. When I returned, things had changed dramatically.

Cities provide an urban landscape and economy which satisfies aesthetically and functionally. Paris is the best case for this. Paris is compact and orderly and easily understood; you can walk Paris in a couple of hours from end to end. It is massive, awesome in scale, with its Tuilleries and Grand Palais, yet is small and intimate when you enter the Marais (the beautiful nineteenth-century palace of the kings of France), or the bourgeois Place de Frustenbourg near Delacroix's studio, or the Jardin de Luxembourg, where nannies and old folks watch the puppet show in the sun.

The problem with cities is that the public and civic parts—Paris had gardens and palaces, museums and plazas—have all been destroyed or abused. There is no place to rest or to move. The economy of movement and communication that connects the city places to each other, and to human use, is destroyed. Rome teaches us an ancient lesson: In the colony of Leptis Magna in North Africa, there is an efficient and orderly city; Old Rome, by contrast, is disorderly, jumbled and layered with the indifference of layers of conquests, cultures, ideas, religions and excesses. The Ancient Rome of technological innovation produced roads, bridges, aqueducts, sewers, harbors, and concrete to span space, inventions still used today. But the efficiency and economy of urban space, which balances nature and the natural environment, is not to be found in Rome, where early capitalism overwhelmed and killed the city, as late capitalism is doing in New York today. Leptis, the city by the Mediterranean, was accidentally covered by the Sahara; now uncovered, it is intact, planned (to export olive oil from the hills of Libya), with a magnificent harbor, streets, agora, theater, forum, and residences. Lessons made, then lost over time.

When I returned to New York from Europe in the late 1960s, I was ready to bring lessons to bear on a new environmental balance. I enrolled enthusiastically in Columbia University's School of Architecture to study city planning, and later explored public policy and government roles at MIT. The challenge of the 1960s at Columbia was to respond to the have-nots, to right civil wrongs, and to make an environment for the future. When Columbia was shut down, the planners moved out of Avery Hall and into Harlem and later to the Dominican Republic. A narrow park (Harlem's only open space) was about to be preempted for a gym. "Columbia must be stopped," was the rallying cry from the students. With the Harlem problem out of the way, the automobile became a target; the Urban Underground was born. A small guerilla army of antipollution activists stopped the automobile show with the battle cry, "The streets belong to the people."

The big war, however, was the war on poverty and the war against highways. Students and advocates lined up to press for better housing and a halt to slum clearance. One by one, the interstate highways planned to rip apart urban neighborhoods—Manhattan Expressway; Route 78 in Newark; the San Francisco Embarcadero; the Chicago Cross-town; the Cambridge Innerbelt; I-95 South, and half a dozen others across the nation—were challenged and prevented.

GOVERNMENT

The lessons of Thoreau on government are threefold: That there must be vigilance and care against the "tyranny of the majority," that the minority's rights must be protected, and that individual conscience is indispensable to the cause of peace, as a way to protest the enslavement of men and stop the abuse of power. But I have believed, from my own experience as a public trustee of natural resources, that our government institutions in a democracy are invented by us to serve the common good, to mediate conflict, and to preserve what we value as our treasure, in public trust.

When I became Commissioner of Natural Resources in Massachusetts, I learned that this was one of the oldest offices in the state, and in the United States. In part, its long history echoed Yankee mistrust of capitalism. But in part, it also spoke to the values of the general population that some common land should be preserved for the common good.

In the twentieth century, however, the guardian of public lands faces a very different set of questions: balancing urban need (its spiraling demand for water, land, and air, and its need to refresh itself from an increasingly degraded urban life) against the need for pristine wilderness preservation. In the twentieth century, people have rushed like lemmings to the seaside, to the mountains, and to the lakes, streams, and ponds. This helps to make laws and create institutions of protection. But it also accelerates pressures.

Walden was one of the first tests—along with South Cape Beach in Mashpee and the old waterways and Merrimack shoreline in Lowell—of how to bring about balance between urban need and preservation. Walden has always had a dual mission, I found, charted by Thoreau: to provide the simple lessons of nature, a stop on a pilgrimage to take in the pond, its multiple life forms and its bond to man; and to use it as it was used over and over again by young and old, in the seasons of fall, spring, and summer, for all times.

▲ ▲ ▲

Bette Woody, an environmental planner, is currently a professor of public policy at the University of Massachusetts/Boston, and research associate at the Wellesley College Research Center. She served as Massachusetts State Commissioner of Environmental Management, and as a staff member with Sen. Edward Kennedy. She is a member of the Walden Woods Project Advisory Board.

If a man walk in the woods for love of them half of each day, he is in danger of being regarded as a loafer; but if he spends his whole day as a speculator, shearing off those woods and making earth bald before her time, he is esteemed an industrious and enterprising citizen. As if a town had no interest in its forests but to cut them down!

"LIFE WITHOUT PRINCIPLE"
HENRY DAVID THOREAU

JOHN O'CONNOR

THE AMERICAN PROMISE

did not become an environmentalist by choice. I was forced.

I grew up 150 yards in back of the second largest asbestos producer in the nation. This corporation made a cold-blooded, calculated decision not to tell us what they had known since the 1930s—that their asbestos was killing us. Not only did they dump their asbestos in the lot in my backyard, but they built a baseball diamond on the edge of their dump and sponsored our Little League, which played on the dump.

The most painful experience of my life, beyond burying my own brother, Raymond, and my younger sister, Katie, was attending the funeral of the second baseman on our Little League team. He died of cancer.

The most painful moment was hearing his mother cry out as they lowered his cancer-eaten bones into the grave: "It's not supposed to happen this way. Mothers are not supposed to bury their children."

It was this experience that made me make the vow that we, as a people, could no longer idly stand by and watch as innocent members of the public die unnecessary, horrible, and preventable deaths.

And that's the key: prevention. Remember, we have available solutions to all environmental problems. The real issue is whether we will organize enough people to break the grip that corporate poisoners have over our sacred democracy. And whether we will win the necessary solutions in time.

Win we must, for our time is running out. I probably don't need to point this out, but unless we get organized and change the factory, farm, automobile, and home, we may leave for our children a landscape of death and disease, and a legacy of contaminated air, water, and soil.

Today, our topsoil is being ruined, the earth is heating up, the ozone layer—the planet's protective skin—is being destroyed, and a synthetic toxic chemical film is building up on all biological life. The birth defect rate has doubled in the last twenty-five years, and the leading cause of death from disease for children under ten years old is cancer.

Part of the crisis in the environment is because of our crisis in democracy. Corporate polluters are using large sums of money to literally steal our sacred democracy. Years ago, if you poisoned someone's well or cattle, you were hanged or went to jail. Today, our weak environmental laws—brought to you by Exxon, Chevron, Dow, DuPont, and Union Carbide—say it's okay to poison and kill people as long as profits are made and a few jobs are provided.

We've got the best Congress money can buy. Corporations are purchasing the services of congresspeople and senators to get the permits to continue the poisoning and polluting. And it's not just Congress. The corporate polluters' influence is felt in the White House as well. George Bush says he's a conservation-ist—but he's really a conversationalist. There is so much hot air coming out of his mouth on the environment that the White House atmosphere has become a variation of the greenhouse effect.

During his campaign, the president said he was an environmentalist. He said Boston Harbor was a problem. And then one of his first acts as president was to cut the funding to clean up Boston Harbor.

Today, we should be saying clearly and with one voice that politicians who fail in their duty to protect the people and our environment must be forced from office and replaced by those who will serve the public interest. Simply put, the solution to our environmental crisis is to take democracy back from the big, moneyed polluters and apply it to the detoxification of the nation's economy. Our homes, factories, automobiles, and farms must be fundamentally transformed, weaned away from their fossil fuel and toxic chemical base to a more livable, sustainable, and less poisonous future.

One idea that must be made part of our environmental solution is the establishment of a Superfund for environmental transition. The nation needs at least $11 billion every four years to clean up and prevent environmental damage. As safe products from renewable resources are phased in, we need reductions in dangerous substances, fuels, and technologies. This Superfund would create the development of and the markets for recycled paper, farm systems without poi-sons, photovoltaic cells for safe energy, nontoxic solvents, and electric and safer automobiles, among other things. It would also serve to guarantee new jobs, continuing income, or education to workers who might lose jobs in the transition.

We the people must set the new parameters of the marketplace. Private enterprise is no longer private if it endangers the life of the planet. A few corporations can no longer be allowed to add more poison to our lives. Private gain through environmental pain must be outlawed.

Remember, the laws don't fully protect you or the planet's life support systems. Therefore, until we change those laws in the longer term, we must use our power as organized consumers to pressure corporations to do better than the minimal standards on the books. If every day is to become Earth Day, here is the new deal: If corporations chemically trespass into our lives, we must exercise our right to know about their plants and products, our right to inspect these dangerous facilities, and our right to negotiate as organized citizens directly with corporations for improvements that do better than the current laws.

The great American Indian nations taught us to live as if the next seven generations mattered. We do not inherit the earth from our grandparents; we are borrowing it from our grandchildren. We owe it to our children and our children's children to leave this land in much better shape than it is today.

The promises we have as Americans will go unfulfilled unless we take drastic action to change our economy. I remember the promise of America: "Give me your tired, your poor, your huddled masses yearning to breathe free." Today, the right to breathe is not guaranteed even under the new Clean Air Act. I remember the promise of America that we the people have inalienable rights and among them are "life, liberty, and the pursuit of happiness." Today life, liberty, and the pursuit of happiness may not be possible unless we change industry and agriculture. I remember the promise of America that we were to be a government of, for, and by the people, not of, for, and by the corporations.

To fulfill the great American promise we must take whatever nonviolent act is necessary to guarantee our children's children's survival. If it takes defiance, we will give corporate poisoners defiance. If it takes marches and protests, we will give them marches and protests. And if it takes asserting our rights against their wrongs, we shall do so, because no corporation should be allowed to endanger our children and our planet.

▲ ▲ ▲

John O'Connor is an asbestos victim and co-author of a recent book, *Fighting Toxics.* He is also founder and executive director of the National Toxics Campaign. He is a member of the Walden Woods Project Advisory Board.

JIMMY BUFFETT

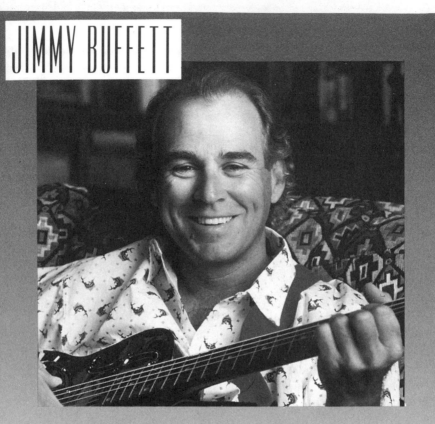

A BOXFUL OF AFRICA

think that we ought to declare a universal "Ten Deep Breaths Day" so that the whole world could stop and everybody just catch his breath. Toward the end of the summer of 1989, I managed to do just that. My idea of a breather was a trip to Africa, where I could spend some quiet time with my daughter before the season of adolescence would swallow her up and make her into a woman, leaving me to ask the question, "Where is my little girl?" Africa seemed to be the right place to spend time with her, out in the bush where the light speed at which the modern world is set on traveling has not quite made its impact. It was a delightful trip, filled, just like life, with ups and downs: beauty, bumpy roads through the black cotton soil, photo after photo of the endless, beautiful vistas of the Abedares, Samburu, Lamu, and the Masai Mara. Lions and tigers and bears. Balloons and baboons. Song and dance and learning Swahili (*Hakuna Matata*). Mosquitos and cheetahs, and souvenirs. Too much stuff for the old duffel bag.

In the six months it took my new belongings to cross the Atlantic and make their way from Africa to South Georgia, major world events became a constant succession of unbelievable stories. It was like a Cubs game, and

Harry Caray would have done the post-game show something like this: "Okay, fans, here's the final wrap-up. Mother Russia, under a new general manager, decided to let the farm teams of Eastern Europe go independent and the game took on a whole new meaning. Romania broke out of a forty-year slump, encouraged by the great late-inning play of their teammates from Germany, Hungary, Czechoslovakia, and Poland. This was after China had decided once again to play hardball to the chagrin of the rest of the teams. We had to take a seventh-inning stretch for Hurricane Hugo and the San Francisco earthquake before winter ball started up in Panama, where General Noriega was traded to the Bush League for an undisclosed amount and players to be named later. Holy Cow."

Holy Cow is right. So much had happened so fast that Africa had become a cherished memory void of dimension. A "thing to do" scratched from the endless list of life, an affirmative response to a question from a reporter or a friend at a party. "Have you ever been to Africa?" I could now nod my head and say yes.

The first of the year, I left the real world and went to the pine woods of South Georgia to be alone. I rode my horse and worked my dogs and thought about the year ahead as I checked my bird feeders to be sure they were full and the snakes hadn't taken over the fast food locations for my birds. Alone in the pines I am just another creature in the woods and I had a flashback to the humility I felt in Africa on a high bluff above the Masai River, where I sipped a gin and tonic and watched the hippos bobbling like big apples up and down in the muddy water and the crocodiles staring at us from the rocks below, knowing that if I fell in, I was just another meal and maybe a smile on the face of a full crocodile. I thought about the day I had watched a three hundred-pound lion paw at our Land Rover as if she wanted to open it up to get to the cat food inside. Africa had reentered my mind.

It was a sign, for when I returned to the house, two huge boxes stood on my front porch. There were smeared letters written in grease pencil with a lot of strange stickers, numbers, and letters, and the words "Kenya-Mombassa-USA" across the side of the boxes, and I attacked them with my Swiss Army knife. Boxes full of T-shirts, carvings, clothing, paintings, jewels, and lots of unnecessary plastic objects (thank you, Nanci Griffith). I put the statues on the table, the paintings on the wall, sorted through the gifts I had brought back for friends, and stared at the tangle of beads, bracelets, and belts which took me most of the afternoon to sort out. I dug down into the bottom of the last box and found what I was looking for. I hopped in the shower, washed quickly so that I could dry off with the dark green towels I had bought at the Mt. Kenya Safari Club. I loved those towels. They were big and fluffy and had elephants and palm trees embroidered on one end. I am a child of the beach and relish the comfort of being wrapped in a big towel, and as I wrapped it around me, I was covered with that wonderful, distant, ancient smell of wood smoke, and my senses came alive with the smells of the bush that had traveled to Georgia in a cardboard box and put me back in touch with the simple world of land, sea, and sky.

▲ ▲ ▲

Jimmy Buffett carries on two careers, as musician (whose hits include "Margaritaville") and author (of the best-selling *Tales from Margaritaville* and of the children's book, *The Jolly Mon*, written with his daughter, Savannah Jane). He is a member of the Walden Woods Project Advisory Board.

> I wish to speak a word for Nature, for absolute freedom and wildness, as contrasted with a freedom and culture merely civil,—to regard man as an inhabitant, or a part and parcel of Nature, rather than a member of society. I wish to make an extreme statement, if so I may make an emphatic one, for there are enough champions of civilization: the minister and the school committee and every one of you will take care of that.
>
> "WALKING"
> HENRY DAVID THOREAU

SENATOR JOHN KERRY

STEWARDS OF THE LAKE AND THE WOODS

When I was growing up in Massachusetts in the 1950s and 1960s, Walden was not yet a cult site for tourists from all over the world. The environmental movement was still a quiet one, and to a young New Englander, some of whose ancestors probably took the side of the good citizens of Concord against the radicalism of Henry David Thoreau, Walden Pond and Walden Woods were very much my own place.

Back then, you could drive or bike up to the site of the pond and wander about the woods, where the stone cairn marking the site of Thoreau's hut stood in its crude glory, and enjoy the casual calm of a place that in spirit had not much changed in the century since Thoreau had packed up his knapsack and moved back to Concord to join—however briefly—the rest of humanity.

The woods then were still rough enough, and quiet enough, for any meditation one might muster. One might occasionally be disturbed by a troop of Boy Scouts in breeches. But as a general matter, the pond did resemble the kind of romantic Eden trod by Wordsworth and the other English Romantics whose tradition Thoreau brought forth to enlightened Americans.

But even thirty years ago, this vision of Walden existed only from certain angles inside the woods and along the pond. Even then, if you wanted to look away from these celestial heights, the boom and hustle of modern America was right there for you on its peripheries.

Just across the road, there was Walden Breezes, a downscale mobile home park, doing solid business for a group of people every bit alive as Thoreau ever was, and producing various kinds of waste that sometimes might accumulate days or weeks before the proprietor could have it all picked up.

There were also postcard and tourist stores, and, as I remember, a growing burden of ever-faster automobiles driven by commuters zipping past Walden on their way to or from work. What had once been dirt was already tarred. What was wood was becoming poured concrete. Concord, once a beacon of civilization unto itself, home to Emerson and the Alcotts, as well as Thoreau, was being transformed into a pleasant place to live for the many whose jobs were in downtown Boston.

And so in this transition period, when teenagers and mothers and children, young couples on the weekend, and families and friends could still come to Walden and just loaf like our good Henry, some of us began to smell the contradiction of Walden's seeming eternity and its unmistakable vulnerability.

War and peace both bring change to the land and waters and air around us. Oil spills, global warming, acid rain, ozone depletion, airborne particulates, sulfides, heavy-metal toxics, polychlorides leached into groundwater—these are as much the byproducts of our civilization as is the beautiful bound volume of Thoreau's *Walden* you may keep cherished in your home library.

As even Henry David Thoreau recognized after a year in the woods, our civilization will not cease to push and prod its way into every corner of the earth simply because any individuals among us choose to live a quieter life. Nature cannot be saved if those who care most about it withdraw to the woods forever.

Thoreau himself became moved to civil disobedience and political activism within Concord after his time of solitude. For me, it is finally that vision of Thoreau—not just child of nature, but also man of the people, both images combined within that one rugged frame—that I hold dearest, and most important.

One of Thoreau's geographic and intellectual neighbors and successors in mid-nineteenth-century Massachusetts was Henry Adams. Adams, heir to the noblesse oblige of one of America's first families, and uncertain of whether he himself could ever live up to his obligations, pondered whether or not mankind was up to the task of adapting to the energy and forces of change that it had itself unleashed.

Adams, distraught by the changes he accurately anticipated, wrote in his autobiography, *The Education of Henry Adams,* that nothing in his education, nothing in his past, provided him with enough wisdom to enable him to meet the challenges that technology had wrought.

The irony of Adams's beautiful autobiography is that, in fact, it was Adams's very sensitivity to the meaning of his American past that made him almost uniquely aware of the need to protect the American heritage and to find a means of enabling it to survive in the environment then emerging.

As the twentieth century comes to a close, the dizzying changes felt by Henry Adams have accelerated. There are times when we despair of our own inability to preserve and protect the things we most cherish from our own childhoods.

But Thoreau and Adams, like John Muir, Ansel Adams, Rachel Carson, and so many others along the way, have left us with not merely a mission, but the markings of a path. That path is the path in which we fear not the future, but insist that the future respect the past.

We did not make Walden what Walden is, but we have endowed this natural place with the weight of our image of it. That image—based on Thoreau's image of Walden, and his writings, and all the writings and images of Walden visitors since, together with our own experience—gives this place a special moral presence in our universe, and that presence gives it a special moral power.

And the truth is, we will need as much moral power as we can find to meet the threats that change and development inevitably bring. As development continues with the immutable push of technological power, we must find within ourselves the moral power to grow and develop as we must—without killing our planet in the process.

Our work together to preserve the Waldens of this earth for the coming generations is quite simply part of the core meaning of our time on earth. If we act as stewards, if we define ourselves not merely as takers but also as preservers and creators and custodians and healers, we will have done something over the course of our lives to improve that which we were given.

Nature in the rough is magnificent, but hazardous for man. Man has not only damaged and deformed nature, but in our multitudinous activity—from horticulture to agriculture to architecture to yes, even development—improved it. It is against our nature to leave the rest of nature alone. Not even Thoreau left things as they were.

If we must change things—and indeed, we must—what we must now learn is to balance the changes with respect for what was, and for what we wish the future to be.

As I write this, mountainous streams of fire are burning in the Middle East, leaving air and sky and sea awash with life-destroying soot. An oil tanker is spilling massive quantites of dark oil into the blue Mediterranean. Alaskan fisheries are still wiped out from the Exxon Valdez. Ever larger holes are being burned in our high-atmospheric ozone, the ecological balance of Antarctica appears threatened by human krill fishing, and the climate of the earth itself may be changing ineradicably because of a mere 150 years of industrial pollution.

So, we do face a challenge.

And even so, Walden Pond's cool waters still beckon us. In Walden Woods, the stones that mark the site of Thoreau's hut remain scattered, but visible, to any passerby who cares to look.

▲ ▲ ▲

John Kerry, United States Senator from Massachusetts, has been instrumental in gaining $100 million in federal aid for the clean-up of Boston Harbor. Since John Kerry was elected lieutenant governor in 1982, he fought to reduce acid rain, through his work on the New England Task Force on Acid Rain. During last year's reauthorization of the Clean Air Act, he sponsored legislation on Acid Rain reduction and fought for stringent regulations. For his service in the U.S. Navy in Vietnam, he received three Purple Hearts, a Bronze Star and a Silver Star. He is an honorary member of the Walden Woods Project Advisory Board.

And this is my home, my native soil; and I am a New-Englander. Of thee, O earth, are my bone and sinew made; to thee, O Sun, am I brother. . . . To this dust my body will gladly return as to its origin. Here I have my habitat. I am of thee.

JOURNAL, NOVEMBER 7, 1851
HENRY DAVID THOREAU

MARIAN THORNTON

"I WOULD FAIN DRINK A DRAUGHT OF NATURE'S SERENITY"

VERSE ONE: BLUEBIRDS, A SYMBOL OF HOPE

A pair of bluebirds has just returned to my meadow from their winter habitat. Which of the two houses in my meadow will they choose? Each bird has inspected both houses; the male has sung a few tentative notes from the rooftops, and all looks hopeful for the summertime, to them and to me.

Bluebirds disappeared from the Concord countryside shortly after I moved here thirty years ago, probably due to fragmentation of their field environment. Last year, however, after years of enjoying the company of swallows and wrens in my bluebird houses, I became aware of a different song and sight. The silhouette was of a slight bird fluttering from the ground to a low branch. As sun broke through the clouds, the bird became an electric *blue!* I was dazzled and pretty darned excited about having bluebirds in my front yard. Beyond that, however, I was also pretty darned excited because these slight birds seemed to indicate more: hope.

Is their return symbolic of a renewed commitment to preserving the natural world? The momentary decline in development activity provides a window of opportunity to secure important open space corridors that can balance human impact. But can we keep that window open, or will we allow it to fall shut, closing out the natural world once more?

Uncertain times like these create a delicate balance, in which intensity and strength of personal commitment can determine the outcome of any project. The positive outcome is the reward; the negative outcome is the unmitigated gall that drives one on to meet other challenges. The fact that we can get opposite outcomes to similar events prompts me to reflect on the consequences of small differences, and the impact of a single person.

VERSE TWO: A WINDOW OF OPPORTUNITY STAYS OPEN

The breeze wicked off the shimmering bay and up through the new green leaves, titillating them into a murmur of delight. The breeze caressed my cheek and the sweet smell of new-mown hay infused my mind, washing away the busyness of the formal lunch I'd just attended. This moment in a summer day auspiciously blended sunlight and zephyr breeze. It was a moment of total satisfaction, the only reward needed for a battle well fought. We laughed, inhaling the sweet smell of success. We stood on a stone wall so integrated with its surroundings that it seemed not a boundary between man and nature, but a natural feature of the New England woods. Through the trees, the house was hardly visible from the bay; its coat of natural colors of wood and stone blended with its surroundings. Even the windowpanes reflected the bay itself.

We rejoiced in the news that this land upon which we stood was to be saved in its natural state in perpetuity as a legacy to future generations, a green umbilical cord to the past. Individuals had felt compelled to argue tenaciously for its preservation, for its worth as open land, for its status as a symbol to people who would never even see it. Not too long ago, there had been another plan for this land. The plan proposed an intrusion of many buildings stuffed onto the land, in a bunch tied by a ribbon of asphalt, licked and stamped with town approvals.

Individual voices pierced and poked through the cloth of confusion and apathy.

Individual voices became clusters of voices, soaring as high as the eagles, and heard worldwide. The window of opportunity was held open by many individuals while nearby the window was closed forever: In a similar time, another opportunity presented itself; a unique piece of land of natural and historic signficance came on the market, with no chance for a bargain sale. . . .

VERSE THREE: THE WINDOW OF OPPORTUNITY IS SHUT

The fall breeze still redolent with harvest swept up the rock-faced hillside with its crown of white pine and hemlock. This furry promontory must have been a natural watchtower for many a red-tailed hawk and many a Musketaquid brave. The panorama of river and fields below left the observer in awe of nature's gifts. As I stood among these trees, I could feel threads to the past weaving me into the fabric of history. Many before me must have stood on this outcrop, this watchtower, alert to activity below, in awe and in quiet contemplation of the passing seasons. From it, I had watched a family of crows knock down a predatory great horned owl, knock him out of the sky down to the field where he stood in utter confusion. Blown out of his perch!

Later that year, I stood in confusion on that same spot, listening to the muffled sounds of dynamite blasting the top off that natural watchtower, "scalping" the natural flora. Newly exposed white rock lay unnaturally in piles resembling heaps of skulls. A haircut had been given to the remaining outcrop as well. Trees lay like matchsticks, in unnatural randomness caused by the cutting tool. With pioneer mentality, the outcrop had been conquered; nature had been overwhelmed. The conqueror had superimposed himself as king, his crown (or crowning blow) an enormous single home for all to see. All had been accomplished professionally and within the law. We have no environmental laws that enforce living in concert with nature.

There is an ache within me. No individual voices raised the alert to protect the historic and environmental fabric of this special place. No individual arms held open the window of opportunity while others rushed in with helping hands, minds and will. From this experience, I realized that victories are sweet, but defeats are the lessons, the eternal reminders, that will provide the energy to fuel the driving force to mobilize individuals and to bring back the bluebirds, that symbol of hope.

▲ ▲ ▲

Marian Thornton is chairman of the Concord Land Conservation Trust, which manages more than five hundred undeveloped acres in Concord, Massachusetts. She founded REUSIT, Inc., a town recycling project, and serves on the boards of The Trustees For Reservations and the Massachusetts Audubon Society. She is a member of the Walden Woods Project Advisory Board.

Measure your health by your sympathy with morning and spring. If there is no response in you to the awakening of nature,—if the prospect of an early morning walk does not banish sleep, if the warble of the first bluebird does not thrill you,—know that the morning and spring of your life are past. Thus may you feel your pulse.

JOURNAL, FEBRUARY 25, 1859
HENRY DAVID THOREAU

PAT RILEY

FOLLOWING DREAMS

In the early seventies, my brother-in-law, Bill Rodstrom, introduced me to the magic of *Walden*. Bill became my link to another time and place and its legacy in our daily lives. He was the seeker and I had an open ear to his quest.

In those unsettled college days, we were ripe for the reading of *Walden*. The philosophy advanced by Thoreau gave us the validation and direction we needed as we sought to define our own life's work. The book wasn't easy reading. It took me three tries before I finally finished it. But for Bill it was the life-changing idea of living alone in a cabin in the woods, reflecting on one's relation to nature and society, that was irresistible. He grew up in the suburbs where nature was something you drove to look at on weekends or vacations, then rushed back pell-mell to seek the hazy comfort of the city. I, on the other hand, grew up in Schenectady, New York, closer to nature and the basketball courts of Central Park. Thoreau painted such an intimate and detailed portrait of "place" in *Walden* that Bill was compelled to see it for himself while I began an insecure, challenging life in a pro-basketball career.

In 1973, Bill was able to take the time off work to make a pilgrimage to Walden Pond. He searched out Roland Wells Robbins, who he knew had discovered Thoreau's cabin site at Walden Pond in 1945. Following Thoreau's description in *Walden,* Robbins built an exact replica of Thoreau's cabin in the woods behind his house in nearby Lincoln. He graciously let Bill stay in the cabin (sparsely furnished with a desk and bed similar to Thoreau's) for several days. As impressionable and reverent as Bill was, he felt the same as if he had been in a great cathedral instead of a tiny ten-by-fifteen-foot cabin. Immersing himself in historic Walden Woods, he tried to imagine the world in which Thoreau lived and the place he loved so dearly. This was a place for contemplation and reflection, where Bill could follow Thoreau's lead and question whether or not we were leading "lives of quiet desperation." Through sharing his experiences, we both drew inspiration from Thoreau so that we could instead chart our own course, so that when we came to die, we would not discover that we "had not lived." This question continues to haunt me as I continue to chart my own course through life.

Bill described his time in Walden Woods and his stay in the cabin as if it were a sanctuary, almost a sacred place. This was a place where the woods and the creatures within were valued for themselves, not just for their use by humans. Walden is the birthplace of wilderness appreciation in the U.S. We owe a lot to Ralph Waldo Emerson for this. He purchased much of the woods around Walden Pond to protect them from the woodcutter's axe. This simple move foreshadowed our National Park system. Emerson also let young Henry live on this land and encouraged him to write. I don't know in whose mind the concept of a benevolent wilderness first brewed, but Thoreau brought forward in *Walden* a "ten commandments" of how to live *with* nature instead of *against* nature. Here was wilderness as tonic instead of wilderness as the dark enemy to be conquered. His mentor, Emerson, may have set the tone of reverence for nature, but Thoreau lived and breathed it. Then, by honing his philosophy so thoroughly in *Walden,* he later influenced generations of naturalists such as John Muir, John Burroughs, Aldo Leopold, Joseph Wood Krutch and others. Emerson was much more famous during Thoreau's day, but it is *Walden* and "Civil Disobedience" that have inspired later naturalists to protect wilderness for its own sake.

Walden also symbolizes a place where people can act according to their hearts, can choose an unorthodox life-style, as Thoreau did. *Walden* is an anthem to individuality and nonconformity—a monument to all those who choose to take a different path or follow the beat of "a different drummer." One passage in the conclusion of *Walden* has given me inspiration and strength for years: "I learned this, at least, by my experiment; that if one advances confidently in the direction of his dreams, and endeavors to live the life which he has imagined, he will meet with a success unexpected in common hours." These words I've used countless times to motivate my players, my motivational speech to audiences, and, mostly, myself. These words have helped me through periods of self-doubt, especially when making major changes in my life's work.

Walden is also the place where civil disobedience had its finest expression. Here Thoreau stood by his convictions and refused to pay the poll tax even when it meant going to jail. With the Vietnam war still raging during our Concord pilgrimage, the concept of civil disobedience took on great personal meaning to Bill while I stayed on my more conservative path. After reviewing the Thoreau cabin's guest book, Bill told me with amazement of the other pilgrims who had stayed in the cabin before, who had come from all over the world to seek this place, including a supreme court justice from India. Thoreau's concept of civil disobedience had influenced Mahatma Gandhi's movement for Indian independence and had come back to Walden. I got a firsthand sense of the worldwide importance of this place.

Bill sauntered around Walden Pond in 1973 and explored Thoreau's favorite haunts in the nearby woods. This included a trip to Brister's Spring (which was still flowing) and to Brister's Hill, both of which are in the area threatened by the Zuckerman development.

What will become of Walden? Bill returned to Walden sixteen years later with his wife Terry to share this special place. They walked around the pond and visited Thoreau's cabin site. Although this time the path around the pond was much more heavily worn from all the foot traffic, the essence of the place remained. But this may not last. Until the historic Walden Woods are protected as park land, the threat of development will be real. I haven't made the journey yet, but I don't have to actually go to Walden if I know that those wild woods are protected for future generations to honor the man that gave so much to us. This place must be protected so that other generations can know that the place that inspired Thoreau is still whole—a place I know I will take my son and daughter to share in this monument of inspiration.

Where would the movements to protect wilderness or the use of civil disobedience to protest injustice be today without Walden?

We owe it to Henry David Thoreau. We owe it to our children. And we owe it to our dreams to preserve this historical place of inspiration.

▲ ▲ ▲

Pat Riley coached the Los Angeles Lakers in four National Basketball Association championship seasons. He is now coach of the New York Knicks.

MICHAEL KENNEDY

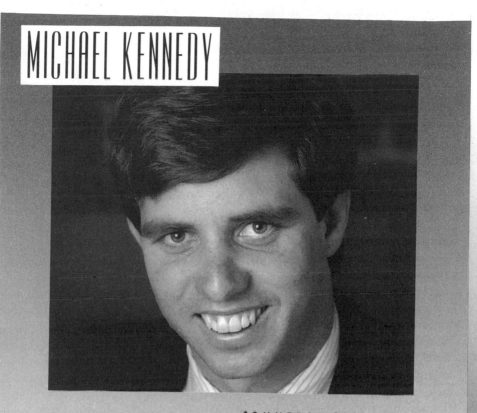

COMMERCE & COMMUNITY:
THE NATURAL PARTNERSHIP

More than a century ago, Henry David Thoreau exhorted man to simplify his life and find truth in his natural surroundings. Writing in the mid–nineteenth century, Thoreau was addressing a community on the threshold of industrialization. The pace of social evolution has surely quickened its step since then, and Western culture is now built squarely and irrevocably on the foundation laid by the Industrial Revolution. As we honor Thoreau for the strength and soundness of his convictions, we must also look for ways to adapt his philosophy of simplicity and self-sufficiency to a vastly different world.

A vast majority of the world's population remains outside the Industrial Revolution. That majority's ancestors never participated in industrialization, and the current generation enjoys none of the last century's "progress." From the tribal villages in the rain forests of South America to the shanty towns of Appalachia, U.S.A., from the teeming cities of sub-Saharan Africa and Latin America to our own inner-city ghettos, human beings are forced to live in poverty and environmental degradation.

It was not until fairly recently in human history that simplicity and harmony with nature were even issues for many of the world's people.

Today, however, rampant industrialization has made the very survival of indigenous populations tenuous at best. Around the globe, the water, land, and air on which they depend has fallen beneath the foot of industrialization. The majority of the world's poor do not own the land on which they live, nor are they empowered to determine how that land is used. They live from day to day at the mercy of forces they cannot control—among other things, famine, disease, and encroaching commercial enterprise.

Economic development—that is, the introduction of commerce and infrastructure and EuroAmerican concepts of community—is not good in and of itself. In fact, the phrase "economic development" would assuredly have been anathema to Thoreau, if it had been current in his day. Thoreau felt that development more often created poverty than progress.

However, it is also certain that, as a pragmatic social activist, he would have been among the first to recognize that we, the beneficiaries of economic development, have an obligation to use the means available to us to effect change for the better. It's not that those of us living in developed communities have found a better way and that we must spread our way of life to the impoverished masses. Today's poor people have been placed in a situation unlike anything in Thoreau's time. The complex, interrelated nature of our world economy and society prevent us from reverting to a preindustrial way of life even if we wanted to. Our planet has a population of more than five billion. Three-quarters of them live in abject poverty. Thoreau was readily able to find a place where he could escape the worst effects of development. But today's poor do not have that luxury. How could we tell twenty million poor people in Mexico City to find a plot of land—a Walden Pond—on which to escape?

In any event, Thoreau did not withdraw from society in order to escape its headaches and problems. His time at Walden Pond was not only a retreat, but also a search for solutions. In fact, his social commentary addressed the multitudes of mankind who faced everyday problems of food, clothing, and shelter. "I do not speak to those who are well employed. . . . But mainly to the mass of men who are discontented," he wrote.

If today's solution to problems of development does not lie in a retreat from civilization, where can we find it? Do we help countries build their economics, raising the standard of living for their people at the expense of the environment? Or do we preserve natural surroundings and neglect the poverty-stricken people that inhabit them? Thoreau advocated a philosophy of peaceful coexistence with nature that I believe we can live with today. Activities that help the poor and that are in tune with nature can and must be conceived and achieved if we are to address the interrelated problems of poverty and environmental degradation. Thoreau was again correct when he wrote, "What is the use of a house if you haven't got a tolerable planet to put it on?"

My brother, Robert Kennedy, Jr., is an environmental lawyer who witnessed firsthand an example of environmental devastation in an underdeveloped nation. While traveling in Ecuador, Bobby saw the immense destruction wrought by international oil companies. Oil rig operators in Ecuador do nothing to carefully dispose of the waste oil that inevitably accompanies the drilling process. Therefore, enormous sludge pits surround the jungle rigs, their contents seeping into the water table. Local Indians are hired to work in the sludge pits. At the end of the day, when the worker emerges covered in slick, black sludge, he is given a kerosene shower to clean him off. You can imagine just how long a worker lasts before he becomes too sick to work. The oil companies then hire new Indians.

In my work as chairman of Citizens Energy Corporation, I have seen many countries rich in natural resources, yet devastated by economic and environmental exploitation and mismanagement. Americans often imagine that the people who live in oil-producing nations must be rich and that their streets must surely be paved with gold. This is sadly not the case. Countries such as Nigeria, Ecuador, Venezuela, the Congo, and Angola have become almost totally dependent on oil export revenues just to maintain their meager standards of living and to remain current with their payments to foreign banks. Just as the United States must have its foreign oil fix, the oil-producing nations of the third world have become addicted to the revenue streams generated by oil. Most of these postcolonial societies lack developed infrastructures upon which to build more diversified economies. Governments in the third world are often left little choice but to turn toward the extractive industries of logging, mining, and oil and natural gas exploration just to keep their countries running.

Citizens Energy Corporation was founded in 1979 to provide energy assistance to the poor, here in the United States and around the world. In addition to our domestic energy assistance programs for the poor, Citizens has conducted programs of technical assistance in many of the oil-producing countries with which we do business. Citizens has established bio-mass and solar energy projects in Central and South America as well as agricultural demonstration projects in West Africa. Here in the U.S., a nonprofit sister company, Citizens Conservation Corporation, has provided energy management services to more than ten thousand low-income apartment dwellers. All of these projects, which are meant to empower the poor, are done thoughtfully and with long-term goals in mind. It is our hope that in some small ways we help provide these people with economic opportunities for today's survival along with tools for building a better tomorrow.

Thoreau addressed his ideas for change to the individual. Today, I address myself to the commercial and governmental institutions of the world. It's time for the international business community to become good corporate citizens of the world and give something back to the communities from whence they derive their economic benefit. Our work at Citizens Energy may not be the answer to the world's problems, but I hope that it is an example of how commerce can work for the betterment of the community and the environment.

Around the world, the tide of economic development will continue to flow. "Progress," if you will, is inevitable. But will it be the kind of progress that puts food in the stomachs of poor people? Will it forge ties of community and understanding between nations? Or will it devastate the landscape and leave people isolated in islands of poverty?

The year is 1991, not 1847. Trying to turn back the clock to a simpler time would be fruitless. We are required to work within the world in which we live, a world of commerce and consumption, hunger and hopelessness. Together, the members of the first and third worlds must forge a new community of man which respects nature and the basic needs of the individual. If we are successful in this effort, all humanity may someday share the simpler, truer life of which Thoreau spoke and perhaps find a bit of Walden in the world around us.

▲ ▲ ▲

Michael Kennedy, son of the late Sen. Robert F. Kennedy, is chairman of Citizens Energy Corporation, which makes energy available and affordable, especially for the poor and elderly. An active member of the boards of the Robert F. Kennedy Memorial, the John F. Kennedy Library Foundation, and the Friends of Boston's Long Island Shelter, he is co-chairman of the Walden Woods Project.

Could a greater miracle take place than for us to look through each other's eyes for an instant?

WALDEN
HENRY DAVID THOREAU

JOHN A. HOYT

IN WILDNESS *IS* THE
PRESERVATION OF THE WORLD

When Henry David Thoreau wrote, "In wildness is the preservation of the world," he eloquently and presciently seized upon a
truth whose relevance to our current ecological crisis we are only
belatedly learning. Indeed, as Thoreau knew, protecting the environment
is essential to our own well-being, and in ruining the world's "wildness,"
we are destroying the natural systems that make life on earth possible.

Although he is now recognized as one of America's best writers and
most creative thinkers, Thoreau's contemporaries largely ignored his writing, dismissing him as an unrealistic idealist, even a crackpot, who vigorously avoided contact with other people. His best known and most
"successful" book, *Walden,* sold only two thousand copies during his
lifetime; *A Week on the Concord and Merrimack Rivers* sold just 215 copies.

"I went to the woods . . . to see if I could not learn what it had to
teach," Thoreau wrote in *Walden.* If today we fail to heed the message
of what he learned in those woods, the future of humanity will truly be
grim, and the "mass of men" will be doomed to truly "lead lives of quiet
desperation."

Deeply ingrained in Thoreau's appreciation of the natural world was a spirituality that perceived the sanctity of nature and saw wildlife and wildness as part of the Creator's handiwork. Thoreau once declared that he believed in the immortality of a pine tree, and in its assurance of ascending to heaven.

From my perspective as a former Presbyterian clergyman, I have serious doubts regarding the immortality of a pine tree. But I do know that pines and other trees allow *us* to attain a kind of immortality, for they help us to live and breathe, and give our species, and others, the ability to "be fruitful and multiply" from generation to generation.

Thoreau correctly saw the elimination of forests and wildlife as a kind of sacrilege, a violation of human stewardship obligations toward the Creation, the desecration of the wildness cathedrals. I appreciate and share with him the feelings of awe and wonder that wildness experiences can generate. Indeed, the Bible and the Judeo-Christian heritage contain a rich tradition of nature appreciation. "The earth is the Lord's and the fullness thereof; the world, and they that dwell therein," observed the psalmist David in Psalm 24. And he exclaimed, in Psalm 19, "The heavens declare the glory of God; and the firmament showeth His handiwork." Psalm 104 declares, "How manifold are thy works, O Lord! In wisdom hast thou made them all; the earth is full of Thy creatures."

The prophet Job, who was a skilled naturalist, advises us to "Stand still and consider the wondrous works of God. . . . The wondrous works of Him who is perfect in knowledge." Thoreau did so, and was inspired to convey a message we would do well to heed today if we wish to have a sustainable and ongoing society.

Were Thoreau alive today, he would be saddened to view the massive destruction we have inflicted on the natural environment he so loved—the profanation, if you will, of God's creation.

But he would also be heartened by the efforts of conservationists, at Walden Woods and worldwide, to stem the carnage and preserve what can be saved for future generations.

In many ways, the fight to preserve Walden Woods represents a struggle taking place around the world—a fight that may determine the future of our beleaguered planet. At Walden, a small but determined group of citizens works tirelessly against overwhelming odds to hold the line against further encroachment on, and to preserve the integrity of, its remaining bit of woods.

Similarly, across the globe, dedicated conservationists are trying to save a bit here, a bit there. But our losses inevitably outnumber our victories. Someday, most of the wilderness, even those parts that we have struggled to preserve, will be gone—forever taking with it much of the potential for the future of generations to come.

As I write these words, and as you read them, tropical rain forests are being cut, burned, and bulldozed at the rate of *one acre every second,* leveling ecosystems essential to the well-being and survival of our civilization.

The trees in these forests absorb carbon dioxide and other pollutants, returning life-giving oxygen to the atmosphere and providing habitat for millions of unique plant and animal species. With fewer trees to absorb the increasing amounts of carbon dioxide we are now generating, global warming accelerates, heating up the atmosphere like a greenhouse. As it reaches dangerously high levels, the polar icecaps will melt, raising sea levels all over the world, which eventually threaten coastal areas on all continents and ultimately, our whole way of life.

Half our prescription drugs come from plants, many from rain forest species. Three-quarters of all anti-cancer drugs are derived from rain forest plants, including the main treatment for childhood leukemia, which is derived from the rare Rosy Periwinkle. In allowing the extinction of unstudied and, in many cases, undiscovered rain forest plants, we may be deprived of numerous cures for cancer and other diseases.

We know that in the wildness of the rain forests lies much of the hope for the preservation of the world, but even this awareness has neither stopped nor even significantly slowed their destruction.

The preservation of wildlife and the protection of animals have been the main focus of The Humane Society of the United States (HSUS), the organization of which I have been president for the last twenty-one years.

Over the centuries, humans have subjected animals to every imaginable kind of abuse—and some that were pretty unimaginable. But in recent years, we have learned that the Bible was correct when it taught us, in Ecclesiastes 3:19, "For that which befalleth the sons of men befalleth beasts, even one thing befalleth them: as the one dieth, so dieth the other . . ."

Clearly, the destruction of so many species of wildlife, and their habitats, has affected the proper functioning of our society, and will have an even more profound impact on future generations. Just as coal miners took canaries into the underground shafts because their sensitivity to poisonous gases caused them to expire while there was still time for the humans to flee, so also should we take heed when we see birds, fish, and other wildlife dying and disappearing all around us; we, too, may be endangered.

Everyone knows that tigers, elephants, and eagles are threatened with extinction. But have you noticed how many fewer butterflies, lightning bugs, and frogs there are today compared to when we were growing up—or just a few years ago?

Acid rain, pesticides, toxic chemicals, and other pollutants not only kill off wildlife but affect the health and lives of humans by damaging and contaminating our environment and food supply. If we allow environmental problems to persist unchecked, they will bring about a drastic decline in the quality of our lives. But by making a few easy, simple changes in our life-styles immediately, we can do much to save our natural heritage of wildness and wildlife, and thereby guarantee our society's security and stability.

For two decades, the HSUS and other conservation and animal protection groups have waged a campaign to persuade the public not to buy fur coats. In the last couple of years we've seen dramatic results. Because American women have largely stopped buying furs, the annual kill of fur-bearing animals by U.S. trappers was reduced by 77 percent in the 1988–89 winter season. This saved the lives of thirteen million animals.

Because American conservationists and consumers have protested the massive killing of dolphins by tuna fishermen, tuna sold in the United States is now largely caught without harming dolphins. Indeed, the major tuna companies proudly proclaim that their cans contain "dolphin safe" tuna. A similar campaign persuaded major cosmetics firms, including Avon and Revlon, to discontinue the painful testing of their products on rabbits and other animals.

So it is possible to make changes for the better, even though the odds are great. We have made tremendous progress in recent years, especially in educating the public about the environmental crisis, and why it is perhaps the most serious crisis our nation has ever faced.

In this last decade of the twentieth century, we are facing what may be our last chance to save our planet. We must immediately turn education into action; we must think globally, and act locally.

There are so many easy, simple things that citizens and consumers can do individually to preserve our environment. Producing aluminum from recycled material uses only 10 percent as much energy as making aluminum from ore. And the energy saved from just one recycled aluminum can is enough to run a television set for three hours. Yet every three months we throw away enough aluminum to rebuild our entire domestic airline fleet.

By using recycled paper and recycling our old newspapers, we preserve trees, save energy, prevent pollution, and fight the greenhouse effect. If just *one* American in ten recycled his newspapers, we could save twenty-five million trees a year. And by recycling our Sunday papers, we could save half a million trees *every week.* Just recycling one Sunday's edition of the *New York Times* would save seventy-five thousand trees.

We can plant trees on our lawns. If every American planted just one tree, over a billion pounds of carbon dioxide and other gases that cause the greenhouse effect would be removed from the atmosphere each year.

And if every commuter car carried just one more passenger, we could save 600,000 gallons of gasoline daily, and prevent twelve million pounds of "greenhouse gases" from entering the atmosphere *every day.*

All this alone won't save the planet. But it would make a good start.

We owe it to our children and grandchildren to let them inherit from us a livable planet. So let's take the easy way out. Because if we don't do these little things now, we're going to have to make some drastic changes and sacrifices in the years ahead. And by then, it may be too late.

Thoreau was right. In wildness *is* the preservation of the world. And in the demise of wildness, it unfortunately appears, may be the dying of our planet.

▲ ▲ ▲

John Hoyt has spent more than twenty years as president of The Humane Society of the United States. He also serves with the World Society for the Protection of Animals, as president of the National Association for Humane and Environmental Education and of the Center for the Respect of Life and Environment, among other animal rights organizations. He is a member of the Walden Woods Project Advisory Board.

But this hunting of the moose merely for the satisfaction of killing him—not even for the sake of his hide—without making any extraordinary exertion or running any risk yourself, is too much like going out by night to some wood-side pasture and shooting your neighbor's horses. These are God's own horses, poor, timid creatures, that will run fast enough as soon as they smell you, though they *are* nine feet high. Joe told us of some hunters who a year or two before had shot down several oxen by night, somewhere in the Maine woods, mistaking them for moose. And so might any of the hunters; and what is the difference in the sport, but the name? In the former case, having killed one of God's and *your own* oxen, you strip off its hide—because that is the common trophy, and, moreover, you have heard that it may be sold for moccasins—cut a steak from its haunches, and leave the huge carcass to smell to heaven for you. It is no better, at least, than to assist at a slaughter-house.

THE MAINE WOODS
HENRY DAVID THOREAU

MICHAEL DORRIS

THREE YARDS

When I was five years old we moved to an old house in the Crescent Hill section of Louisville. The property was oddly shaped for an urban lot, and the backyard measured almost one-third of an acre. It seemed to me then—and still does, in memory—a vast, lumpy expanse, a veldt big enough to plant trees or till a garden or run in a straight line long enough to be winded. The story went that a century before this property had been the city dump, and indeed a bit of digging was always rewarded. Over time I collected worn sherds of blue glass, broken tools, bits and pieces of detritus that, in its bounty if not its perfection, struck me as treasure worth preserving.

The backyard was a place of record, from the spreading oak against whose trunk I stood each birthday for a measuring snapshot, to the clovery dell where I retreated to write in my diary. The geography was generous and precise: a fire pit for burning trash and autumn leaves, a plain on which neighbor children and I staged theatrical performances—our parents assembled on the bleachers of the porch steps, a tangle of my grandmother's roses—a different variety planted every Mother's Day.

Our house wasn't rich, our neighborhood was unremarkable, but I was wealthy with privacy, affluent with quietude. By merely walking out the door I could reach a green island where the sounds of traffic were muted and, when I lay flat upon the earth, clouds were all there was to see.

Much later, in my twenties, I lived alone in a small cabin perched on a bluff overlooking Cook Inlet. I was in Alaska to conduct my first stint of anthropological field work, observing the changes wrought in an Athapascan Native community by the discovery of off-shore oil deposits. Doubly isolated by remote location and by my inability to speak the local language, I spent many hours each day sitting at my table, staring through my one glass window at the grey-blue waters. As the seasons altered, the light changed from day to night and the surface from rough-waved to an opaque frozen marsh that reached all the way east to Kenai.

The ocean is a taciturn companion, giving up less than it takes. At first its sweep drained rather than replenished my enthusiasm: It seemed simply too big, too alien, too beyond calculation. In contrast to the benign, mowed lawn of my childhood lot, this crooked finger of the Pacific was a wall that seemed to separate me from everywhere I wanted to be—until one sunrise when the tide was turning. From that bright, sparkling-smooth mirror shone a single piercing idea: to do something about my loneliness, to initiate a process that eventually resulted in the adoption of my eldest son. Contemplation of the depths had, without my realizing it, reached bottom and become buoyant. Ever after in that spot, whether on cloudy days or sunny, the sea looked familiar as tomorrow, and now, when I cast my thoughts back a quarter century, its face is the one I most clearly recall.

For seventeen years I've lived as an adult with my family in a rambling New England farmhouse fronted by a dirt road that carries little traffic. Our six children have played among the stone fences that transect the property, dodging the thorns of raspberry bushes and hiding from each other behind the weave of grapevines that drape the giant elm. The land, in its known history, has been put to many uses—fed sheep and cows, nourished crops, gone to seed. My wife and I are the latest to be married within its boundaries, in a grove of slender willows.

We have a photograph of our place taken in the nineteenth century. Some of the farm's prior tenants stand in the yard beneath trees that were young to them, but gnarled and ancient to us. They would be surprised and pleased at our improvements: a new pond fed by underwater streams, concrete laid upon the dirt of their basement floor, a second well. But these are superficial changes, scratches on the surface. The smell of alfalfa in August is the same as it was. The wind through the pines sounds just as clean. The rocks still rise through the soil and must be harvested every spring before the furrows are dug.

Wherever we go from here, a part of us will stay rooted in this patch of earth, buried like a cache, ready to be redeemed by memory or by return. Domestication is a product of habit, a series of adjacent yards whose only fences are the limits of imagination, the length and circumference described by a line of sight in any direction.

▲ ▲ ▲

Michael Dorris is author of *The Broken Cord,* a nonfiction book about fetal alcohol damage, and the novels, *A Yellow Raft in Blue Water* and, with his wife, Louise Erdrich, *The Crown of Columbus.*

What are the natural features which make a township handsome—and worth going far to dwell in? A river with its water-falls—meadows, lakes—hills, cliffs or individual rocks, a forest and single ancient trees—such things are beautiful. They have a high use which dollars and cents never represent. If the inhabitants of a town were wise they would seek to preserve these things though at a considerable expense. For such things educate far more than any hired teachers or preachers, or any at present recognized system of school education.

I do not think him fit to be the founder of a state or even of a town who does not foresee the use of these things, but legislates as it were, for oxen chiefly.

It would be worth the while if in each town there were a committee appointed, to see that the beauty of the town received no detriment. If here is the largest boulder in the country, then it should not belong to an individual nor be made into door-steps. In some countries precious metals belong to the crown—so here more precious objects of great natural beauty should belong to the public.

"HUCKLEBERRIES"
HENRY DAVID THOREAU

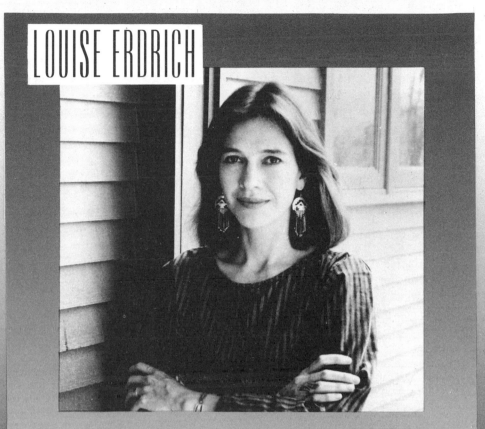

LOUISE ERDRICH

THREE PONDS

The foundation of our old farmhouse was laid right across from a tiny pond that would never be more than four feet deep, a catchall for runoff water with no exit, a stagnant, exciting, sala-mander-breeding kidney of coffee-colored water. Periodically, we've scraped it down to the ledge, hoping that by some miracle the water will clear, maybe a little beach will form, a swimming hole of sorts, but it remains itself—secretive, sprouting quick alder and aspen at its edges. As for pond number two, that's down the hill, on someone else's land, and last night when we went to visit it and listen to the spring peeper's dense electronic whine, we noticed it was in that intermediate stage of develop-ment—it is not quite a pond any more, in fact it is almost past being called a bog. It is nearly dry land, a thick-grown area of cattails and sumac and mud that practically boils with frogs and must attract a number of frog-eaters, judging from the evidence—everything from raccoon and fox tracks to skunk and bear scat. And then, last of all, there is the new pond, the human-made pond, the big, beautiful, new expanse of water that took us such a short time, in the scheme of things, to grow.

Two years ago it was an old field, and that is what it had been for over two centuries. The grass that grew upon it fed the flock of sheep the poorhouse indigent tended, and the cows and horses of the long succession of farmers that did their best with its sloping rubble. The shoots of grass must have been eaten to the quick each summer, the ground picked over for rocks, planted some years. By the time my husband, Michael, bought this farm, it sprouted a crazy tangle of vintage fences, half-sunk concrete water troughs, and the bases to vanished barns. He grew a garden there with scientific accuracy, and courted me with zucchini bread. We had no time for it, though, once we married, and we gardened closer to the house, in smaller beds. The field went to grass, then hay, then goldenrod, asters, burdocks. Finally, one day, we looked at it and we saw water in a trough lit by sun, white birch reflected like fingers—we saw a pond.

It took two years and a lot of heavy equipment before the pond was made. Last year it was completed, and this is its first spring of existence. But in all stages of its making it has been a place that taught us more than we expected to find out about the woods around us, forty acres of second growth, the pines now teenagers at eighty or ninety years.

When it was empty of water, for instance, it was as interesting a place as you'd want to find. As soon as the topsoil was scraped off and piled aside for later, to be replaced like frosting on the built dikes, the killdeer arrived. They laid their eggs in shallow cups in the ground and scissored sharply through the air when anyone stepped too near. In a hiatus of excavation work, as the rains came, they raised their young and then they disappeared. The dozers returned, did their work, and in the dry fall with the streambeds no more than trickles, the tiny pool in the bottom of the pond attracted, from the woods, all of the inhabitants that keep themselves invisible.

First there was the mysteriously large dog track, which was not that of a dog at all, but the print of a coyote. Having once been eradicated from this area, coyotes seemed to have moved north and mixed to some degree with the Canadian gray wolf before they returned in the 1970s, attracted by the plethora of winter killed deer whose numbers had grown even past those which blaze-orange–clad humans could eradicate. There is now an open season on the coyote here, with radio collar hunting legal, and over the door of the local general store the stuffed head of a coyote, its tongue painted pink, snarls feebly at a line of fishing hats. They're shy creatures to begin with, and the snarl is wishful thinking on the part of a hunter. Out here, coyotes have become almost preternaturally elusive, and have even lost their tendency to howl. They have fallen silent, and somehow they have survived. I was delighted to see the track, for I would rather have coyotes in the woods controlling the deer herd than most of the hunters I meet gearing up with coffee and ammo and cheap licenses all November. My windows have been blasted out by hunters, but no coyote has ever leapt through.

Raccoons, hand delicate and spiny, waddled to the water, fat on berries and acorns. A doe, a fawn, traveled down every morning. Three hen turkeys gabbled past occasionally, a blue heron stalked speculatively along the edge of the growing pool, and then, long after most of the local birds had flown south, we saw the lone Canadian goose.

Because they mate for life, and are usually gregarious creatures, this one was obviously in mourning, immersed in a sumptuous sorrow. By night, the great bird bedded in the new-grown rye grass, by day, it surveyed its own personal pond, now filling rapidly with the runoff of fall rains, and it had lots to eat: cracked corn, oatmeal, barley, suet and whole grain bread. Each morning of that long, warmish, sunny, New England fall, we rose in the clear air and checked the goose. And there it was, day after day, its neck an abrupt black periscope. It didn't fly, it didn't swim, it just paced. Back and forth, along the side of the pond; it strode back and forth like any widow or widower trying to out-walk loss.

Then it was gone, and before the grass could even turn from green to brown, the snow came and hid the banks and made the pond a white-on-white sculpture that did not freeze hard, in this oddly warm winter, until about the middle of February, when my parents came and when my father, a man of startling energy, rose just after dawn each day to shovel paths and runways in the packed snow and make of it a temporary maze for skating. And so, for that short time, the pond was a floor, a solid place. Just two weeks after that, the shovel fell through, dark water welled to the surface. Rains came. The ice became a porous slush and then sank in sheets beneath a suddenly warm April sun.

Today, I see my husband at the side of the pond, sitting in a blue chair and reading the paper, and as I look at him and write these words it seems to me that this is what transformations are about. He now sits in a kind of room, an outdoor room, its focus a watery and living place. All night, all day, already, it is filled with the furious barks of wood frogs. Tiny water striders skim the surface. Plants have sunk their roots into the banks. Soon it will be time to garden the pond by adding fish, a bucket or two of trout spry. It is as though the field has been turned upside down, inside out, into its opposite, for where hoofed animals grazed, now fish will rise; where dry bales were cut, now waves lap, and where the ground once absorbed the human glance now it gives back doubled images— dark pines in banks, an old sugarbush of ragged maples, ash, beech, and the butter yellow grass springing thick and sudden.

▲ ▲ ▲

Louise Erdrich has written four novels, *Love Medicine*, *The Beet Queen*, *Tracks* and, with her husband, Michael Dorris, *The Crown of Columbus*. She has also written two volumes of poetry, *Jacklight* and *Baptism of Desire*.

JOHN McALEER

A WALK ON THE GURNET

During the last days of July 1851, Henry Thoreau, visiting Duxbury in his native Massachusetts, fished the waters around the Gurnet and explored the seven miles of pristine beach which stretched from the lighthouse to Green Harbor, where Daniel Webster's rambling estate lunged forward to confront the tribunal of the sea. Within the year, Webster was dead. Today the lighthouse still stands, on the edge now of all that remains of that once formidable promontory known to the Pilgrim fathers as Gurnet's Nose. Soon it will topple into the sea. But the Gurnet remains.

On weekends, throughout the year, setting out from my house on Webster Island, I walk the Gurnet. In the morning, when the tide is right, companioned by a neighbor's German shepherd, who likes to carry smooth stones in his mouth (and insists that I select them), I look at the sea, studying its varying moods. Sometimes I walk after dark with only the stars for companions, or lights which, when the sea is rough, seem to bob like a fairy coronet on the surface of the waves. They are, in fact, no gossamer vision, but the lights that illumine Pilgrim, Plymouth's controversial nuclear installation.

At the start of my journey I look away from the sea wall, which runs parallel to the shoreline for a distance of two miles. Thoreau never saw this wall because it was built only in the present century to protect summer houses which were strung along the beach, bit by bit, year by year, in defiance of the sea. Veritable fortifications, they call to mind Henry Beston's observation that the white man has never truly adapted to this environment but, instead, has occupied it only in a military sense. By an act of will I can discount the wall and its intermittent, bunkerlike access openings. The graffiti that summer visitors have left behind is another matter. SMOKE THE CORN, we are instructed. Elsewhere, a science lesson awaits us: THERE IS NO GRAVITY. THE WORLD SUCKS. Next a philosopher speaks out: WHERE THERE IS NO LOVE, PUT LOVE, AND YOU WILL FIND LOVE. Or a vigilante: WHO WATCHES THE WATCHMAN?

I like the way the sea lodges its protests against the intrusions of man. At one place the wall has been breached by a northeaster. Farther down the beach, the jetty, built to shield the pleasure boats in the marina, shows toothless gaps where the battering rams of coastal gales have lifted five-ton stones out of their settings. Yet, in its contest with the jetty, Nature has received scars too, the intercepted waves have left the beach ribbed with sandbars.

I stop to confer with a young woman who has taken seven Cub Scouts on a nature walk. "It's funny the things they care for," she confides. "There was a clammer. He had to go down a foot for the big clams he got. The boys had questions but he didn't answer them. Maybe he didn't have a license to dig, or thought we had designs on his clamming grounds. They found a dead mackerel gull. And a dead skunk, too. What they relished most were the bones of a blue shark, and the teeth! Whatever was dead, they liked best. I wonder if all boys are like that?"

Not boys only. The night before, in the dusk, I met a man with a metal detector. He had tried to turn away but I didn't take the hint. I told him I'd seen someone the week before passing a detector over graves at Governor Winslow cemetery. "Ghouls!" he said. "Some places they ban it. They dig holes and never fill them up again." Did he ever find anything? "I'm an armchair treasure hunter," he explained. "For anything more you have to go out to the wrecks. Lots of wrecks along this beach in the old days. Not so many in our time." He seemed regretful.

Sometimes I'd walk with Anna. Bruce, her husband, had drowned while white-water rafting in British Columbia, six years past. She was walking Bruce's dog, Velvet. The dog was epileptic and sometimes, she said, had three or four seizures in a single night, and she'd jump up out of her sleep to help him. "You see, he was Bruce's dog," she reminded me. She carried rubber gloves and plastic bags on the chance that Velvet relieved himself on the beach. "It's not nice to soil the beach," she'd tell him, and then she'd put the results in a bag to throw into a trash container. Even if he furtively sought the dunes, she cleaned up after him. As an environmentalist, she was one of a kind. Other clean-up types came too, sometimes all in a group. They dangled heavy-duty green trash bags and gathered up every alien object in sight, even clamshells. Yet afterward, they ran their dune buggies through the dunes. "Thanks to us," they said, "the place looks transformed now." And so it did. The poverty grass never looked so down and out.

Another Gurnet regular is old Earl. He is a green-bagger, also, but a specialist. "I pick up beer cans," he told me. "The redeemable ones only. That's how I pay for the parking sticker I need to leave my car in public parking." I pointed to signs that promised heavy fines for those bringing beer onto the beach. "Cans float in on every tide," he said. "Fishermen throw them overboard. Duck hunters, too. Drinking is the biggest part of their sport." We heard sounds like muffled firecrackers, carrying a distance across the water. "They're out there now, shooting at ducks," he said. "Half the time they're so far out, or far in the bag, they never see where their ducks fall. When I was young we killed birds for food. That big expanse of rock at Brant Rock, the rock that gives the place its name, was where the brants were. None there now. Hasn't been since Depression times in the thirties. A lot of people must have been hungry then because brants are an oily bird and as tough to chew as rawhide."

At Powder Point I stopped to look at a gathering of gulls, mostly ringnecks, the ones some people call priest gulls because of their collars. They were scavanging at the water's edge. I was surprised to see what looked like a fledgling among them, then saw it was a duck. He sensed my interest and ran into the surf, swamped by the waves breaking over him. One wing hung limp but he wouldn't let me help him. When I came back that way an hour later I looked for him. The gulls were gone and so was he. But then I saw him above the tide-wrack, where he had crawled up among heaped stones exposed by the spring tides. He let me pick him up now. His neck had been creased by a bullet, the flesh harshly abraded, his right wing blood-drenched. With a handkerchief I cleaned his wound and closed it as well as I could. I carried him, cradled in enfolded hands, back to Webster Island, talking to him cooingly all the way. I'd protected him from dogs that run the beach, given him water, a handful of blueberries, and a downy bed lined with sweet grass. What next? I wasn't sure. At least he knew some other living creature understood his plight. I pitied the plight of all birds shot wantonly out of the sky. He drank some water but an hour later, when I went to see how he fared, I saw he had fallen into the bowl and drowned in it. The water was pinkish from the blood that washed from his wound. So far as I could tell, my efforts had counted for nothing—or worse.

But that night, as I walked along the beach at water's edge, I saw two wavering ribbons of geese, tapering their flight against the smudges of twilight, courageously unfurling in the torment of the winds that bucked their progress. I looked up at the pinpricks of stars as they appeared and remembered Thoreau's observation that darkness is necessary if we are to see the light of heaven. I needed this darkness, this graphic sense of man's depredations of Nature, to shame me to a fuller awareness of the benefactions Nature bestows on us.

The Gurnet that Thoreau knew is not now as he beheld it. Far from it. But the sea still beats upon the shore and caring mortals, with fumbling assurance, still come there hoping to do what they can to assist Nature's efforts to restore this plundered planet.

HOMAGE

When the sky itself will bend to kiss
The hem of dear Earth's tattered robe,
Take heed!
If heaven stoops to reverence Earth,
Can we, as men who came from dust,
Forbear to show a kindred trust?

▲ ▲ ▲

John McAleer was befriended by Mahatma Gandhi while serving in the U.S. Army in India during World War II, and became a student of Emerson and Thoreau. He has been a professor at Boston College since 1965. His sixteen books include *Artists and Citizen Thoreau* and *The Matter of the Red Man in American Literature.* He is past president and current director of the Thoreau Society, and a member of the Advisory Board of the Walden Woods Project.

The ocean is but a larger lake.

CAPE COD
HENRY DAVID THOREAU

JACK NICHOLSON

SOLAR ELECTRICITY

Somewhere back in the sixties or early seventies, when utopian ideas seemed somehow more pragmatic or at least possible, I was lured to a chain-linked hilltop commune high in the Santa Monica Mountains. What had attracted me was a friend telling me that this group of young science-oriented people, led by a man purported to be Joseph Heller's pilot in World War II (in my book, this made him Yossarian), were working on some ideas that would revolutionize the world by practical application of solar electricity. The group had an idea that since the NASA program had used photovoltaic solar batteries as source electrical power in its launches, solar electricity, if made cost efficient, could generate enough electric power (an unlimited amount, actually) to convert H_2O to hydrogen which could then replace petroleum as a fuel base for automobiles, and, of course, many other things. The concept was reinforced by the fact that almost any current internal combustion engine could be converted to run on hydrogen for roughly $300. I later saw a demonstration of such a car, and was filmed for television inhaling the exhaust of this engine which was, of course, pure steam, or water from which the hydrogen had originally come. Which brings me to the gap between hard physical science and public relations.

Good ideas sometimes get lost; they also get rediscovered. Man's first real good idea, you might say his first technological leap, happened around two million years ago with the use of stones for tools and weapons. From the use of stones, it took a million and a half years before man's next big idea became a techno leap: making fire.

On a planet with a rapidly dwindling supply of wood, there are two billion people burning it to make their meals. That's half of the world's annual wood harvest—going up in cooking smoke. This fuel problem has been around for quite a while. About 2,400 years ago, the Greeks had virtually burned up all their forests in order to warm their houses and cook their meals. A few hundred years later, the Romans would do the same thing.

But the Greeks, followed by the Romans, solved that problem. They sent their ships up to a thousand miles away to bring back wood from places that had it. Some of the local denizens of targeted forests probably resented the foreigners taking their wood. The smart ones probably tried to sell it, the stubborn ones fought to protect it. Some folks back in Greece thought the loss of life wasn't worth it. "No Blood For Wood." There had to be another way to keep their homes warm. There was. The first use of solar energy became a technological idea.

The Greeks, followed by the Romans, designed planned communities with streets and buildings facing south to take advantage of the sun's warmth to heat their homes. They introduced architectural innovations that allowed the low-slanting winter sun in, but kept the too-hot overhead summer sun out.

The use of solar energy disappeared during the Dark and Middle Ages. During the Renaissance, some fertile minds began to tinker with the idea again. The Industrial Age produced some innovators that did more than just tinker.

In 1839, it was discovered that sunlight could produce electricity. (Experiments in electricity had been going on for over a hundred years, so what it was and how it worked was well-known.)

In the 1860s and '70s, a French inventor named Augustin Mouchot developed a solar motor that could pump water, distill alcohol, cook food, pasteurize wine, and make ice.

In the same era, John Ericsson, an American engineer and designer of the ironclad Civil War battleship The Monitor, prophesied that the development of solar power would avert an eventual global fuel crisis.

In 1888, Charles Fritts, an American inventor, made the first solar cells. These small, thin, selenium wafers could generate an electrical current when struck by sunlight.

Then, after the Second World War, the U.S. space program, as previously mentioned, discovered that solar cells were the lightest and most compact power source available to supply the energy required for satellites in space.

We came to the modern photovoltaic cell. Photo means light, voltaic refers to electric. A photovoltaic cell is a semiconductor device that is capable of transforming sunlight energy (photons) into electrical energy (electrons). Conveniently, the PV cell is not made of some rare and exotic material that would make price and availability a problem. The primary ingredient of most photovoltaic cells is silicon. Silicon is made from silica. Silica is a hard, glassy mineral found in quartz and sand. Since silica is the primary constituent of more than 95 percent of the rocks on Earth, it is therefore one of the most abundant elements in existence.

The belief of this sixties Santa Monica group was that the large petroleum interests were more than willing, in fact, they encouraged studies, discussions, press releases, etc. about solar energy. The reason for this, however, was only to confuse and distract public attention from the real revolutionary concepts of solar electricity. Solar electricity is a term which I had never seen mentioned in mass media and wouldn't until the inauguration of Jimmy Carter, the only president ever to allocate federal spending specifically for solar-electrical study, which was not administered by the petroleum industry.

Then Ronald Reagan became the new president. His first move was to tear down the solar panels that Carter had installed on the roof of the White House. His second act of leadership was to have the Department of Energy cut the funds and tax incentives for solar exploration and development. Reagan liked nuclear. George Bush, an old oil man and nuclear advocate, has followed his mentor's lead.

Further study of the funding of this issue logically produced the theory that since there were no jobs outside of a small group of solid state physicists at Eastman Kodak, which had some investment in photovoltaics for use in light meters for cameras, there was no professional exploration of the principal application of solar electrical principle. No avenue open to the thousands of solid state physicists, engineers, etc. who graduate annually from our universities. They could teach the ideas, but had nowhere to apply them.

We vacillate about our environment because every meaning has a little movement all its own. We don't correlate. There are green groups for everything. Some want to save rain forests, whales, redwoods, dolphins, the ozone layer, national monuments, and on and on.

The result of this shotgun consciousness is lack of focus in the murky waters of the debate concerning the health of our world. Henry David Thoreau said, in the first chapter of *Walden*: "One generation abandons the enterprises of another like stranded vessels." The stranded vessels that this generation is about to abandon are the dangerous and nonrenewable sources of energy that previous generations sailed by. Thoreau concluded *Walden* with three profoundly simple lines: "Only that day dawns to which we are awake. There is more day to dawn. The sun is but a morning star."

No issue is more compelling than the air we breathe, be it hot or cold, be it hawk or human. The idea of hydrogen-powered economy, with solar electricity as the fulcrum, immediately purifies the air we breathe and returns to the atmosphere the element, water, from which the hydrogen is drawn. It is only cost and applied engineering that stands between the world and a pure and limitless energy supply. The magic has already occurred. Now it's up to us.

Solar electricity. Solar electricity. Solar electricity. There. I've said it again.

AUTHOR'S NOTE John Hackett is gratefully acknowledged for his assistance in researching this chapter.

▲ ▲ ▲

Jack Nicholson is a film actor and director who is presently living in Los Angeles, California.

> If one listens to the faintest but constant suggestions of his genius, which are certainly true, he sees not to what extremes, or even insanity, it may lead him; and yet that way, as he grows more resolute and faithful, his road lies. The faintest assured objection which one healthy man feels will at length prevail over the arguments and customs of mankind. No man ever followed his genius till it misled him. Though the result were bodily weakness, yet perhaps no one can say that the consequences were to be regretted, for these were a life in conformity to higher principles. If the day and the night are such that you greet them with joy, and life emits a fragrance like flowers and sweet-scented herbs, is more elastic, more starry, more immortal,—that is your success. All nature is your congratulation, and you have cause momentarily to bless yourself. The greatest gains and values are farthest from being appreciated. We easily come to doubt if they exist. We soon forget them. They are the highest reality. Perhaps the facts most astounding and most real are never communicated by man to man. The true harvest of my daily life is somewhat as intangible and indescribable as the tints of morning or evening. It is a little star-dust caught, a segment of the rainbow which I have clutched.
>
> *WALDEN*
> HENRY DAVID THOREAU

KATHI ANDERSON

A RIVER AND A POND

t's springtime at Walden—my favorite time of year. The tiny leaves on the oak trees are just beginning to open up. A flock of red-wing blackbirds clustered in a nearby pitch pine is noisily squawking while the spring peepers are engaged in a lighthearted chorus of their own. A warm breeze catches the rays of the sun, turning the surface of the water into a million sparkling diamonds.

I slowly make my way along the trail that encircles the pond and leads to Thoreau's Cove. It was here, in 1845, that Henry David Thoreau built his small cabin and began to chronicle his two years and two months of residence at Walden Pond in what has become one of the greatest literary masterpieces of all time.

Thoreau's cabin has long since disappeared, but it is marked by a series of sturdy granite posts with an interlocking chain. Nearby lies an enormous cairn. Stones of all shapes and sizes have been placed here by visitors to Walden through the years—people from across the world who added a stone to the pile in a humble gesture of respect for the man whose literature and philosophy inspires and endures nearly 130 years after his death.

A slight incline leads from the pine forest surrounding the cabin site down to the pond. There's a young child perched at the water's edge whose attention has been captured by a small minnow swimming only inches from the shore. The minnow pauses, suspended in liquid space, then darts away with a sudden swish of its tail. Elusive, these little fish—a useful trait, since it permits some of them to become big fish. The little boy squeals with delight and runs to tell his mother about the great discovery he's made.

Alone now with my thoughts, the vision of the child and the minnow have conjured scenes of my own childhood. My fascination with nature began very young; my fondest memories relate to the outdoors and to wildlife. They have been a guiding force throughout my life, and I think they have brought me to Walden, just as Walden brings them back to me.

I remember sitting on a stone wall staring into the water, mesmerized by a school of "shiners." Only about two inches long, these fish generate a bright flash of silver when they turn on their sides. It seems like there are thousands of them swimming, shining, just below my feet, which are dangling precariously over the edge of the wall. The tide is unusually high and almost touches my toes. I am very tall for a ten-year-old.

It's early evening, and the full moon is beginning to rise over the hills across the river. I take a deep breath of salt air, which fills my lungs with an aroma more overpowering than the profusion of lilacs which grace the backyard. I glance over my shoulder to see my mother turn on the porch light—a signal that it's nearly time for me to go inside.

Our summer house is not very large. In fact, it's really only a cottage— somewhat more spacious than Thoreau's cabin, but not much—five simple rooms, no telephone. These things aren't important. What is important is that our cottage is surrounded by some of the most breathtaking beauty that nature can offer. The Westport River in the 1960s: My own definition of paradise.

I rise from my vantage point on the wall and walk out on the dock, which extends about fifty feet from the shoreline. Peering between the wood slats, I see the rocks below, which are covered with seaweed, creating a haven for mussels, eels, and an abundance of periwinkles and hermit crabs. The seaweed that grows on the rocks is long and stringy, with air-filled chambers interspersed along its length. They make a loud pop when you squeeze them, not unlike the bubble-wrap that envelops fragile packages.

Perched at the end of the pier is a lone seagull who has claimed this territory as his own. We've named him Sammy. He has an insatiable appetite for fish heads and other unsavory entrails discarded during the process of cleaning the striped bass and bluefish my father brings home after a day of sport fishing off Cuttyhunk Island. Sammy's blessed with a keen sense of aim. At least once a week, he leaves his calling card on the bow of our boat.

As night falls, I return to the cottage. Lying in bed, the sounds of summer fill my head. In the complete absence of cars, people, and similar distractions of civilization, the nonhuman world of the river comes alive. Crickets, tree toads, and the occasional whippoorwill fill the twilight air with their song. The June bugs hum and buzz against the screen of the window. In the distance, I can hear the periodic plop of a fish breaching the water as it attempts to escape the jaws of a larger predator. In the silence, the overpowering noise of nature lulls me to sleep.

A new day begins with the arrival of the neighbor's two cocker spaniels, looking for a handout. They are rarely disappointed by mother's abundant assortment of refrigerated leftovers.

We stockpile a collection of our own edibles into the cooler and load it into the wooden skiff. It's mid-morning, and the tide is receding rapidly. We push the skiff into the shallows and row out to deeper water. My father starts the small, five-horse motor and the boat skims across the surface. Careful not to stray from the depths of the channel, he chooses a route that takes us into the middle of the river near a series of small islands. The rocky shore leads up to a collage of gnarled undergrowth interspersed with tall pines. Atop the highest branch of the tallest tree sits a magnificent osprey. These islands are one of the few remaining habitats for these birds, nearly driven to extinction by the haphazard and uncontrolled application of DDT. The osprey holds a fish in its talons; it's perched near an enormous nest, which likely houses a set of hungry mouths.

We move downriver to our destination—a shallow, muddy area where there is an abundance of quahogs. These large clams live just below the surface of the mud. We climb over the side of the boat and lower ourselves into the cool water. It's so shallow here that the water barely covers my knees. The eel grass is very thick. It tickles as it sweeps past my legs while I walk along. Sinking up to my ankles in the mud, I cling firmly to the side of the boat, pushing it ahead of me as I walk. Feeling for quahogs with the soles of my feet, I am frequently rewarded by the touch of a smooth, round firmness in the soft mud. Reaching down into the water up to my shoulder, I retrieve the prize and place it along with its companions in a pile in the bow of the boat.

Suddenly, my father lets out a loud yelp and yanks his foot out of the water. Firmly attached to his big toe is the claw of one of the largest blue crabs I have ever seen. Tenacity is this crab's middle name. It's not about to let go. Its free claw jerks wildly back and forth, snapping, searching for another victim. Finally, with a swift movement of his leg, my father hits the crab (and his foot) against the side of the boat, probably inflicting more pain on his foot than on the crab. Momentarily stunned, but essentially undaunted, the crab relaxes the grip of its pincers and drops into the water. It scurries off, moving along in its uniquely crablike way.

We return with five dozen quahogs. The shells of the largest ones will be filled with quahog stuffing (a spicy blend of seasonings, sausage, bread crumbs, and chopped quahogs), then tied shut with string and baked to a crispy delight. The smaller ones will be made into a delicious chowder.

Suddenly, a movement along one of the trails leading into Walden Woods jolts me back to the present. It's an older couple, walking silently, arm in arm, lost in their thoughts. They remind me of my parents. I wonder what memories Walden has summoned for them.

And what special memories of Walden will the child with the minnow take away with him?

I've heard that you can no longer take quahogs from many parts of the Westport River. Septic runoff from overdevelopment along the river and the use of pesticides and herbicides have contaminated the shellfish beds. The blue crabs are less abundant now. Even the eel grass is dying off. Nights on the river are filled with the sounds of speedboats and jet skis.

I return from Thoreau's Cove along the same winding path I took to get there. But what path will we choose to follow at Walden? Will we take the course that we have selected so many times before? Or will we choose a new direction—a tougher road, perhaps, but one that holds for us a greater and more enduring reward?

Continuing along the path, I look ahead and notice that I am following in the footsteps of the older couple. Several paces behind me comes the young child with his parents, still smiling from his first experience with nature.

▲ ▲ ▲

Kathi Anderson, now the executive director of the Walden Woods Project, previously served on Senator Edward Kennedy's legislative staff for thirteen years.

Our village life would stagnate if it were not for the unexplored forests and meadows which surround it. We need the tonic of wildness.

WALDEN

GREGORY PECK

WALDEN WOODS: A SACRED TRUST

When I was a student attending the University of California at Berkeley, I read a considerable amount of Thoreau and Emerson. Despite the good-natured, but relentless, raillery of my companions, I doggedly pursued a degree in English literature (referred to by my slide rule-toting friends as a degree in "bullshit"). I couldn't read enough of the New England Transcendentalists. I was amazed that so much wisdom could have emanated from the same small Massachusetts town.

Much has changed in California since my days at UC Berkeley, and much of it has not changed for the better. Unlike those who recently transplanted themselves to the West Coast, I am a native Californian, so I remember a time when there were no smog alerts, when the freeways were not jammed with automobiles, when the coastline near Los Angeles was not marred by wall-to-wall development.

Well over a century ago, Thoreau wrote that "there is a subtle magnetism in Nature, which, if we unconsciously yield to it, will direct us aright. It is not indifferent to us which way we walk. There is a right way, but we are very liable from heedlessness and stupidity to take the wrong one." How right he was. On far too many occasions it seems we have ignored our instincts or have deliberately chosen the wrong path because it was more convenient or less strenuous.

Thoreau, Emerson, and their transcendentalist contemporaries predicted with frightening accuracy the difficult choices which would ultimately confront humankind. They foresaw the damage that would be wrought upon the environment should we fail to strike a delicate balance with nature. Emerson said, "To the senses and the unrenewed understanding, belongs a sort of instinctive belief in the absolute existence of nature. In their view, man and nature are indissolubly joined."

The failure to recognize our unalterable link to the natural world has resulted in an onslaught of environmental degradation. The ramifications of our relentless assault on nature are staggering:

- Ninety percent of our Pacific Northwest's ancient forests have been cut.
- The tropical rain forests are disappearing at the unfathomable equivalent of one football field per second.
- The earth's atmosphere is being depleted of its protective ozone layer at twice the rate which scientists predicted. During the next fifty years, over twelve million Americans will develop skin cancer and over 200,000 will die.
- Over one hundred endangered species of plant and animal life are becoming extinct each day.
- The United States is losing one to one-and-a-half million acres of farmland each year to nonagricultural use.
- Thousands of lakes in the eastern United States—including at least 10 percent of all those in the Adirondack Mountains—are too acidic to support fish. Acid rain research has implicated airborne sulfates in at least fifty thousand premature deaths each year.

The root cause of many of these critical environmental problems can be traced back to rapid and indiscriminate overdevelopment. I suggest that the time has come for us to reevaluate our priorities to determine whether that new shopping mall down the street is worth the destruction of twenty acres of wetlands; whether that new hotel downtown will place too high a demand on our drinking water supply; whether that new high-rise will overburden our sewage systems; whether that new office park will destroy too many acres of forest.

I am not proposing that we call a halt to all forms of development. On the contrary, there is a need for growth; but that growth must be conducted in a selective fashion with careful evaluation. It can no longer be achieved at the expense of the environment.

Development projects have not only had a deleterious impact on environmentally sensitive areas, but also threaten sites which hold historic significance. From the battlefields at Gettysburg, Manassas, and Fredericksburg to the woods around Walden Pond, condominiums, shopping centers and office buildings are eroding our national heritage. It is evident that our nation—whose heritage is briefer than most—has not yet fully realized the value of historic preservation. Americans don't walk on a Great Wall which was built by our ancestors over two thousand years ago. We don't gaze upon the magnificent Taj Mahal constructed in 1648, or upon the great pyramids built under the reign of the pharaohs in 2200 B.C. We believe that our national treasures will always be there for future generations—that the loss of an historic site here or there won't really matter.

Nothing could be further from the truth. If we begin to haphazardly surrender our Waldens to the greed of developers, we will be letting our history slip away like so many grains of sand through our fingers. It will disappear gradually, undetectably, until one day we will realize our folly and it will be too late. Neither the environment nor our national heritage can be recreated or rebuilt. It endures only through careful and conscientious stewardship. It is a sacred trust.

"When we walk, we naturally go to the fields and woods: what would become of us, if we walked only in a garden or a mall?" (Henry David Thoreau, "Walking")

▲ ▲ ▲

Gregory Peck won an Academy Award for his work in *To Kill A Mockingbird*, and has received four other Oscar nominations for his more than fifty motion picture roles. He received the American Film Institute's Lifetime Achievement Award in 1989. In addition to acting, Mr. Peck has produced or co-produced such films as *To Kill A Mockingbird, The Guns of Navarone,* and *Captain Newman, M.D.*

In September or October, Walden is a perfect forest mirror, set round with stones as precious to my eye as if fewer or rarer. Nothing so fair, so pure, and at the same time so large, as a lake, perchance, lies on the surface of the earth.

WALDEN
HENRY DAVID THOREAU

JIM HIGHTOWER

BACK TO THE GRASSROOTS

People have the power.
The power to dream,
            to rule,
            to wrestle the world from fools.

                        Patti Smith, "People Have the Power"

What is our national environmental policy?

It's always fun to ask your member of Congress, because, no matter how convoluted the answer, the obvious quickly becomes apparent: We don't have a policy.

Oh, sure, there are environmental agencies and laws, programs and regulations, commissions and studies, but they are pouring out more foam than beer. They do not add up to a comprehensive and determined commitment at the top to *just do it*, to stop the pollution.

Absent this, the polluters and their arsenal of lawyers, lobbyists, PACs, and PR flacks are able to wind in and out of the process, tying environmental enforcement into knots.

Instead of action, we get delays, hedging, circumvention, obfuscation, deception . . . and more pollution. We get George Bush saying with a straight face that America must go slow on any plan to prevent global warming, and we get the Congress cooking up a backroom consensus with polluters on legislation to reduce toxic air pollution.

We know from experience that "go slow" and "consensus" are artful dodges for protecting profits and preserving the status quo. And, as a farmer friend of mine put it, "status quo" is Latin for "the mess we're in."

The good news is that a huge majority of Americans are growing restive with the half-steps and rationalizations of their leaders. A recent *New York Times* poll found that 84 percent of the people believe pollution is serious and getting worse, 71 percent want action to protect the environment even if this requires more government spending and higher taxes, and 74 percent say that the environment is so important that improvements must be made, regardless of cost.

No longer is environmentalism the domain of balloon-flying ex-hippies and Republican bird-watchers. It has become a personal cause of the workaday majority:

• people who pack up their families for a day at the lake or the local springs, only to find they can't let their kids go into the water because it has been contaminated by upstream development;

• suburbanites living in modest homes in distant housing developments who notice that their roses died after neighboring cotton fields were sprayed for the eighth time this year, that their cat got sick about the same time, and that their children have developed unusual rashes;

• farmers who increasingly worry about what these chemicals really are, what they're doing to the horned toads and whippoorwills that used to abound, what they're doing to the soil and water, and what they're doing to their own families' health;

• workers in petrochemical plants who learn that their life will be ten years shorter than normal because of the toxicity of their workplace, even as the top bosses of their corporation are trying to bust their union, cut their health plan, and loot their pension fund.

To put the environment of us all over the profits of a few, we must reach out to people like these. We can tap not only into their anger at "the mess we're in," but also into their vision of what could be, rallying them into a powerful grassroots political alliance for the environment.

My Aunt Eula, who used to farm in East Texas, told me years ago that "the water won't ever clear up until you get the hogs out of the creek."

There's our problem: The hogs are in the creek, muddying our environmental, economic, and political waters. You don't get a hog out of the creek by whining "pretty please," but by putting your shoulders to it and shoving it out.

We need a clarion call for the shoulders of all people with goodwill and environmental commitment. The Powers That Be always try to keep us apart, but this is a cause that can bring together seemingly disparate people to forge a common sense majority—environmental activists with small business, small business with labor, labor with family farmers, family farmers with suburbanites, and so forth.

People like this already are teaming up locally and regionally. On one hand, they are making changes in their personal lives and in their communities to reduce pollution—from developing curbside recycling and energy conservation programs to buying organic food and nontoxic household products.

On the other hand, Mad-as-Hell indigenous groups are sprouting up like wildflowers throughout the country to fight local environmental outrages. They bear blunt acronyms like S.M.E.L.L., CAN-IT, H.A.L.T., CAP-M AND WHOA! Their membership cuts across all the standard separations of race, partisanship, and class. They do not shrink from confrontation with power, and they tend to align themselves with the more combative national groups, such as Citizen Action, Clean Water Action, and National Toxics Campaign.

They are founded by ordinary people like Rita Carlson, a homemaker who came to environmental activism the same way most people are finding it—from personal experience. Until recently, she lived twelve blocks from the Union Carbide plant in Texas City. Each week, 160,000 pounds of toxic chemicals spew from that plant. There are eight such chemical factories in Texas City, and twenty-nine in neighboring communities along Galveston Bay. Thirty percent of the nation's chemicals come from these twenty-nine plants.

Alarmed by illnesses in her family, Carlson began her own investigation and found a cancer hot spot in Texas City. On one street of twenty-two homes, seventeen families have cancer. In some houses, both husband and wife have cancer. Cats die of cancer here. Children have kidney transplants and others have holes in their sinuses eroded from breathing the polluted air. Carlson has a tumor in her sinuses and her son has abnormal lymph glands.

She has now moved out of state to try to save her family's health. "They say we are only screaming women," Carlson says. "I think the reason you see a lot of women more involved in environmental issues is because it's the women who have to rock the sick babies at night."

The national majority for a resounding environmental victory is right in front of us, in the Rita Carlsons. Critics say that these folks are fine as far as they go, but they are mostly naive, myopic NIMBYs who care passionately about their local problem, but little for the more stupefying issues of rain forest depletion and global warming.

Hogwash. These are people who have informed themselves, emboldened themselves, and girded themselves to flay against distant powers, to endure local ostracism and to try to make democracy work. They are acting locally, but they are thinking globally. They are winning more than they are losing, and they are our best hope for a green future.

Our environmental movement must be in Washington, of course, tending to business as best we can. But our emphasis needs to shift from there to the countryside. Instead of trying to coax the Washington power structure into doing what's right, we can build a new power structure out here that can demand what's right, and get it.

This means getting back to Thomas Jefferson's notion that ours was to be a nation of "citizen governors"—we *are* the government. Voting biennially, writing letters to Congress, and sending others to lobby for us is only part of this citizenship. It also requires us to organize at the grassroots so we can run against the bastards and eventually become the Congress.

This level of democracy takes a lot of grunt work, and it calls for a long-term strategy, but there will be no "green" revolution without a "democratic" revolution to nurture and sustain it. Put another way, you can't have a mass movement without the masses.

It's the only way to wrestle our world from fools.

▲ ▲ ▲

Jim Hightower is chairman of the Financial Democracy Campaign, which works with consumer, labor, farm, church and community groups to insure a just resolution to the S&L crisis and other financial industry reform efforts. He was formerly Texas Agriculture Commissioner and chairperson of the National Democratic Party's Agriculture Council. Hightower has written two books with Susan DeMarco, *Hard Tomatoes, Hard Times* and *Eat Your Heart Out.*

A town is saved, not more by the righteous men in it than by the woods and swamps that surround it.

"WALKING"
HENRY DAVID THOREAU

MERYL STREEP

CHILDREN ARE OUR FUTURE; GIVE THEM LIGHT AND LET THEM LEAD THE WAY

In 1981, a group of mothers in my small town in Connecticut formed a group called Mothers and Others to respond to specific dangers posed by pesticides on produce. Since then, Mothers and Others for a Livable Planet, under the aegis of the Natural Resources Defense Council, has broadened its scope to build popular support for numerous environmental reforms—governmental, institutional and personal—that are needed to sustain a livable planet for our children. In large measure, we are now focusing our efforts on two global issue areas: sustainable food production and global warming.

On the matter of food production, Mothers and Others is a noted advocate for sustainable low chemical techniques of farming and has led a consumer campaign to encourage the market availability of organic and low-input produce. In 1989 we published a popular guide, "For Our Kids' Sake," advising consumers on how to protect their families from pesticides in produce. We continue to push for legislation that will ensure safer farming techniques and a safe food supply for all.

Regarding global warming, Mothers and Others has begun a collaborative effort with the American Conservation Association to create the

Children's Earth Fund. The Children's Earth Fund is being formed to help kids take action to save the planet's resources. In response to their concerns, and with confidence in their ability to make a difference, the Fund seeks to help our children organize and become more effective; to inspire grown-ups by their example; to persuade leaders in government to take the difficult steps required; to build bridges between different peoples; and to raise funds for the earth's safe-keeping.

Of special concern, and the focus for Children's Earth Fund, is the peril to the planet's future posed by global warming and far-reaching climate change and by the growing disparity between rich nations and poor that damages not only the environment, but also the prospects for world peace.

In its first year, CEF is eager to demonstrate the concerns and determination of children to preserve the planet in time for the Earth Summit in June 1992. Toward this end, CEF will implement the following programs:

1. "The Carbon Challenge," in which an estimated one million kids will each pledge to reduce their homes' CO_2 emissions by one ton. In January 1992, this army of children will petition President Bush to commit the United States as a *nation* to the same percentage reduction, a step he has resisted in the past, but one that is needed for a strong Convention (Agreement) on Climate Change to be adopted at the Earth Summit. The one ton reduction is readily achievable as documented by The Audubon Society and others, and would be accomplished through steps ranging from use of energy efficient lighting and insulation to tree planting.

2. "Pennies for the Planet" will be collected in a student fundraising drive matched by corporate gifts that will include Rainforest Crunch (similar to the Scouts cookies). The proceeds will be used to contain global warming by: (a) saving U.S. forests, like the California redwoods and ancient forests of the Northwest, and (b) being applied to overseas rain forest protection, tree planting, and the subsidized spread of solar cookers in temperate areas to reduce woodburning for cooking purposes.

3. "An Earthbridge" will be formed, classroom to classroom, with students exchanging concerns and hopes for the Earth Summit. Kids who are interested in having a direct impact on their future now will be encouraged to join the Earth Rangers and to petition the policymakers with this pledge:

MY PLEDGE
As an Earth Ranger, I _____, will do my part to save the planet from getting TOO HOT. My family has agreed to send up to the sky, *one ton* less

carbon gas (CO_2) from our home this year and twice that later on (that's 20 percent less than what most homes now send up).

MY PETITION

1. Dear President Bush: As our leader, will you join us and send up to the sky 20 percent less carbon gas from the White House?

2. Mr. President, please go to the June 1992 Earth Summit and promise that the United States—now the source of more carbon dioxide than any other country in the world—will do its part and send up 20 percent less carbon gas by the year 2000. Also, please ask all the world leaders to help save our planet's lungs—the rain forests we are losing so fast. When you lead them in a big rescue, could you help save our forests, too, and say "yes" to recycling?

3. And Congress, can you and the President please be brave enough to say "no" to cars that waste energy (and wasteful lightbulbs and buildings, too)?

_____ is hereby recognized as an Earth Ranger, who is working to save the planet from getting too hot from the threat of global warming, oil pollution and energy waste by sending up to the atmosphere from home one ton less carbon dioxide gas (CO_2) this year and twice that by the year 2000 (equal to 20 percent of the average household's CO_2 emissions), and by urging the President of the United States to send up less CO_2 from the White House and committing the nation at the June, 1992 Earth Summit to emit 20 percent less CO_2 by the year 2000.

We, as parents, are hopeful, but sometimes daunted by the size and scope of the environmental problems we see down the road in our children's future. Our children, on the other hand, bring with them the empowerment of their own optimism and the belief in their own omnipotence that only belongs to the young. By putting the means at their disposal, and giving them a voice, we form the strongest coalition imaginable with our children, the past with the future, knowledge with faith, a covenant they'll keep with their children that may help close up the hole in the sky.

▲ ▲ ▲

Meryl Streep is an actress, the mother of three (maybe four tomorrow) children, and a co-founder of Mothers and Others for a Livable Planet.

ARUN GANDHI

A BALANCE BETWEEN OUR NEED AND OUR GREED

I was twelve years old when I received my first definitive lesson in environment, ecology, and concern for others. This was in 1946 while living with my grandfather, Mohandas K. Gandhi, in India. Much of Grandfather's philosophy was derived from what he found useful in the writings of Thoreau, Emerson, Ruskin, Tolstoy, and others. He experimented with what he learned in his life and, in turn, influenced others around him. Grandfather believed firmly that if one was not able to mold one's life according to lessons learned, then there is something wrong with education.

In 1946 World War II had just come to an end and the international community was dumbstruck by the devastation caused by the two atomic blasts over Nagasaki and Hiroshima in Japan. During this period, people were more concerned with survival than ecology and environment. These words had not become a part of normal vocabulary.

Yet, Grandfather was convinced that the survival of our civilization, our culture, and our Independence depended "not on multiplying our greed but upon restricting our need." His life and his philosophy were centered around this maxim.

At twelve, I was still too young to understand the importance of his message. We lived in a large community called an *ashram,* where families lived and worked together sharing what they had or what they produced. The *ashram* had a common kitchen where men and women cooked the meals for all those who lived in the *ashram.* It was teamwork at its best. All the duties were divided. While one team did the cooking, another washed the clothes and the dishes; a third worked on the farm to produce fruits, vegetables, and grains needed for survival; yet another swept and cleaned the yard and the common bucket toilets used by the more than a hundred people who lived in the *ashram.* Everyone ate and prayed together. The only time most people parted was at night, when adults needed privacy. Often children slept together on string beds under the canopy of a starry sky.

One day, after my lessons, I decided it was time I got a new pencil. I was tired of the one I had. It was now about three inches long and I thought I had used it long enough. Impetuously, I flung it into the bushes, determined to ask Grandfather for a new one. That evening I did, and learned a lesson I haven't forgotten since.

"Why do you need a new pencil?" Grandfather asked. "If I remember correctly you had a pencil this morning."

"Yes, Bapu." I said. Bapu is the Indian term for Grandfather. "I had a pencil but it was too small, so I threw it away."

"Oh my," Grandfather exclaimed. "That wasn't a very wise thing to do."

He looked out the window. It was getting dark. Grandfather rummaged through his little desk and brought out a flashlight.

"Here," he said. "Take this and find the pencil."

I thought he was joking. Apparently, he was not. There was something about Grandfather that commanded obedience. No one that I know would ever question his motives. I took the flashlight and walked out obediently.

It was hours since I had randomly flung the pencil somewhere in the tall grass and bushes. How would I ever find it with a flashlight?

I was terrified of snakes and scorpions and did not know which of the three I would find first. Mumbling a prayer, I poked the grass and bushes desperately with a stick. It was almost two hours before I found the pencil. All the while I muttered angrily at Grandfather's seeming obstinacy.

With tremendous relief I ran into Grandfather's room. "Look," I said almost triumphantly. "Isn't it small?"

Grandfather took the pencil, carefully turning it around as though inspecting something of great value. Then he looked at me and said, "No. I don't think this is small. I am sure you can use it for another eight or ten days if you are careful."

I was stupefied. Grandfather saw the look on my face and smiled. "You must think I am crazy," he said with his arms around my shoulders. "I could have given you a new pencil, but I want you to learn some lessons from this episode."

I was curious. What on earth could I learn from a discarded bit of pencil?

Grandfather explained how many billions of pencils were manufactured in the world and how many trees are chopped for the wood. Trees, he said, serve a useful purpose and if we go on chopping them indiscriminately because we have wasteful habits then one day the earth will have no trees left.

"Imagine," he said. "If there are ten million children like you in the world who throw perfectly good pencils away how much of the world's resources are wasted?"

I was never good at mathematics, but I could imagine the mountain of discarded pencils.

"There is something else I want you to learn from this," Grandfather went on. "There are millions of poor children around the world who live in so much poverty that their parents cannot afford to buy them paper and pencils to get some education. They are poor because we are wasteful. If we learn to use the world's resources carefully then we will be able to share them with more people."

The message was firmly embedded in my mind and, when I grew up, I understood more thoroughly the profundity of Grandfather's vision. He not only lectured on these and other subjects but insisted we practice them in our lives.

This was what *ashram* life emphasized. We learned to live in simplicity, cared for each other, shared whatever we had, worked together to produce and to consume. The idea was to utilize everything to the maximum.

Every day we carried the hundreds of buckets of urine and nightsoil into the fields and emptied them in trenches which were then covered and allowed to lie fallow until the waste had been absorbed. We worked through the fields systematically. We also refurbished the soil with compost made from kitchen and garden waste.

We improvised our life-style so that we could live with the least amount of furniture. We sat on the floor to eat so that we could live without a dining table and chairs; at night we spread our mattresses on the floor so that a bed became redundant; during the day the same mattresses were piled judiciously in the living room and covered with colorful bedspreads to make comfortable sofas for visitors. We had short-legged stools with flip tops to use as desks and store our books. They were high enough so that we could sit on the floor and write on the table. They were small and light enough so that we could carry them to any part of the home.

Life was simple and uncomplicated. There was never any need to buy furniture, nor change it to suit prevailing fashions. It saved not only money, but a considerable amount of wood. Ecologically, the Indian life-style before Westernization was ideal.

In other words, what Grandfather tried to teach us was that we cannot continue to waste and hope to conserve environment and ecology. Conservation must begin with the smallest things at the youngest age. If we allow children to grow up believing they can throw away useful things because they cost so little, how can we expect them to grow up conscious of the need to conserve?

Grandfather used to tell us: "You must learn to save pennies in order to conserve dollars." In other words, we need not only to learn, but to put into practice what we learn.

Eastern nations that had a tradition of simple living have succumbed to Western influence and its wasteful habits. In order to be considered civilized in Western terms, their life-style has become Westernized. They need more furniture, among other things, and need to change it more often. This means a greater destruction of forests for timber than is necessary.

Forests in developing countries are being destroyed at an alarming rate in part because a vast section of the poor population find wood to be the cheapest fuel for cooking and heating their huts during winter. In the past, the poor in India used cow dung cakes for fuel. Cow dung plastered on mud walls and floor also provided excellent insulation against the cold. But this tradition too became a victim of Western influence and mores. First, and probably more significantly, the Western model of high-tech industrial development was responsible for change in Indian traditions. Also significant was Western ridicule of the Indian custom in which the cow is considered sacred.

To a society as advanced as the United States, considering an animal sacred must appear to be utterly primitive. But consider two important facts. First, that the cow was, still is, a very important animal for human beings. It provides milk, labor in the field, cow dung for fuel and heat and, when it dies, skin for leather, to name just a few benefits. It is, therefore, important that poor farmers take good care of the animal. Second, it must be remembered that Indian society for several centuries has been influenced by religion more than anything else. So, it is understandable that reverence for the cow became a religious tradition.

When Gandhi said Western society had become too materialistic and, therefore, wasteful in its habits, he was expressing his concern for environment. He saw the disaster coming and tried to caution India from joining the race to extinction. But the glitter and glamor of Western life-styles was too tempting to be rejected. Gandhi did not want India to remain stagnant in ancient tradition, but to modify those traditions to suit changing life-styles.

Ultimately, the only way we can save the earth from being destroyed is by changing our habits. We need to become less wasteful and more concerned not only for nature but for other people and places. The planet can be saved only in its entirety and not in segments. The West cannot save its portion of the planet and remain complacent. We have got to save it all or lose everything. The process of saving not only has to start now, it has to start with you and me.

▲ ▲ ▲

Arun Gandhi, a grandson of Mohandas K. Gandhi, is currently director of the Gandhi Institute for Non-Violence and Peace and the M.K. Gandhi Foundation. These Memphis-based groups work for racial emancipation, world peace and harmony in human relationships, with a special focus on South Africa, India and the United States. He is a member of the Walden Woods Project Advisory Board.

> There are a thousand hacking at the branches of evil to one who is striking at the root.
>
> *WALDEN*
> HENRY DAVID THOREAU

PAUL C. PRITCHARD

ONE POND, MANY PARKS

Each town should have a park . . . a common possession forever.

Henry David Thoreau

For a nation to have conceived of such a public cause as the national parks, it took more than just one person, more than one philosophy, and more than the inspirational qualities of one place. Nonetheless, the more than 120 nations that now cherish the ideal of national parks owe Henry David Thoreau and Walden Woods an infinite debt of gratitude, perhaps one as "bottomless" as Thoreau regarded Walden Pond itself.

Thoreau's beloved Walden Woods became the fountainhead of the conservation ethic in America, an inspiration to mankind the world over. Walden is now the mecca of modern-day environmentalism and a pillar in the foundation of national parks. As Joseph Wood Krutch once wrote, "The quietness of Walden Pond sounds through the world." Today, nearly 120 years after the establishment of Yellowstone National Park, and during the seventy-fifth anniversary year of the National Park Service, the quietness of Walden still resonates—just as the cracked Liberty Bell really still rings at Independence National Historical Park, and a moving stillness still cloaks Appomattox Court House National Historic Site. From Walden, and from all the cherished places in our national park system, an unfathomable power surges; something from far below the trees and mountains and beyond the book learning of history. From one pond, and many parks, comes a people's quiet sense of place.

But just as in nature, silence does not necessarily mean stability. The simple truth is that a nation and a planet mired in a deep environmental crisis needs the message of Walden—ecology, economy, civility—more than ever before. If we fail to release and capitalize on the strength of such places, our cherished havens and their enduring values—including the national parks and the human spirit they celebrate and nurture—will surely perish. That is the challenge that Walden offered Thoreau and he offered us. If we have ignored it, we have done so naively. It is before us now again, as both the national park system and Walden Woods face new and unprecedented threats. It is now late in the twentieth century, and we have little time to act to protect and enhance Walden, and to secure its lesson for this and future generations. We must not fail.

As Walden Woods has seen the years pass, and grown in importance, it has been almost like a forgotten parent of the national park ideal. Congress, on August 25, 1916, verbalized a unique vision, sprung from Thoreau and his predecessors, that has guided the creation and preservation of our system of national parks even to this day: " . . . to conserve the scenery and the natural and historic objects and the wildlife therein and to provide for the enjoyment of the same in such manner and by such means as will leave them unimpaired for the enjoyment of future generations."

Those words captured two principles that would shape the mural which we know today as the national park system. The first principle is the nineteenth-century heritage of Emerson and Thoreau, who saw that nature was essential to man's understanding of his full potential. The second principle is a precept of democracy, expressed in the Constitution, born of the concept of equality: that these special places be preserved for and accessible to all, not just a privileged few.

Both principles are reflected in the mandate for the National Park Service: to preserve symbols of the character of the nation. The NPS role has been and still is to provide for the protection of a heritage found in the American landscape, and in the settings of the events of historical significance of its diverse peoples.

Well before the world's first national park was established at Yellowstone in 1872, there were forces at work that served as the pigment for this new phenomenon. Ancient societies had deified the natural world, preserved gardens, revered unique wildlife and open spaces. But, for the most part, really protected areas had been kept mainly for the privileged classes. Not so for America's national parks. To this day, the unfolding drama of the system has been the effort to maintain that universal role, rather than allowing the preservation of our heritage to become focused on any sector or interest to the exclusion of the general welfare.

By the time of Thoreau's adulthood in the mid-1800s, the Industrial Revolution was beginning to change the face of much of the world, bringing the railroad to Walden Woods and unsightly development to Niagara Falls. The belief in an American Manifest Destiny propelled our society forward. Sensitive minds such as Emerson's and Thoreau's saw aspects of these movements as evil, disruptive influences on nature and on the manner in which mankind was meant to live and understand itself. Though it was intrinsic in Native Americans' religious practices and powerful reverence for Mother Earth, Thoreau's escape to Walden Pond was modern America's first historical connection between a specific natural place and the human discovery of self.

During the same era, European and American painters began to reflect the majesty and mystery of our western landscapes. The Civil War followed, brushing more human drama across the nation's tapestry, and also encouraging reflection and the growth of national self-awareness. These forces—combined with the emergence of new professions such as landscape architecture, through which leaders like Frederick Law Olmstead, who launched such efforts as Central Park—further forged the Walden-based attribute that Olmstead saw as distinguishing mankind from the other animals: the "contemplative faculty."

As the nineteenth century came to an end, a handful of national parks and historic sites—including Yellowstone, Yosemite, Sequoia, and Gettysburg—comprised a loose-knit amalgamation with no fixed home in the federal bureaucracy. They did, however, still represent our society's rich inheritance, its creative lust, its struggles with itself, its conflicting values, and its evolving sense of self-worth.

Gradually, another legacy of the Thoreau citizen-naturalist also matured; the importance of relating visitors' experiences at parks directly to their own lives helped create the profession of "interpretation." Thus could Freeman Tilden, the creator and muse of environmental education in the national parks, trace his inspiration to Walden Woods.

Since the establishment of the unified National Park Service, the national park system has grown and matured. The system now numbers some 357 units, protecting diverse natural and cultural resources from the Anasazi ruins at New Mexico's Chaco Canyon to the home of freed slave Frederick Douglass to the Yorktown battlefield to Palo Alto (a battlefield in the Mexican War Thoreau went to jail to protest) to the wetlands of Florida's Everglades (once considered worthless) to Alaska's thirteen-million–acre Wrangell-St. Elias National Park and Preserve. Each addition has helped America find a stronger and stronger voice, and recognize the breadth of its heritage, just as Thoreau discovered and found eternal meaning even in the smallest new details of the world around him.

In his lecture on "Huckleberries," Thoreau also wrote of the crucial role parks can play in preserving the simple quality of life in every community: "It would be worth the while if in each town there were a committee appointed, to see that the beauty of the town received no detriment." Over a hundred years later, the legacy of the Land and Water Conservation Fund commenced, acting on a broad plan for the nation's park and conservation goals, and bringing benefits to every state and nearly every locality. The logic was inescapable: The public should benefit from the depletion of the nation's natural wealth by dedication of some of the proceeds for parks.

In the 1970s, national parks were thrust into urban America for the purpose of providing park facilities where people lived. Golden Gate in San Francisco, Gateway in New York City, national lakeshores and seashores, all gave the National Park Service new access to the people and to the agendas of their public leaders. Today, this aspect of Thoreau's legacy is all around us—in the hundreds of state and local parks, protected river and trail corridors, and patches of green offering opportunities for contemplation and renewal. This legacy continues to grow, even in Thoreau's own New England stomping grounds. To the protected landscapes of Minute Man National Historical Park in Lexington and Concord, Sudbury's Great Meadows National Wildlife Refuge, and diverse privately held lands, Congress is considering adding protected corridors along the Concord, Assabet, and Sudbury rivers.

But there is much more work to do, much more to save, at Walden and around the nation. As we celebrate the seventy-fifth anniversary of the National Park Service, interest in conservation has been rekindled. However, the issues that face the Park Service are extensive, and parallel those faced by Walden Woods. How can the Service develop a science program that understands and protects declining plant and wildlife species? (How healthy is the ecology of Walden Woods?) Does the national park system need concessions operating within its boundaries when the parks are rimmed by growing communities with businesses serving the same clientele? (Does Walden need the same?) Can the U.S. achieve the goal of setting aside 5 percent of its landscape when we lag behind other nations in doing so? When do you close the gate to one-too-many visitors? How will the park system meet the needs of Americans with growing ethnic and racial diversity? (How do we ensure Thoreau's message remains valid for all Americans?)

The condition of Walden Woods is a microcosm for our society, and still has the power to focus the *zeitgeist* of the nation on public health issues, toxics, pollution, loss of open space, and other effects of unbridled economic growth. Our concern for parks and Walden Woods must be guided by the words of Newton Drury, director of the National Park Service (1940–1951) and a defender of the parks from some of the most serious proposed raids on their resources: "If we are going to succeed in preserving the greatness of the national parks, they must be held inviolate. They represent the last stand of primitive America. If we are going to whittle away at them we should recognize, at the very beginning, that all such whittlings are cumulative and that the end result will be mediocrity. Greatness will be gone."

If there is one problem with the Thoreau legacy it is debunking the myth that Thoreau cared only for retreating to the woods, alone, to plant his beans. Saving Walden Woods, saving the parks, saving the planet, will require a team effort that builds on the concerns and energies of individual citizens working collectively. Walden must be made more relevant to our everyday lives, as it inspired John Muir, Gandhi, and the courageous Chinese students in Tianenman Square, and through them, became relevant to millions worldwide.

"In some countries precious metals belong to the crown—so here our precious objects of great natural beauty should belong to the public," wrote Walden's sage. The national parks *are* America's crown jewels; Walden is another precious stone, but without a setting. But unlike the icy shine of diamond, or false warmth of inanimate gold, the mural that is our parks is never finished, it evolves constantly. Its relevance to the nation depends on the creativity and the commitment of people like Thoreau, who have helped craft one of man's most important self-portraits, a reflection of the highest values of humanity. It is now our commitment to uphold.

Distressed by the bite of the woodcutter's axe on his beloved Walden Woods, Thoreau once lamented that within a greater vision, "All Walden Wood might have been preserved for our park forever." Over a century has flown by; where are we now and where are we headed? Roads, landfills, and development have pushed into Walden Woods, and displaced some of Thoreau's legacy with asphalt and disrespect. But amazingly, much beauty still remains. Certainly enough so that the resources and the spirit—along with the promise, the opportunity, and the hope for the future—though tattered, still remain.

▲ ▲ ▲

Paul C. Pritchard is president of the National Parks and Conservation Association, the 300,000 member organization that protects U.S. national parks. Previously, he was a deputy director in the Department of the Interior, and director of the President's National Heritage Trust Task Force.

MARY KAY PLACE

FROM THE BIG CHILL TO THE BIG PICTURE

In 1982, I participated in a movie about a group of baby boomers who attend the funeral of a mutual friend who has committed suicide. During the course of the weekend together, they reflect on their lives and the loss of their sixties idealism. In *The Big Chill,* I played Meg, a single career woman who, after a disillusioning experience as a public defender, joins the corporate world as a real estate attorney. She jokes that her clients have gone from raping people to raping the land. Meg expresses a sense of loss from the bonds of their community of friendship and the sense of a shared commitment and goals.

Meg, and most members of the group, have either dropped out or sold out on their former idealistic values. Sam, a TV star, confesses his feelings of mistrust of people and Meg agrees that it's a "cold world out there. Sometimes I think I'm getting a little frosty myself." She seeks "warmth" from Nick and wants him to father her child. He is impotent since Vietnam and unable to comply. Sam, who is already a father, feels guilty about his lack of attention to his own child. He also declines Meg's offer of fatherhood. She wants nothing from the men, just their sperm. She will raise the child on her own.

Meg's frustration in finding a man hit a chord in many career women of my generation. I was constantly stopped on the street by women who related to that predicament, whose longing for intimacy and partnership was thwarted by the inability to find the "right" man. Meg thinks she might not even want a man any more, just a baby. By playing Meg, I was able to try on all of her emotions, processes, and decisions. I wore them and lived in them for three months. They aroused disturbing feelings. Pretending to be Meg, I learned a lot about myself.

I became conscious of my own alienation. Like Meg, work had become my family. I had no time to pay attention to the nagging feeling of separation from some core that I couldn't articulate. Meg thought a baby would bring her the connection, the intimacy, the "heart" she missed in her life. I realized that I needed to discover my *own* path to wholeness. I intuited that for me, this missing element would have to come from within before I could share it with someone else, whether that was a man or a baby.

The emotions that erupted from playing Meg could not be ignored or "busied" away. Like it or not, my unconscious took this opportunity to speak to me. I began a descent into the dark, scary, mysterious depths of my being, not realizing it was the beginning of a journey toward finding a new sense of connection. I went from the outer-directed, work-centered, masculine journey, into the inner-directed, still waters of the feminine journey.

So why in the Sam Hill am I telling this story in a book about ecology? My experience, Meg's "frostiness," Nick's impotence, Sam's mistrust, a friend's "burnout," a neighbor's heart disease, a couple's divorce, the isolation of an elderly woman on the street, a newborn baby's addiction to crack, a teenager's bulimia, have become everyday occurrences. These are human examples of a culture that is in need of healing and transformation. Now a growing group of scholars and researchers are arguing that there are real connections between the diseases in us and our society, and the host of environmental tragedies that are ravaging our earth.

In her book, *A Passion For This Earth*, Valerie Andrews writes about the eighteenth century philosopher, Leibnitz, and his book, *The Monadology*. In it he said that the whole of life is reflected in the smallest unit of reality or, in our context, what is happening among individuals is happening societally and to the entire planet.

The effects on the planet may not be quite as easy to see as personal problems in our daily lives, but they're there, and getting worse. Thomas Berry writes in *The Dream of the Earth*, "our entire society is caught in a closed cycle of production and consumption that can go on until the natural resources are exhausted or until the poisons inserted into the environment are fed back into the system." We are making the land and air and sea so toxic that the very conditions of life are being destroyed. Due to our abuse of the planet, hundreds of thousands of species will be extinguished before the end of the century. This scenario is so unthinkable that, as Berry suggests, "a disturbance exists . . . on a greater order of magnitude than we dare admit to ourselves or even think about."

How did we get in this state of dis-ease? In our race for power, control, position, more, better, newer, faster, our culture has worked itself into an all-consuming, undisciplined, and out-of-sync existence.

In *The Chalice and the Blade*, Riane Eisler describes two basic models of society: the dominator model (patriarchy or matriarchy), which ranks one half of the population over the other, and the partnership model, which involves the principle of linking rather than ranking, where diversity is celebrated and people aren't broken down into inferior or superior groups.

Recent anthropological studies suggest that the partnership model is not just a theory, but has a basis in history. Marijua Gimbutas, in *The Goddesses and Gods of Old Europe*, gives evidence of a matricentric society between circa 7000 and 3500 B.C. It was an earth-centered, agricultural, highly artistic and creative, Goddess-worshiping, egalitarian male-female society. Then came the Aryan invasions, and along with them a patriarchal model of social organization. This system was based on male dominance, male violence, and a generally hierarchic and authoritarian social structure. Four patriarchal structures have dominated Western history over the centuries: the classical empires, the religious establishment, the nation-state, and now the modern corporation. In all of these structures, males have dominated through systems based on power, control, and methods of warfare.

The dominator model is now deeply embedded in our cultural traditions, in our religious traditions, in our language, in our entire value system, and its negative effects are accelerating. Berry, Eisler, and many others suggest we must move toward a more encompassing, holistic mode of existence. We must move toward a partnership society, and that means including the feminine values that were once a part of our culture—feminine values which, while largely ignored, remain an important part of our collective unconscious.

When I've mentioned this concept of balancing the masculine with the feminine, I've noticed resistance from some of my men friends. The hair goes up on the back of their necks—oh no, some feminist rap. This is not another divisive concept, but an inclusive one. Masculine forces have been at work in our culture to the exclusion of a counterbalanced feminine force. These archetypal forces are creative, and men and women contain both the masculine and the feminine. But there is much evidence that the predominance of masculine forces has become counterproductive—life-taking rather than life-giving—and needs to be balanced by the nourishing, nurturing energy of the feminine.

This does not mean that men should become like women, but that the whole culture, men and women, should begin to appreciate and discover values that are more intuitive, relational, and interdependent. In *The Heroine's Journey*, Maureen

Murdock writes, "we need the moist, juicy, green, caring feminine to heal the wounded, dry, brittle, overextended masculine in our culture." We all share the blame for what has happened to our planet and must work together in partnership to reach a new way of being.

In moving toward partnership ways of being, as both men and women, we also need to discover our own authentic voices. We need to learn to form relationships with our unconscious, to "hear" the inner wisdom and guidance it can offer. Our bodies are conduits for this information, but through excessive food, alcohol, drugs, sex, and busyness we numb our bodies, and its signals are unable to reach our consciousness.

I have learned that my "gut alarms" are powerful signs and when I ignore them, trouble is sure to follow. As I become more in tune with my body, I am increasingly grateful for its guidance. But I have to remember to be still and slow down so that I can "feel" its messages. When I get caught up in the busy, doing, linear, rational mode, I begin to feel split apart, off-track, disconnected. I know I need periods of solitude, gardening and hiking in nature. Meditation and prayer also help me reconnect to my body and to a spiritual Source, the Self deep within. Being present in this realm has proven to be a comforting and nurturing experience, but alas, in depressions and burnout, it can also be frightening entering the unknown, where all seems to be arid and desertlike, devoid of meaning.

Experience has taught me, however, that hanging on through the darkness (and it has *not* been easy) pays off. In the darkness lie seeds of renewal and rebirth. I have learned the importance of patience and process, two values that are not appreciated or respected in our fast food, instant-gratification culture. I have a new understanding of faith and trust. I have begun to see that the rhythms and cycles of nature are a part of not only my personal rhythms but of all living creations on this earth. There is reciprocity and interdependence linking all living things. And while I continue to struggle on the inner path, I also experience a yearning to move beyond myself into the community for connection and relationship.

But this partnership business is not easy. Just think about the state of man-woman relationships. So often we are split apart by addiction, codependency, poverty, success, fear, illness, emotional unavailability, projections, alienation, and the inability to communicate. So how do we get together? What is the key? I wish I knew. But in my efforts, which range from the insane to the ridiculous, from the unconscious to the more conscious, I have learned a few things about what does not work. Seeking fulfillment or wholeness from a mate is impossible. Ultimately, he can not and will not fill the black hole. This is my responsibility. And we're in trouble if I try to be his mother or he tries to be my father.

Some experts suggest that by taking the inner journey and coming into relationship with our inner, opposite, archetypal masculine and feminine forces that unconsciously drive our actions, we are less likely to project those forces onto our mates. Others say we need to discover and heal the secret wounds of childhood, so we will not act out and repeat the dysfunctional family dynamics in our adult relationships. New hope comes from acknowledging, grieving over, and accepting all the denied hurts and fears, and finally forgiving those that delivered them.

If I have the courage to look at my shadow side and acknowledge all the ugly, horrible, negative parts of myself that I have denied and driven into my unconscious and accept them, then their power over me begins to fade. When I begin to accept, with love, all the negatives in myself, I am more willing to accept the parts I'd like to criticize in my mate. In discovering who I truly am, I am more capable of allowing my mate to be who he truly is. The more my authentic self emerges, the more a healthy relationship is possible—based not on dominion or control of one over the other, but on a partnership of equals with diverse gifts, perceptions, and abilities. And getting back to Leibnitz's theory, it follows that as we learn to accept the diversity in our own partners, our children and families, we also can celebrate the diversity of our neighbors—whether they live across the yard, the tracks, the state, or the world.

So by finding our authentic voices, we find the freedom to change the focus from self to others. And we respond to the need to serve a larger purpose. In community and partnership we can begin the difficult task of effecting change for our culture and our planet. And in spite of the enormous magnitude of our challenge there is hope.

There is hope in the growing ecology movement, where the focus is on moving from our human-centered reality to a nature-centered reality.

There is hope in our increased consciousness and awareness of what we have to do to heal ourselves, our community, and our planet.

There is hope in moving toward a partnership society and the feminine, eliminating the warfare system.

There is hope in reconnecting to the earth and becoming its lover again. But we can not love what we do not know. We must spend time with nature and experience the mystery of her rhythms and cycles of birth, death, and rebirth. We must teach our children to respect these mysteries and to have reverence for the sanctity of the earth, as our Native American people have always known.

There is hope in listening to the earth. We must come into communion with Mother Earth and rediscover her life-giving energies. Like the wisdom of our bodies, the body of the earth can aid and direct us in our mutual, interdependent journey back to wholeness. In the depth of her wounds lie the seeds of healing. We must let go of the illusion that we know what is best for earth. Our greatest hope is in forming a partnership with the earth, letting the earth become our guide.

. . .

I would like to acknowledge the following authors whose scholarship, research and insights informed this article:

The Heroine's Journey, by Maureen Murdock (Shambhala Publications, 1990)

The Dream of the Earth, by Thomas Berry (Sierra Club Books, 1988)

The Chalice and the Blade, by Riane Eisler (Harper and Row, 1987)

Fire in the Belly, by Sam Keen (Bantam Books, 1991)

▲ ▲ ▲

Mary Kay Place is an actress living in New York City.

Not till we are lost, in other words, not till we have lost the world, do we begin to find ourselves, and realize where we are and the infinite extent of our relations.

WALDEN
HENRY DAVID THOREAU

ROBERT BLY

SEEING WHAT IS BEFORE US

Thoreau was capable of true patience in observing the nonhuman world, and he exclaims in one passage, "Would it not be a luxury to stand up to one's chin in some retired swamp for a whole summer's day?" If we've read Thoreau, we know that he would be perfectly capable of it. He walked two hours each day and noted with the most astonishing perseverance and tenacity the exact days on which wildflowers—dozens of varieties—opened in the forest. In 1853 he notes in his journal, "My Aunt Maria asked me to read the life of Dr. Chalmers, which, however, I did not promise to do. Yesterday, Sunday, she was heard through the partition shouting to my Aunt Jane, who is deaf: 'Think of it: He stood half an hour today to hear the frogs croak, and he wouldn't read the life of Chalmers.' "

His neighbors saw him stand motionless for eight hours beside a pond to watch young frogs, and all day at a river's edge watching ducks' eggs hatching.

Thoreau felt invited to observe the detail in nature, and he did not receive this invitation from Wordsworth or Milton; it came to him as a part of his genius. When he was twenty-one he wrote in his journal, "Nature will bear the closest inspection. She invites us to lay our eye level with her smallest leaf, and take an insect view of its plain." There is something brilliant in the last clause, advising us to take a low-lying, or insect, position when we look. One day, while he lay on his back during a soaking rain, he saw a raindrop descend along a stalk of the previous year's oats. "While these clouds and this sombre drizzling weather shut all in, we two draw nearer and know one another," he wrote in his journal (March 30, 1840). R. H. Blyth declared this sentence to be one of the few sentences in the English language that was a genuine haiku.

Emerson said this of Thoreau's patience in his "Biographical Sketch":

It was a pleasure and a privilege to walk with him. He knew the country like a fox or a bird, and passed through it as freely by paths of his own. He knew every track in the snow or on the ground, and what creature had taken this path before him. One must submit abjectly to such a guide, and the reward was great. Under his arm he carried an old music-book to press plants; in his pocket, his diary and pencil, a spy-glass for birds, microscope, jack-knife, and twine. He wore a straw hat, stout shoes, strong gray trousers, to brave scrub-oaks and smilax, and to climb a tree for a hawk's or a squirrel's nest. He waded into the pool for the water-plants, and his strong legs were no insignificant part of his armor. On the day I speak of he looked for the Meryanthes, detected it across the wide pool, and, on examination of the florets, decided that it had been in flower five days. He drew out of his breast-pocket his diary, and read the names of all the plants that should bloom on this day, whereof he kept account as a banker when his notes fall due. The Cypripedium not due till to-morrow. He thought that, if waked up from a trance in this swamp, he could tell by the plants what time of the year it was within two days. The redstart was flying about, and presently the fine grosbeaks, whose brilliant scarlet "makes the rash gazer wipe his eyes," and whose fine clear note Thoreau compared to that of a tanager which has got rid of its hoarseness . . .

His power of observation seemed to indicate additional senses. He saw as with microscope, heard as with ear trumpet, and his memory was a photographic register of all he saw and heard.

We need to understand that Thoreau received through Emerson and Coleridge, through the Eastern spiritual books he read, among them those of the Indian poet Kabir, and through Goethe, Schelling and other German writers, the doctrine that the spiritual world lies hidden in—or moving among, or shining through—the physical world. Nature is one of the languages that God speaks.

He spoke in Hebrew—New Englanders had always known that—but the truth of the soul's interior abundance, while not denying that, added that He also spoke the local language called nature.

Since the physical world conceals or embodies a spiritual world, if one studies facts in nature, one might be able to deduce or distill from many physical facts a spiritual fact. Robert Frost, who is Thoreau's greatest disciple, hinted at that in his poem "Mowing":

> There was never a sound beside the wood but one,
> And that was my long scythe whispering to the ground.
> What was it it whispered? I knew not well myself;
> Perhaps it was something about the heat of the sun,
> Something, perhaps, about the lack of sound—
> And that was why it whispered and did not speak.
> It was no dream of the gift of idle hours,
> Or easy gold at the hand of fay or elf;
> Anything more than the truth would have seemed too weak
> To the earnest love that laid the swale in rows,
> Not without feeble-pointed spikes of flowers
> (Pale orchises), and scared a bright green snake.
> The fact is the sweetest dream that labor knows.
> My long scythe whispered and left the hay to make.

Thoreau remarked in his journal on February 18, 1852, "I have a commonplace book for facts, and another for poetry, but I find it difficult always to preserve the vague distinction which I had in mind, for the most interesting and beautiful facts are so much the more poetry and that is their success. They are translated from earth to heaven. I see that if my facts were sufficiently vital and significant—perhaps transmuted into the substance of the human mind—I should need but one book of poetry to contain them all." So one can translate certain facts "from earth to heaven." Scientists, because they do not know Kabir's truth of the double world, do not translate. Scientific study of facts in Thoreau's time did not encourage the scientist to cross over the threshold between worlds. But Thoreau is able to cross from earth to heaven: "I see that if my facts were sufficiently vital and significant—perhaps translated into the substance of the human mind"—they would become poetry.

We understand that Thoreau's observation is not a simple-minded cataloguing of detail. Behind his persistence lies the promise, grounded in his vast reading, that, in Coleridge's words, "each object rightly seen unlocks a new faculty of the Soul." What is it like, then, to look at an object rightly? Suppose one watched ants fighting. Eyes see surprises, polarities, nuances; the observer's language, if he or she wrote of the battle, would have to contain those nuances, so that the reader could also see rightly. We notice in the following passage that Thoreau provides "embraces", "sunny valley" and "chips" as nuances among the violence: "I watched a couple that were fast locked in each other's embraces, in a little sunny valley amid the chips, now at noonday prepared to fight till the sun went down, or life went out. The smaller red champion had fastened himself like a vise to his adversary's front, and through all the tumblings on that field never for an instant ceased to gnaw at one of his feelers near the root, having already caused the other to go by the board; while the stronger black one dashed him from side to side, and as I saw on looking nearer, had already divested him of several of his members. They fought with more pertinacity than bulldogs."

How good "pertinacity" is here! The swift changes of mood in animal encounters, the intricacy of instinctual gesture, the mixture of comical and tragical, require a vocabulary that can go from high to low in an instant, that can move from dark to light and back, from metallic word to fragrant word, from a slang phrase to words from the Middle Ages or the eighteenth century. American democracy suggests that good writing about nature requires only a simple heart; but bravery of soul, immense learning, and cunning in language—none of them simple—are what nature writing requires.

We recognize that Thoreau's account of the ant battle is not pure observation without human imposition; while he observes details, he is also declaring that men's proclivity is mechanical and antlike: "Holding a microscope to the first-mentioned red ant, I saw that, though he was assiduously gnawing at the near foreleg of his enemy, having severed his remaining feeler, his own breast was all torn away, exposing what vitals he had there to the jaws of the black warrior, whose breastplate was apparently too thick for him to pierce; and the dark carbuncles of the sufferer's eyes shone with ferocity such as war only could excite."

"Assiduously" is essential here. Long, "unnatural" words suggest the fierce intensity of the insect world, in which no one is "laid back" in the California way. Thoreau places "feeler," a word a child might use, near "vitals," an adult word that evokes complicated feelings, including fear. He mingles with that "black warrior" and "breastplate," words that carry a Middle Ages fragrance, and they prepare for the astonishing phrase "dark carbuncle of the sufferer's eyes."

Thoreau writes with equal cunning when he composes less tendentious description—for example, when he describes a squirrel chewing on successive ears of corn. His language then imposes fewer human analogies, becomes amazingly quick-footed, and his nimble rhythms seem transparent to the animal's consciousness.

Thoreau attempts something new in American literature. He does not agree with earlier New Englanders that the world is fallen, and a dark ruin, but believes by contrast that the world remains radiant from the divine energy that shines through it. A few days before he died, a family friend asked him "how he stood affected toward Christ." Thoreau answered, as reported in the *Christian Examiner* in 1865, that "a snow-storm was more to him than Christ." He is suggesting, I think, that even in the 1860s, so far into the nineteenth century, the snowstorm is still luminous with spiritual energy; and Christ is not needed to lift it back up into radiance. The snowstorm and God had never quarreled.

Thoreau trained himself over many years to see. His training involved a number of disciplines. The first was constant labor. His journals are so immense that they must have required, during his short life, two or three hours of writing each day, over and above the walks he wrote about. Second he aimed to become just, and in this struggle followed the ancient doctrine, contrary to scientific doctrine, that certain secrets of nature reveal themselves only to the observer who is morally developed. The alchemists founded their penetration of nature on their moral character. Concentrating on a "low-anchored cloud," Thoreau wrote:

> Drifting meadow of the air
> Where bloom the daisied banks and violets,
> And in whose fenny labyrinth
> The bittern booms and heron wades;
> Spirit of lakes and seas and rivers,
> Bear only perfumes and the scene
> Of healing herbs to just men's fields!

▲ ▲ ▲

Robert Bly is a poet, storyteller, translator and lecturer. His eight collections of poems include *The Light Around the Body,* winner of a National Book Award. This essay originally appeared as the introduction to the 1986 Sierra Club book, *The Winged Life: Selected Poetry and Prose of Thoreau.*

"No truer American existed than Thoreau."

"THOREAU"
RALPH WALDO EMERSON
(DELIVERED AS A EULOGY TO THOREAU IN 1862)

KIRSTIE ALLEY

THE ROMANS, THE MAD HATTERS AND.......WALDEN 1991?

Sweet Thames, run softly, till I end my song.
The river bears no empty bottles, sandwich papers,
Silk handkerchiefs, cardboard boxes, cigarette ends
Or other testimony of summer nights.

T.S. Eliot
"The Waste Land," 1921

Eliot was starkly prophetic about the environmental problems we face today. He drew on the past as well as the present to create new insights. He said, ". . . the conscious present is an awareness of the past in a way and to an extent which the past's awareness of itself cannot show."

How often can we look at what was routine and customary centuries ago, only to see it as absurd today? Yet this very perception is a learning process. What superstitions made people believe the world was flat? Why did doctors drain blood from people to "cure them?" Why were Christians thrown to the lions in the Coliseum? Hopefully, as the human race we don't just change these things, but we look at ourselves, and learn a few lessons.

When it comes to the care of human life and the environment we don't have to look very hard at the past to see lessons we can use today. It is not clear though if we learn environmental lessons well. Fifty years from now will building condos in Walden Woods, or paving the Amazon, look as outrageous as bloodletting or a flat globe do today? They should. There seems to exist something that occludes man's ability to learn from past environmental mistakes.

Historians theorize one of the major reasons for the decline of the Roman Empire was its penchant for wine. The wine might have been bad enough, but it was the lead in the wine goblets that poisoned Rome's leaders. The lead lowered I.Q., increased neurological problems, disabled potential great minds. We see the same thing going on today with school children from the lead in their water and air. I saw a story recently about a woman who was having terrible mental problems. She went to every physician her husband could find. The concerted medical opinion was that she was crazy. Her husband refused to believe this. He took a list of her symptoms to the library and started to trace their cause. He found that she had every symptom of lead toxicity. He had a harder time finding a physician who would even do a simple blood test for lead. Finally, a test showed her blood levels were dangerously high. It turned out that she drank coffee every day from porcelain cups that were not properly made and leached lead. Her husband, fortunately, didn't drink coffee. She was treated and her symptoms went away. Rome revisited?

Lewis Carroll's immortal phrase, "mad as a hatter" was borrowed from the Middle Ages. Centuries ago, when big, felt hats were in vogue, hatters made the felt stiff by rubbing a solution into the felt. The solution contained mercury. It was absorbed through the hatter's skin and made them "mad." People in villages knew if you worked in a hatting factory, you would be "mad as a hatter." A few months ago, I saw a "60 Minutes" report that questioned whether the mercury in our dental fillings might be doing the same thing.

Why don't we learn from past environmental mistakes as we seem to from other human errors? Why would someone build a condo on environmental holy ground? Why would a company try to place a toxic waste dump on sacred Native American soil? The answer is common to a goblet, a coffee cup, a felt hat, a dental filling—money. There is nothing wrong with money or commerce, but when money obfuscates care for human life or the environment, it turns to greed.

Probably no industry epitomizes greed more today than the petrochemical cartels. But unlike the owner of a hatting factory in the Middle Ages who had to change his manufacturing practices or go out of business, these conglomerates proliferate their poison. With vast sums of money they can afford scientists, lawyers, lobbyists, politicians who perpetuate their greed, and discredit any opposition. They are self-sustaining.

This is no conspiratorial theory, this is happening today in your grocery store, in your home, and on your TV. David Steinman, a member of the National Academy of Sciences, recently wrote an important book, *Diet for a Poisoned Planet*. This book details the amount of poisons, pesticides and other additives that contaminate our food. It offers helpful suggestions. Raisins were one of the foods that Steinman found had some of the highest pesticide levels. No wonder. Cesar Chavez has been saying this for years. You take a grape and dry it, and the chemicals on it are going to be even more concentrated. Steinman hadn't even published his book when an agricultural association put up a half a million dollars to kill the book. When Steinman did a "Today Show" interview, the phone campaign was so intense, the network never aired the interview. C. Everett Koop even started talking about "how safe" American food is. I know he did a lot of work to help people quit smoking, but I have no idea what vested interests fund the think tank Dr. Koop works for today. Steinman's book still made the best-seller lists in many cities. This attack was just greed perpetuating greed.

In the United States 2.7 billion pounds of pesticides are applied to crops every year. Less than one-half percent of these ever hit a bug. For years farmers have been sold a propaganda line—their crop yields will suffer if they don't use chemicals. Yet reports show that the amount of crop losses from pests are fundamentally the same now as before farmers started using all these chemicals. Some chemicals can actually deplete the nutrients in the soil, and hurt the farmer in the long run.

Chemical company influence-buying went so far that for years farmers *had* to use chemicals or they were denied farm subsidies by law. This was like the fox serving as security consultant to the chicken house, and getting paid for it! This was rigged for greed.

In the office of the Director of the United Nations Environmental Programme, Dr. Noel Brown, there's a picture of an airplane crop-dusting pesticides over an African field. A woman with a baby on her back is in the field. This image vividly reminds us how chemicals are exported for profit to third world countries even when they are banned as too harmful for use in the United States. A report that examined U.S. Customs documents showed that in 1990 chemical companies were exporting these poisons at a rate of 2.5 tons per hour to poorer countries. The pesticide chlordane made by Velsichol Chemical Corporation and used to kill termites, was banned in this country in 1988. According to the National Academy of Sciences there is "no safe" dosage level of chlordane. Velsichol, after the U.S. ban, increased its exports of chlordane by more than ten times. In this same period customs records showed a St. Louis, Missouri chemical company using a generic name exported over twenty-one million pounds of pesticides. The only chemical company in these records located in St. Louis, Missouri is Monsanto Chemical.

Another chemical company, ICI Americas, provided a spurious 1980 report on the "safety" of molinate, a herbicide used in rice fields. Despite new, credible findings this year that molinate causes reproductive damage, the State of California allowed the use of one million pounds of the herbicide.

Serious questions have been raised about the scientific integrity of the California State Health Department's approval for aerial spraying of malathion last year. Now new reports show that aerial spraying can be harmful to sensitive people. Other inside reports from the federal Environmental Protection Agency (E.P.A.) indicate that Monsanto Chemical researchers falsified safety studies on dioxin. These studies were a cornerstone for setting human exposure levels for one of the most deadly chemicals known to man. Dioxin is found in everything from Agent Orange to disposable diapers and milk cartons.

A Texas lab that analyzes pesticide residues on foods for eleven chemical companies is under E.P.A. and U.S. Justice Department investigation for falsifying testing data, and showing lower than actual concentrations of pesticides on food.

There is a federal law which requires a grocer to clearly display a notice at the point of sale of fruits or vegetables if they have been waxed. The wax makes the apples and cucumbers shiny. Grocery stores do not comply with this law even though it carries fines and jail terms. After all, who would buy apples with shellac on them? When the FDA was called, they first denied knowing about the law. Then after finding it, they said it was the state's responsibility to enforce it. When the state of California was called, it said that it was L.A. County's job to enforce the law. I think the county had one part-time person who had no time to think about it. To make matters worse, fungicides are normally put in this wax as preservatives, and not even reported by law.

These instances defy all common sense. This is not "commerce" or "providing jobs." This is getting paid to slowly poison people as chemical guinea pigs while covering it up with lies or fast talk. This is greed.

The facts don't lie:

• The National Academy of Sciences has estimated that there will be more than one million deaths in our lifetime from pesticides.

• The World Health Organization reports approximately three million pesticide poisonings a year worldwide.

• There are more than fifty-five known or suspected cancer-causing pesticides that can leave residues on our food.

• Studies have shown increased childhood cancers from using household pesticides.

• Federal studies have shown measurable pesticide residues in the tissues of most Americans.

• Cancer kills nearly twenty-five percent of Americans. One hundred years ago, before the use of petrochemicals, it killed about three percent.

As harrowing as all this might sound, and as formidable as the chemical interests may appear, they really are paper tigers. Their strength is not their own, nor even their money. Their strength is derived from us, the consumer, the person on the street. It is our money that supports them, it is our vote that elects them, it is our enlightenment that can defeat them. If we demand pesticide-free foods, if we elect leaders who will not bow to vested interests, if we protest (in the streets if necessary) the poisoning of our third world neighbors, if we refuse to accept false studies from chemical manufacturers and demand dishonesty be prosecuted, if we purchase only non-toxic alternatives, if we decry all personal or institutional investment in companies that profit from environmental destruction, if we insist that our health and our children's health is protected . . . we can win. We can each make a difference.

In 1968, Rene Du Bois, the celebrated scientist and environmentalist, said:

"The greatest danger of pollution may well be that we shall tolerate levels of it so low as to have no acute nuisance value, but sufficiently high, nevertheless, to cause delayed pathological effects and spoil the quality of life."

Whether it is the greed of the goblet maker, the condo developer, or the chemical cartel, we can learn these lessons, and make this a better world.

▲ ▲ ▲

Kirstie Alley is an actress, activist and environmentalist. After recovering from a pesticide poisoning herself, she led public protests against misuse and overuse of pesticides. She produced "Cry Out," a children's environmental booklet used across the country, and a national public service announcement radio campaign for the environment. She is founder of the Alley Foundation, dedicated to environmental education.

The morning wind forever blows, the poem of creation is uninterrupted; but few are the ears that hear it. Olympus is but the outside of the earth every where.

WALDEN
HENRY DAVID THOREAU

TODD N. TATUM

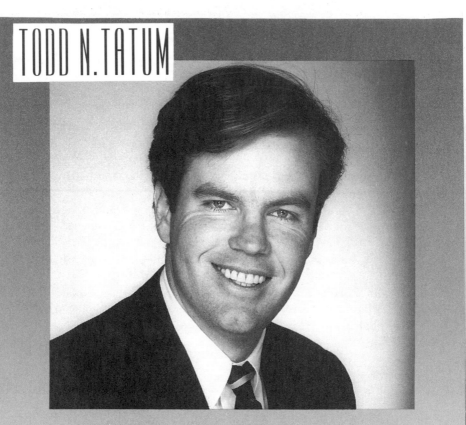

THE NEW CALL TO ARMS

t seems like an average Monday morning. I'm leafing through the *Los Angeles Times* looking for articles I thought would be on the front page. I was sure there would be huge pictures and headlines describing the events that would be happening in order to celebrate the biggest environmental awareness day of the year. But they're missing. Even though it's April 22, it just seems like an average day.

Why did Earth Day 1991 come and go almost unnoticed? Sure, there were a few schoolchildren and serious environmentalists who actively observed it. But the emotion I felt on Earth Day 1990 just wasn't there. If you were one of the many who did actively observe Earth Day, then you know what I mean. People all across the world seemed to care so much, I was sure the feeling would at least last twelve months. It was obvious how fast many of us forget, or don't want to remember, the problems that the Earth Day 1990 efforts made us all aware of. Even though the organizers of the 1990 event tried to project the idea that every day should be Earth Day, this idea just didn't make it through the year.

Why wasn't this one day event celebrated by many more people? Why are people less concerned with the problems in their own backyards than with events on the other side of the globe? I know everyone shared concerns for the Persian Gulf war, yet only a small percentage of our population have willingly made the sacrifice to join the armed services. There are many who say they would gladly serve their country in a time of need but are unable due to age, family, and numerous other commitments. Many of these same people become passionate about their patriotism and what they would do if given the chance. Well, their chance is now!

When I founded the Citizens Volunteer Corps a year ago, I wasn't really sure if a volunteer group could address the problems that each and every community faces. But the notion that one person has the power to make significant change is something I truly believe in. The power of the people is confirmed in breathtaking fashion every day as we witness extraordinary events around the world. Yet, the "people power" that works toward change here in our own backyard is rarely acknowledged. It is more glamorous for the world press corps to focus on the revolutions taking place in Eastern Europe and other parts of the world. But what about the men and women who clean up our beaches after an oil-tanker spill? Or the people who start a neighborhood recycling program? How about the tireless volunteers who work for Greenpeace and other environmental groups? Every day these "small revolutions" are helping to save our planet. But they aren't enough.

How often have we heard: "What can I possibly do to help the earth? This is a job for the government or business community, these problems are their fault anyway." Or: "Well, it isn't really *that* bad!"

We as a people must begin to believe that being a resident of this planet involves certain duties as well as privileges, and that every citizen must exhibit a sense of responsibility to his or her community, country, and planet. While we witness extraordinary events around the globe, let's open our eyes to the environmental problems at home. A day should not go by in which every one of us has not taken the time to help make our planet a better place to live.

Answering this call to arms doesn't take much. It could mean buying products that can be recycled and making sure they are recycled after you use them. Taking the time to write your legislators concerning environmental issues. Being aware of your water consumption and cutting back on your use of this precious resource. Teaching a younger person the importance of these environmental issues. These are just a few of the practices every citizen must begin to take seriously.

In the early 1960s, President John F. Kennedy said, "One person can make a difference, and everyone should try." It is up to you and me to take charge of problems in our own communities and make our neighbors aware of what they can do to help. At the Citizens Volunteer Corps we have started a small recycling program to encourage our volunteers to become involved in local environmental issues. Being based in the High Desert of Southern California doesn't offer a lot of opportunities to work on the kind of environmental problems we see others work on around the country. The problems we face are water shortages, destruction of the natural landscape and overflowing landfills. Although these are very urgent issues that everyone in this community must begin to face, I wasn't really sure if anyone would care enough to help a voluntary recycling program. But we now pick up recyclable items each week from over 150 separate homes and businesses. I hate to think how many tons of recyclable items would go to our landfills if we hadn't taken the first step by starting our program. Such programs also need to be expanded—especially to include kids. If we begin teaching our young children the importance of environmental concerns, our future generations will realize their responsibilities to the environment.

What I've come to realize is that each of us needs to adopt a life-style that proves his or her commitment to our environment. And that if I can begin to do this and persuade others around me, then everyone can. But the most important act that all of us must do is vote for candidates who echo our beliefs. This is the only way to bring about permanent change. It isn't enough to actively point out the problems; we must have legislators who will make laws to reflect the needed changes.

I believe in the idea that we must act locally to make changes globally. This might mean some real commitments to those who aren't used to standing up for their beliefs. Martin Luther King, Jr. said, "An individual has not started living until he can rise above the narrow confines of his individualistic concerns to the broader concerns of all humanity."

Let this be our new call to arms! Let each of us answer this call by making the commitment to do our part to help change this planet. Let's make Walden our shining example of what each of us is capable of doing if we join together.

▲ ▲ ▲

Todd Tatum is president/founder of the Citizens Volunteer Corps, which is dedicated to providing people of all ages the opportunity to perform volunteer community service work. He previously spent two years as executive/legislative assistant to Rep. Joseph P. Kennedy II. He is a member of the Walden Woods Project Advisory Board.

A lake is the landscape's most beautiful and expressive feature. It is earth's eye; looking into which the beholder measures the depth of his own nature.

WALDEN
HENRY DAVID THOREAU

DIANDRA M. DOUGLAS

DEYA—CHANGE COMES TO THE GLOBAL VILLAGE

I am bounding down a tiny path in a small mountain village in Spain. Moving like a gazelle—or how I imagine a gazelle would run, because I've never really seen one. The leaps make me feel free. There is a loud rushing sound in the air, the *torente*, and over its roar I can only faintly hear the birds and the leaves whispering their secrets.

The *torente* is one of the two jewels of our village, the other being the pristine blue Mediterranean Sea. I call them jewels because they are always bestowing gifts on the Deyans!

I'm on my way to see Matias. I think of him as a wizard but he doesn't know it. He has a small farm toward the end of the valley.

Matias, upon my arrival, has just finished making the most incredible labyrinth I have ever seen—it is a maze of walls and rivulets. It stretches around us for as far as I can see. Mula, who has helped him diligently in this endeavor for going on twenty-three years, stands sweaty in front of a wooden plow under a tree. I've arrived just in time. Matias raises a small wooden board and miraculously a steady stream of water obediently follows its path through the maze, delivering the *torente* to every tomato, carrot, and lettuce in the garden. When he feels they've drunk enough, Matias quickly sends the *torente* back to its usual course down the ravine. He lets me help him pull a few weeds, but only the ones that really must go, he explains, since the remaining ones will flower in the spring. He carries on his own private, continuous battle with the ever-encroaching wilderness. I call it "wildness," but he corrects me and says "wilderness," with an experienced warrior's mutual respect for a competent enemy.

Now it is time to go and milk the goats and pick some olives. As a special treat I've brought along some cocoa I have stolen from the cook at home so we can mix it with the warm milk in an old tin can we've brought along.

It's almost 11:30 and I have to get back to Miramar in time for lunch. I've begged Matias to lend me Mula, knowing that if we keep a steady trot I should be able to make it home in about 1½ hours Spanish time.

As I head up the little path toward the main road I can see her. I don't really know how old she is, though Matias says over eight hundred. I wonder who wants to count that far, anyway, and for what reason? I don't really know how many little stone houses make her up; not too many but just enough. She's backed up against two tall mountains sprinkled with olive trees. The Puig protects her from the rear. They're so high that I don't know anyone who's been to the top, even though I have heard some say they have.

The largest structure is a beautiful old church on a little hill. It presides impressively over the village with a graveyard that's walled-in, which I think is considerate as I do not like to look at it very much.

I can barely glimpse the sea down the ravine. My mother told me Deya was so far up the valley to protect it from pirate raids. Too bad it makes the walk to the beach a good two hours. In summer it is grueling.

From my perspective on Mula, Deya looks almost like she was carved out of the mountain or created simultaneously with the mountains themselves. She really belongs there, part of the very nature of things. And she is in her own way part of it, because each and every person there for generations respected what nature gave. In exchange for working hard to keep things as they were, they survived and even thrived. How can you improve on paradise, anyway, I thought. All the Deyans knew every important tree, *torente,* and path to good fishing spots. Nobody wanted it any different, including me.

Suddenly I could hear the trumpeting of a conch shell. Jaime, the fisherman, was trudging up the path with a little reed basket full of about a dozen differently colored and shaped fish.

After carefully poking and examining the beautiful colors of his catch, I congratulated him, and it was time for us to part. He had to sell his fish in the village before they spoiled in the sun. Already there were a lot of *senoras* standing on their steps waiting for him because they heard his trumpeting in the distance. I, too, had to pick up my pace or face the consequences from Magdalena, our cook, if I was late for lunch. Jaime offered me a fish of my choice. I picked a little red one and placed it under my blouse to keep the dust of the road off it until I arrived home. Along the way, to pass the time of the journey, I tried to teach Mula the *piaf* and *passage* I had learned from my riding teacher, but she was having difficulties with the rhythm.

Once in a long while, a car full of *extranjeros* (the literal translation being "strange ones from another place"—better known today as tourists), would stop the car and stare at Mula and me, as they had probably never seen a dancing plow mule before.

Miramar was a magical place, a large sprawling villa built on a high bluff above the sea, surrounded by small formal rose gardens and promenades with fountains. A small chapel graced the end of the garden at the far left. People always said the house and the chapel were haunted, but I didn't believe them. In fact, the chapel terrace, when lit with candles, was my favorite place for spaghetti parties with my friends. It had such a beautiful view.

After lunch, when everybody would leave for *siesta,* I would go to my room and uncover my "box"—a small battery-operated record player about half the size of a normal record. In fact, it was very difficult to balance a record on the small spinning table. We had no electricity but I didn't miss it. The hot water and refrigerators ran on gas and the flicker of the flames in the little crystal oil lanterns cast a warm yellow light. Each room possessed a beautiful enamel stove with delicate decorations, all of which were sent from Austria to provide heat about one hundred years before my time. There were also more candles than I ever successfully counted, and every time Magdalena asked Pedro, her helper, to light them or blow them out, it brought a frown to his face.

I liked the candles because it always felt to me that we were living in some kind of a church. When the possibility arose, my mother decided not to install electricity, for to do so, she thought, would "change the feel" of our house. When I was not scurrying around the beach hunting for shiny shells in the crystal-clear water or in the company of Matias, I had many lonely afternoons as a child. I had no brothers or sisters and lived a good distance from any reliable source of playmates. Matias, my favorite friend, was pushing sixty, so he had many chores to face during the day. I was eight and presumably my childishness bothered him from time to time.

Surprisingly enough, I did not gravitate to the company of my parents, as one would have thought, or the company of the people who worked in our house, but rather to the large windows in our study which so perfectly framed the mountains into a masterpiece canvas, looking to me as if it could only have been painted by God. I would carefully set up my box at the very edge of the window and play Stravinsky's "The Rite of Spring." The beauty of the mountains which I knew so well, and the majesty and awesomeness which nature instilled in my young spirit, even at that age, kept me captive at the sill of the windows hour after hour. I am not quite sure what I thought of during those long hours—

probably some childhood Prince Charming fantasies. But, I was always conscious of the fact that it was the overwhelming presence and the force of nature itself which held me to my spot. I would examine every rock formation, every tree, the thousand different colors and hues of green which I slowly discovered, the way the light shone on the cliffs, playing tricks as the sun moved across the sky, and the aroma of the woods that drifted through my window on a cool, fresh breeze.

Finally Magdalena would burst into the room shouting orders, annoyed by the slow, jerking sounds emanating from my box. The batteries, after many hours, had lost their juice and I, lost in reverie, had not even noticed.

Towards the close of that summer, television arrived at the cafe in Deya—well, a form of television. At exactly 4:00 P.M. on Saturday afternoons, all the children would fight for cane chairs under a sole, suspended television. Finally someone would turn it on. At first there was nothing but fuzziness and static sounds. Then suddenly, as if by magic, an episode in black and white of "The Big Valley" with Barbara Stanwyck, set in the American West, would appear. We were all spellbound till, too soon, the one-hour show would be over and the television shared nothing but snowy interference till the following Saturday at 4:00 P.M. Soon the bar man would chase us out and a huge cowboy range war would break out on the main street. I played along reluctantly, but felt secretly that this game did not seem to fit Deya. But times were changing and I was a witness.

At the end of the summer, my mother informed me I was now grown up and had to go away to boarding school in Switzerland—as she put it, "to make sure I would be well educated." In my mind, it turned out to be quite the contrary. In fact, I felt that Geneva, with its multitude of people I did not know, traffic, noise, crime, and dirty air taught me little of interest or use. School was only marginally better. However, despite my protests I was to remain there seven more years.

Now I have my own child and I still return to Deya each summer. But I can barely stand to visit Matias now. He is now pushing his late eighties, and there is such a sense of tragedy in his eyes. His first question to me is always, "What has happened to the *torente*? It's been all dried up for so many years now. What's happened in the village? Indeed, in the village everybody seems so strange. Nobody chats to each other on the streets. They throw garbage in the streams and on the beach." I never seem to be able to answer his questions satisfactorily and so I promptly suggest a change of topic. But I think about it and it bothers me.

Deya formed the basis of much of my value system with respect to a life balanced among man, his spirituality, and nature. It became my reference point for a balanced life and I took it for granted that it would always be there. Deya, as so many other magical and beautiful parts of the world, has suffered with time the arrogance and destructiveness of man. The scars are clearly visible and too numerous.

Deya was my Walden Pond and Walden Woods—a place magical and powerful enough to make us stop and bow and slowly learn to see the humble majesty of nature—and Deya, like Walden Woods, represents to me the plight of the environment across our small planet. It is as if some deteriorating virus of unimaginable power and resilience has taken hold of all that is wild, pure, and beautiful and intends to destroy the very force of nature herself on which ultimately all man, animal, and plant life depends for survival. That virus is man himself, practicing denial of all the issues he urgently needs to address, so as to perhaps ultimately perish by his own avoidance—by his own hand.

So it is clear we can no longer accept the slow, methodological destruction of our environment for short-term interest and material gain. Thoreau, even in 1845, was crying out to individuals to reexamine their lives, to balance real needs against an obsession with the accumulation of personal wealth which left man with "no time to be anything but a machine." His most important message to us is that all men have the right to hope for a better life for themselves and their children. In fact, we have more than a right, we have a responsibility to do so.

To me, one of Thoreau's most important messages was that "the beginning of all reform is the spiritual perfection of each individual." And of course this personal quest is what encouraged him to move to Walden Woods and seek isolation from society. Thoreau's example of life at Walden has exemplified how one individual can successfully pursue a life endowed with a higher code of basic values and content.

As early as 1845, Thoreau foresaw the destructiveness that the Industrial Revolution, if unchecked, would wreak not only on our environment but on the well-being of the human consciousness.

In *Walden*, Thoreau offers us a courageous example of how one can attempt to "realize one's divinity to fulfill one's potential for ideal existence in the real world." He always writes of the "ideal," and of how one can achieve this ideal, whatever it may be: "I learned this, at least, by my experiment; that if one advances confidently in the direction of his dreams, and endeavors to live the life which he has imagined, he will meet with a success unexpected in common hours. He will put some things behind, will pass an invisible boundary; new, universal, and more liberal laws will begin to establish themselves around and within him; or the old laws will be expanded, and interpreted in his favor in a more liberal sense, and he will live with the license of a higher order of beings. If you have built castles in the air, your work need not be lost; that is where they should be. Now put the foundations under them." Thoreau's words of 150 years ago mean more to us today than one might have ever imagined. The difficult task now is to get each individual to understand the critical role he or she plays in being able to make a positive difference. However small the gesture, everyone has the power to make a difference. Whether one's involvement is donating money and/or time, the commitment will bring public attention and support to various pressing environmental issues. For it seems there are too many of us for Mother Earth to sustain, as man has not yet learned respect for the planet and the delicate ecosystem that bore him.

Thoreau summons all of us, individually and then collectively, to bring about a halt and hopefully a reversal of man's destruction of his own small planet. We must band together not only as a nation with a collective consciousness, but also as a global community, for the actions of each and every one of us, as we have seen, eventually affect our global neighbors.

The question I keep asking myself is, can mankind as a species evolve at this point in time the intellectual capacity to see the plight of our ecosystem and place environmental conservation in a position of prominence in his priorities? As a species, our technological, industrial, and destructive capabilities seem to have far outweighed our wisdom and foresight. My only hope is that the innate dignity that I must believe we possess as a species will strike a chord of urgency and create a new awareness in society. Hopefully the citizens of this tiny planet, with a unanimous cry, will demand and implement the changes necessary to ensure a toxin-free and well-balanced ecology, and we will enhance not only the quality of our own lives, but also the lives of future generations.

The struggle to preserve Walden Woods in 1991 is part of that effort. Thoreau, a pioneer of environmentalist thought, compels us to act. He strongly believed in the morality and responsibility that all must bear to preserve nature and their own sense of spirituality. This very philosophy was born under the protective branches of Walden Woods, which are now threatened by development. To me, the loss of Walden Woods would represent not only the loss of a beautiful forest, but the annihilation of the very thread of hope in which Thoreau believed so strongly. It is not only Walden Woods which is threatened but every forest, every little village in the mountains like Deya, every endangered species, and, in the end, our very existence. We dare not leave such a heritage of destruction to posterity.

▲ ▲ ▲

Diandra M. Douglas is an independent film producer, a freelance writer, and contributing editor at *Mirabella* magazine. She is a member of the Walden Woods Project Advisory Board.

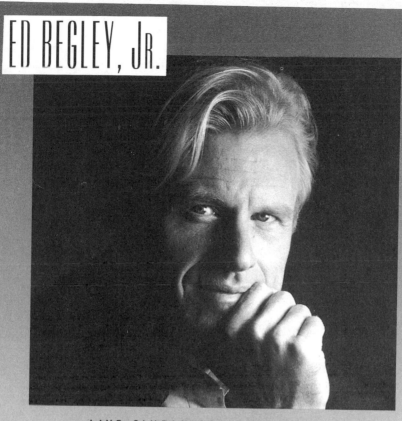

ED BEGLEY, Jr.

LIVE SIMPLY SO OTHERS CAN SIMPLY LIVE

Among the many hidden blessings that come with an association with the Walden Woods Project is the opportunity to rediscover Thoreau. Though we have now traveled much further down the path upon which Henry David feared we might be headed, our basic problems remain the ones he confronted: Man's vain attempt to gain dominion over nature, our refusal to heed clear signals of danger, and on a much deeper level, the absurd notion that material things will ease the longing in our souls. (It's gotta be rough when you slap the final stone in place on the Taj Mahal or the Trump Tower, or you carve out the last bit of moustache hair on Mount Rushmore, and you're still left feeling unsatisfied.)

The idea of respect for nature predates Thoreau by quite a few years. In the five thousand-year-old Book of the Dead, one's eternal fate could be decided on the basis of two questions: Did you ever pollute the River Nile or cut down a fruitful tree?

But I'm surely getting ahead of myself. It's probably not essential that we comprehend the big picture just now. We really need to discuss something else: Since our environmental problems have been painfully apparent for some time, why isn't everyone leaping into action? Why aren't consumers scrambling for the string bags and the compact fluorescents? As is usually the case with matters of great importance, the demons of deceit are our biggest enemies.

There are basically two old lies about the environment that stand in our way. The first, the older lie, has very little power any more. That's the notion that everything's under control. Lies of that ilk, which flourished in the 1950s, don't hold up as well today. "Better Living Through Chemistry" took on new meaning after Love Canal and Bhopal. Add to that the Exxon Valdez and Persian Gulf spills, the ever-growing hole in the ozone layer, needles and porpoises washing up on the Eastern seaboard, orphan garbage scows with no place to dump their cargo, and it gets rather difficult to deny that there's a problem. You'd need to be a lingering spelunker to be unaware of how bad things have gotten out there. I'll bet even Terry Waite has a pretty fair notion of how much damage has been done in the last few years. So the old lie that it's business as usual should no longer be a threat.

The second, and the far more dangerous fib is that there's nothing that can be done. Many seem to feel that it's too late, that the damage is irreversible—or that government and the big corporations are in bed together, so why bother? People have a wide range of reasons for their inaction, but when you examine them closely, none of them really cuts it.

Who makes air pollution and hazardous waste? *Who* makes the decisions at the giant corporations that we seem to battle at every turn? *Who* makes the choice to develop a site as important as Walden Woods? To quote the Chevron ad that can be guaranteed to make my lunch spin, *"People do."*

Well, then, people can also *un-*do. So why don't they? If you accept the fact that the wonderful book *Fifty Simple Things You Can Do To Save the Earth* is a national best-seller, you've got to assume the multitude of do-gooders that bought it simply haven't read it! Or worse still, *have* read it, but prefer getting their exercise driving a car to the gym rather than simply bicycling and breathing clean air. *Have* read it, but prefer buying the more-expensive-in-the-long-run General Electric bulbs to compact fluorescents because they're so fond of companies like G.E., and want to make sure they keep cranking out killer weapons and power plants. *Have* read it, but prefer to keep their homes like an ice box in the summer and like a sauna in the winter, knowing our wasteful ways will soon make global warming a certainty. (Perhaps there's a method to their madness. The notion of being able to grow mangos in Manitoba does have a certain appeal.) But the more likely scenario is that folks are as overwhelmed by the scope of the solutions as they are by the scope of the problems. They're hard-pressed to tackle the Mount Everest of environmental ills that we face not simply because they fear such a long hard climb, but because for now, they are stuck at base camp, deciding which mountaineering gear is appropriate for their needs.

One way that people have decided to embark on this journey is through recycling. It's the way many of us began on the environmental path after the first Earth Day back in 1970. But I quickly discovered that recycling alone was not enough. We're not going to turn this thing around by loading up the Volvo with old copies of the *L.A. Weekly* and spent Evian bottles once a week. That might be an important first step, but it will not get us to our final destination. We're going to have to be a lot more aggressive if we wish to make any real headway. The way to do that is in the hands of the three million-odd good souls who plopped down $4.95 for the book I mentioned earlier. If just those who currently have the book in their possession would remove it from under the short leg of the kitchen table, open it, and *try* one of the suggestions each week, things would change. If they would then recycle the book by passing it on to a friend, the results would be staggering: Marked reduction in gas consumption and deforestation. No need for any new power plants. No need for any new landfills. Air fit to breathe. Water fit to drink, and plenty of it.

I think part of the problem is the title of the book. *Fifty Simple Things You Can Do To Save The Earth.* We don't need to save the earth. The earth is going to be just fine. It's survived the past 4.6 billion years, and it will surely survive anything we can throw at it. The title should be *Fifty Simple Ways To Save Your Ass.* It is *our* fate that's in jeopardy, along with the fate of countless other species. That's what is at stake here. Will we survive and flourish or choke and eventually suffocate in our own detritus? The choice is ours, and personal action is the key.

Many feel that we should put our faith in government or industry to solve these problems. These are entities made up, after all, of people. But after twenty years of empty promises from both groups, it becomes clear that this effort can and must be undertaken on an individual basis. To await some breakthrough from groups that are that cumbersome would surely be a mistake. We must act alone, but welcome all who join us. As Margaret Mead said, "Never doubt that a small group of concerned and dedicated individuals can change the world." Indeed, it's the only thing that ever has.

▲ ▲ ▲

Ed Begley, Jr. began his acting career on "My Three Sons," spent several years as a stand-up comedian and has appeared in dozens of motion pictures, but he's best-known for his portrayal of Dr. Victor Erlich on "St. Elsewhere." He is a board member of the Environmental Leadership Forum, the League of Conservation Voters, Earth Communications Office, Californians Against Waste, the American Oceans Campaign and the Walden Woods Project Advisory Board.

FLOYD RED CROW WESTERMAN

CHIEF SEATTLE SPEAKS

The following letter was written almost two hundred years ago. It speaks of the prophecy of pollution and decay in America. We have always heeded the warnings of our ancestors. Chief Seattle wrote this letter to Washington when his people were being forced to the reservation "concentration camp," and forewarned America about the way Americans were living then. The images of this letter are most appropriate when we see the global environmental problems of today.

—Floyd Red Crow Westerman

How can you buy or sell the sky, the warmth of the land? The idea is strange to us. If we do not own the freshness of the air and the sparkle of the water, how can you buy them?

Every part of this earth is sacred to my people. Every shining pine needle, every sandy shore, every mist in the dark woods, every clearing and humming insect is holy in the memory and experience of my people. The sap which courses through the trees carries the memories of the red man.

The white man's dead forget the country of their birth when they go to walk among the stars. Our dead never forget this beautiful earth, for it is the mother of the red man. We are part of the earth, and it is a part of us. The perfumed flowers are our sisters; the deer, the horse, the great eagle, these are our brothers. The rocky crests, the juices in the meadows, the body heat of the pony, and man—all belong to the same family.

So, when the Great Chief in Washington sends word that he wishes to buy our land, he asks much of us. The great Chief sends word he will reserve us a place so that we can live comfortably to ourselves. He will be our father, and we will be his children. So we will consider your offer to buy our land. But it will not be easy. For this land is sacred to us.

This shining water that moves in the streams and the rivers is not just water but the blood of our ancestors. If we sell you land, you must remember that it is sacred, and you must teach your children that it is sacred and that each ghostly reflection in the clear water of the lakes tells of events and memories in the life of my people. The water's murmur is the voice of my father's father.

The rivers are our brothers, they quench our thirst. The rivers carry our canoes and feed our children. If we sell you our land, you must remember and teach your children, that the rivers are our brothers, and yours, and you must henceforth give the rivers the kindness you would give any brother.

We know that the white man does not understand our ways. One portion of land is the same to him as the next, for he is a stranger who comes in the night and takes from the land whatever he needs. The earth is not his brother, but his enemy, and when he has conquered it, he moves on. He leaves his fathers' graves, and his children's birthright is forgotten. He treats his mother, the earth, and his brother, the sky, as things to be bought, plundered, sold like sheep or bright beads. His appetite will devour the earth and leave behind only a desert.

I do not know. Our ways are different from your ways. The sight of your cities pains the eyes of the red man. But perhaps it is because the red man is a savage and does not understand.

There is no quiet place in the white man's cities. No place to hear the unfurling of leaves in spring, or the rustle of an insect's wings. But perhaps it is because I am a savage and do not understand. The clatter only seems to insult the ears. And what is there to life if a man cannot hear the lonely cry of the whippoorwill or the arguments of the frogs around a pond at night? I am a red man and do not understand. The Indian prefers the soft sound of the wind darting over the face of a pond, and the smell of the wind itself, cleansed by rain or scented with the pine cone.

The air is precious to the red man, for all things share the same breath: the beast, the tree, the man, they all share the same breath. The white men, they all share the same breath. The white man does not seem to notice the air he breathes. Like a man dying for many days, he is numb to the stench. But if we sell you our land, you must remember that the air is precious to us, that the air shares its spirit with all the life it supports. The wind that gave our grandfather his first breath also received his last sigh. And if we sell you our land, you must keep it apart and sacred, as a place where even the white man can go to taste the wind that is sweetened by the meadow's flowers.

So we will consider your offer to buy our land. If we decide to accept, I will make one condition. The white man must treat the beasts of this land as his brothers.

I am savage, and I do not understand any other way. I have seen a thousand rotting buffalos on the prairie, left by the white man who shot them from a passing train. I am a savage, and I do not understand how the smoking iron horse can be more important than the buffalo that we kill only to stay alive.

What is man without the beasts? If all the beasts were gone, man would die from a great loneliness of spirit. For whatever happens to the beasts soon happens to man. All things are connected.

You must teach your children that the ground beneath their feet is the ashes of our grandfathers. So that they will respect the land, tell your children that the earth is rich with the lives of our kin. Teach your children what we have taught our children, that the earth is our mother. Whatever befalls the earth befalls the sons of the earth. Man did not weave the web of life, he is merely a strand in it. Whatever he does to the web, he does to himself.

Even the white man, whose God walks and talks with him as friend to friend, cannot be exempt from the common destiny. We may be brothers after all. We shall see. One thing we know, which the white man may one day discover—our God is the same God. You may think now that you own Him as you wish to own our land: but you cannot. He is the God of man, and His compassion is equal for the red man and the white. This earth is precious to Him, and to harm the earth is to heap contempt upon its Creator.

The Whites, too, shall pass; perhaps sooner than all other tribes. Contaminate your bed, and you will one night suffocate in your own waste.

But in your perishing, you will shine brightly, fired by the strength of the God who brought you to this land and for some special purpose gave you dominion over this land and over the red man. That destiny is a mystery to us, for we do not understand when the buffalo are all slaughtered, the wild horses are tamed, the secret corners of the forest heavy with the scent of many men, and the view of the ripe hills blotted out by talking wires. Where is the thicket? Gone. Where is the eagle? Gone.

▲ ▲ ▲

Floyd Red Crow Westerman, Native American activist and country folk singer, has appeared in a number of motion pictures, including *Dances with Wolves, The Doors,* and *Renegades,* and on TV in "Son of Morning Star" (in which he portrayed Sitting Bull), "L.A. Law" and "Northern Exposure."

Among the Indians, the earth and its productions generally were common and free to all the tribe, like the air and water—but among us who have supplanted the Indians, the public retain only a small yard or common in the middle of the village, with perhaps a grave-yard beside it, and the right of way, by sufferance, by a particular narrow route, which is annually becoming narrower, from one such yard to another. I doubt if you can ride out five miles in any direction without coming to where some individual is tolling in the road—and he expects the time when it will all revert to him or his heirs. This is the way we civilized men have arranged it.

I am not overflowing with respect and gratitude to the fathers who thus laid out our New England villages, whatever precedent they were influenced by, for I think that a 'prentice hand liberated from Old English prejudices could have done much better in this new world. If they were in earnest seeking thus far away 'freedom to worship God,' as some assure us—why did they not secure a little more of it, when it was so cheap and they were about it? At the same time that they built meeting-houses why did they not preserve from desecration and destruction far grander temples not made with hands?

"HUCKLEBERRIES"
HENRY DAVID THOREAU

ARLO GUTHRIE

WALLED-IN BEINGS

Everyone now knows that all human beings are people. However, it is important to understand that we live in a universe filled with people, few of which are human.

There are spirit people, animal people, plant people, rock people, and zillions of other kinds of people, too. A person is a temporary condition of a permanent non-being. If you are being, you're probably a person. Everything that is has personhood.

Children know this, though they may not express it this way. The mistake children make is that they place human senses around all persons, whether they are human or not. Children are not aware of limitations arising from human-ness, and so cannot understand the limitations on other beings—that they have to be themselves. They assume that every person thinks and feels what they do. Do fish laugh? If you are young enough, of course they do!

It is important to understand that all beings can be bound by their senses, imprisoned in ego bodies which confine their understanding of what truly exists by what they perceive themselves to be. These ego bodies create a false reality. Average people, for example, do not laugh at fish jokes. It's not that fish aren't good at telling jokes either.

It is equally important to know that all beings can be freed from this prison of their own points of view. Different traditions have different thoughts on how this takes place, but most agree that freedom from the illusion of a separate, and therefore partial, reality takes some effort and that the effort is well spent. But that is a story for another time. It is enough to realize that everything that is is a person.

The variety of people who inhabit a place can make it special. During 1990, many human people gathered near Walden Pond to rescue the area from the construction of an "office park/housing development." I went because I wanted to find out for myself what an "office park" was. I couldn't figure it out just from the words. I went for other reasons, too.

I imagined that surely some of the tree, rock, and pond people who were known by Henry David Thoreau might still be there. These kinds of persons generally seem to have long lifespans, especially when humans aren't progressing in the area.

Not being known for having made much progress lately myself, I couldn't believe that I posed much of a threat to anyone within the Walden domain. And, after all, I was coming to help rescue the domain from destruction. And so I imagined that it would not be difficult to strike up some conversation with the local beings, and maybe learn a thing or two.

Not surprisingly, when I arrived there were a lot of humans talking with each other. We had a nice champagne brunch and listened to lots of speakers. Photographers were everywhere, trying to get that special photo of Don Henley, Bonnie Raitt, or all of us together. Interviewers asked questions like, "What's so special about Walden Woods?" or "What about housing for poor people?"

To his great credit, Don Henley was polite. He had envisioned the rescue operation from the beginning, and had now to put up with the politics of persuasion—not an easy task. Although brunching with the brunch-set was not my particular forte, I knew that the cause justified any small inconvenience on my part. I did, however, note, with a sense of awe, how much the survival of the universe depended on brunching with the right people.

If anyone acknowledged the local beings who surrounded us that afternoon, I was not aware of it. Certainly no one addressed them publicly. It was as if the rocks and trees, as if the earth and the sky were simply there—a nice pastoral scene where we humans made our plans and celebrated our little victories.

What a shame that we thought of ourselves as being alone there, surrounded as we were by beings who, after all, provided the reason for our being there in the first place. It was these very beings who inspired at least one man toward liberation. If nothing else, Henry David Thoreau sought to be free.

Like all beings, we share in the deceptive bondage of personhood. In sharing the illusion we also partake of the dreamlike reality of freedom or liberation. We are each other.

Too often, it seems that those of us most motivated to rescue our environment find it difficult to rescue ourselves. This alone may provide us an occasional laugh in a world dominated by gloomy and excessively serious people. Beings who cannot control themselves often attempt to control everything around them.

A person addicted to eating potatoes may move to Antarctica to avoid them, but, if he does not consume his desire, it will grow and he will breathe his last breath with potatoes on his mind. He will immediately be reborn in Idaho. It's fun to wonder about the nature of things. It may also lead to conclusions which nurture an awe that is truly inspiring.

Perhaps the time is coming quickly when we will begin to discover what the environmental movement is truly about, or just as importantly what it is not about. It is about the commonality we have with all beings, and the struggle we share to peer beyond the restrictions that time and space impose upon our apparent separateness. It is not about the fear of mutual destruction, preservation, or restoration.

If we are here only to preserve ourselves, we will be disappointed quickly enough. Our lives, as they appear to be, are shorter or longer, but nevertheless, finite. Everything that is born must return to apparent death. Nor are we here to preserve the world for our children. We are our children!

When we begin to consider these things, we may approach an understanding that loosens the grip of a fear that binds all persons to countless cycles of births and deaths.

This is not the *goal* of an environmental movement, it *is* the environment wherein all movement takes place. This is the path which all beings must wander, and we will wander it all the more joyfully when we begin to grant to other beings the same respect, compassion and love which we desire for ourselves.

In other words, be wary of environmentalists who have no sense of humor. Be skeptical of those who do not laugh at fish jokes. And as my father, Woody Guthrie, said often, "This world is your world. Take it easy, but, take it."

▲ ▲ ▲

Arlo Guthrie, the son of Woody Guthrie, has been performing onstage as a musician and storyteller since he was thirteen years old. He has made thirteen albums, from 1967's *Alice's Restaurant,* which contains his anti-draft anthem, to his most recent, *Someday,* made for his own independent label, Rising Son.

PAUL TSONGAS

WALDEN: OUR LIVING HERITAGE

Walden Pond. Why bother? It's really nothing more than a small body of water. There are tens of thousands of larger ponds and lakes all over America. If Walden Pond falls to the developers, it won't be the first one to go, and it sure won't be the last. Hey, let it go.

To some, this is the voice of pragmatism. Saving Walden Woods to preserve Walden Pond is like much ado about very little.

But that view is essentially acultural. It's a perspective that attaches no value to a tree beyond its leaves and branches; no value to the pond beyond the total volume of its water. It implies that everything is temporary. What has gone before has no present relevance. And what is here today will not matter to those who come after us.

This view is modern man exhibiting his most detached self. It is not only destructive of physical beauty, it has become simply unsustainable as a way of life, if what we care for is long-term human survival.

We are not merely a collection of two-legged animals enamored with cars and VCRs and ATM machines. We did not arrive here sanitized, like chicken parts in the supermarket. We are a people, merely one link in a chain that stretches back to days beyond memory. We are the link that connects that heritage to the generations that will follow, and we desperately need the wisdom brought by continuity with our ancestors.

Preserving Walden Pond declares that some things matter because the people who believed in them lived there. Walden Pond is where one travels in order to experience and honor the values of Henry David Thoreau. His insight into human behavior and his sense of being are captured on the printed page. But they reside also on the land and in the water which nurtured him.

This land and this water must be sanctified not because it is the prettiest land on the most impressive pond, but because this is where Thoreau's contemplation took place. This land and this water are the site of values that have shaped the thinking of both world leaders and unnoticed citizens. There is a greatness to the legacy of Henry David Thoreau, and Walden Pond speaks to our respect for that greatness, our need to keep it alive.

But all this is so obvious.

So why is it such a battle? And why is it such a lonely battle? And why is it that the idea of preserving Walden Woods has not resonated across the country like a clap of biblical thunder?

Walden Pond and Walden Woods, part of our heritage and part of the intellectual fabric that bonds us together and makes rich our national experience, was for a long time the preserve of the Middlesex County Commissioners. Their primary interest was to stock the pond every summer with patronage. It was part of the spoils system that was, sadly, very much a Massachusetts tradition.

A Middlesex County reform slate (of which I was part) was elected in 1972 and it transferred Walden Pond to the state's Department of Natural Resources. We wanted the supervision of the pond to be in the hands of people who knew how to nurture it and cared enough to do the job. Then-governor Francis Sargent, an ardent environmentalist, received the property with great enthusiasm and he and his successors, including Michael Dukakis, have sought to restore its integrity.

Walden Woods is the buffer that protects the pond and provides the ambience that makes the Walden Pond experience meaningful. The drive to preserve Walden Woods is the precondition for preserving Walden Pond. Indeed, when Henry David Thoreau walked, he did not walk through the water, he walked through the woods. He contemplated while journeying in the woods, not while immersed in the water.

This relationship between Walden Woods and Walden Pond isn't truly appreciated by many who live in Massachusetts, nor by many who make political decisions in Massachusetts. The prevailing sense has been that Walden Pond was all that we needed to preserve. Walden Pond was essential, while Walden Woods was a frivolous add-on. That view cannot be allowed to prevail.

When I was a Peace Corps volunteer in Ethiopia, I lived amongst people whom Americans perceived as relatively backward, not "sophisticated," as we were. Yet, in reality, these people lived closer to the earth and had a resonance with it. They were avid environmentalists but never saw themselves that way. They were merely being at one with their surroundings. Those of us who live in this modern, rich society can learn a lesson from them, and it is akin to the lesson of Thoreau's *Walden: We are all human beings. We are all inhabitants of this earth and the traditions that are part of this earth.*

Because Henry David Thoreau so beautifully articulated these ideas in this place, there are few places more sacred to the intellectual history of America— and, indeed, to the world as a whole. Walden Pond and Walden Woods are part of us—one of the best parts. We intend that they will be preserved.

▲ ▲ ▲

Paul Tsongas, currently a candidate for President, was a U.S. Senator from the Commonwealth of Massachusetts. While serving in the Senate, he co-authored the Alaska Lands Act. A member of the Recycling Advisory Council, he is the author of *The Road From Here: Liberalism and Realities in the 1980's* and *Heading Home.* He is co-chairman of the Walden Woods Project.

Let your walks now be a little more adventurous; ascend the hills. If, about the last of October, you ascend any hill in the outskirts of our town, and probably of yours, and look over the forest, you may see—well, what I have endeavored to describe. All this you surely *will* see, and much more, if you are prepared to see it,—if you *look* for it. Otherwise, regular and universal as this phenomenon is, whether you stand on the hilltop or in the hollow, you will think for threescore years and ten that all the wood is, at this season, sere and brown. Objects are concealed from our view, not so much because they are out of the course of our visual ray as because we do not bring our minds and eyes to bear on them; for there is no power to see in the eye itself, any more than in any other jelly. We do not realize how far and widely, or how near and narrowly, we are to look. The greater part of the phenomena of Nature are for this reason concealed from us all our lives.

"AUTUMNAL TINTS"
HENRY DAVID THOREAU

WHOOPI GOLDBERG

TALKING LOUD AND SAYING NOTHING: AN EXERCISE IN CIVIL DISOBEDIENCE

I sort of knew what the night was going to be like by looking at the sort of people who were in attendance. Not that I'm a snob per se, but I guess the older I get, the easier it gets to say to oneself, "This is not my cup of tea," but hell, by then it was too late. I was there being greeted and kissed and spoken to and pressed for my opinion about a movie I hadn't seen yet. Pre-movie there was lots of food, jewelry and perfume in the room, and the man I brought with me was not ready for this, nor really was I, as I had been told it was to be a screening, a simple, low-key affair. Oh, well, to each his own.

We walked in to be seated and as I looked around, there were maybe four other black folks in the theater. Now when I was growing up, I never counted black folks. I never wondered how many of us were anywhere because growing up as I did in New York, there were all kinds of people everywhere. Oddly, it was not until I got to California that I heard of, and became really good at, spotting boundary lines, color lines and ethnic stop signs. I think, too, because I'm such a mutt—Catholic, Jew, black, German, Chinese, female—it never occurred to me to spot-check for color, but, sadly, now I do.

So in the screening room, I began to wonder why there were not more of us around. I mean the film was about South Africa and apartheid and directed by a black woman, a fact repeated at least a dozen times before I sat down, kinda like a reverb chamber, "A black woman directed. This is a first. No black female has ever directed a studio film. A breakthrough film." Hosanna. "Well," I thought, "people had the right to pat themselves on the back." This apparently *was* a big breakthrough. It put film into the hands of a black woman, and, by God, she made a movie. Sort of like getting your dog to do a really simple, but stunning trick. I guess they were relieved she didn't get some kind of soul period and fuck up their movie. I immediately realized that it was just me being crabby, and I wondered if anyone knew how sad it all sounded to me. But then I had to stop myself and say, "These people are people who believe in the right things, they do the right stuff, and maybe there are no black women directing," so I stopped being so critical for a couple of minutes.

The lights began to dim and a very nice lady got up to speak and she talked about the movie and the fact that this was a big breakthrough (with a black woman directing it), and I crunched down deeper in my chair and bit my lip, and she talked about South Africa and about the way black people were being held down by the whites there and how we here, in the theater, had to send a big message to South Africa that we (who were there in the theater) were more enlightened and would not sit back and allow this bigoted behavior on their part. She went on to say, with a quivering voice, that we would not be free until South Africa was free. What!! We won't be free?? Did she know what she was saying? What she was asking? I was stunned. And my friend who was with me poked me so I could join the rousing applause, but I couldn't lift my arms. They were like silly putty, I couldn't quite get them to work. We would not be free until South Africa was free! I wanted to yell to her. "Free," that's a word that you have to savor. It's the knowledge that you have that you can do or be anything. I had it put into my head all my life that I was a part of a special group. A batch of American blacks that were truly blessed because we were living truly free. We had access to any school, any water fountain, any seat on any bus, free to pursue any destiny. I was free to be anyone I chose and I walked with that knowledge. And now I was being asked by someone who never had to wonder about freedom to say that I would not be free until the wrongs were righted in their minds.

I wondered where everyone was before South Africa became a popular cause because South Africa's history has never been pretty and she wanted to be bound until the tides of apartheid, as she recognized them, were lifted. What did she mean? I wondered. And a small voice said inside my head, "It was a figure of speech, a metaphor. Lighten up, eat some popcorn, stop thinking." But another voice piped up in my head and wanted to know what my problem was. Didn't I understand what she was saying and what she meant? "Yes," said yet a third voice. "Well, so what's the big deal?" And a small, weird voice explained that this fight for freedom has been fought over a long period of time by people much simpler than we, and that the road to freedom here in the United States was paved with little girls in churches blown to pieces, students both black and white killed and disposed of like so much garbage. Freedom here was about the men and women on the front lines, ordinary people in extraordinary circumstances. They paved the way for my freedom. And what I finally figured out listening to all of this in my head, and trying to define why this woman's small speech set my teeth on edge, was that the only way to free people was by declaring loud and clear: I am free and I am waiting for you and I will help you see freedom. I will help you want to taste it, not by re-binding myself, but by basking in the pond of freedom, because as long as freedom is a goal, people will move toward it. Whoa, I said to myself, more popcorn, quick. I had to wonder also whether the fact that she was a white woman bothered me. Was I judging her too harshly? Because, really, she was a woman whose enthusiasm for the people of South Africa abounded. I'm still exploring the answer to that question for myself. I know I was not enthusiastic about the film, but that's OK, because we're all entitled to our opinions.

So, as we poured out of the theater, a lot of people were really freaked out. There is something about the sight of policemen shooting children that is too much for most people, but it's very effective because in cinema the images are constantly moving. But to understand, we have to remember that so many children have died in the fight for freedom. I wanted to scream at everyone, "Remember, it's here in our own backyard!" I wanted to ask them how many blacks or Hispanics or Asians did they know or employ. How many doors have we ripped open and kept open? I made the mistake of saying this to someone who had tears in his eyes as he said to me how moved he was to see what apartheid was like. Needless to say, he didn't want to share any more hors d'oeuvres with me. I guess I wasn't quite as sympathetic as he wanted me to be, or maybe I confronted him too hard for dropping the ball here in the United States. As a last resort, I asked someone else what freedom was. His answer was right, strangely, and true because he said freedom is the absolute ability to walk away when you don't give a shit anymore and that's exactly what he did. I sighed, popped another pig in a blanket in my mouth, said "Good night" to my friend and stepped out into the night, and I decided that I would be free for the rest of my life and fight within the bondage that is my mind.

▲ ▲ ▲

Whoopi Goldberg made her auspicious motion picture debut in "The Color Purple." Her performance as Oda Mae Brown in "Ghost" earned her an Academy Award for Best Supporting Actress. She is also known for her tireless humanitarian efforts on behalf of children, the homeless, human rights, substance abuse and the battle against AIDS.

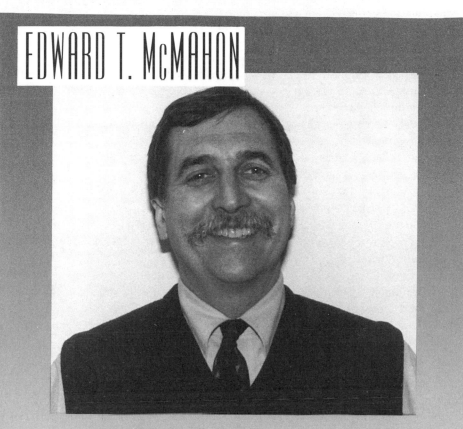

SCENIC AMERICA: CAN IT BE SAVED?

"Nothing except love is so universally appealing as a view," historian Kenneth Clark once observed. And in America, the views most of us see are from the road. Unfortunately, the scenic views and vistas that belong to all of us are slowly disappearing.

When I leave Washington and head for Alabama, where I grew up and where most of my family lives, I pick up Interstate 85 just south of Richmond, Virginia.

Today I-85, like much of America, is being transformed: forests, farmlands, and scenic vistas going or gone, replaced by flashing signs, metal self-storage sheds, cut-rate motels, discount towel bazaars, drab fast-food franchises, and, for hundreds of miles, billboard after monstrous billboard.

These days when I finally reach my home in Alabama, I feel saddened and depressed, my eyes and mind and soul abused by the horrors along the highway. "Don't look," a friend advised. "That's progress," said another. "You can always fly," said a third.

Yet there is another America: serene, unspoiled, still worth fighting for. Walden Pond is one such place and there are many others.

Like many people, I have never visited Walden Pond, but like millions of other Americans, I know the value of wilderness and appreciate the need to restore the harmony between man and nature. In 1973, when I returned from military service, I visited my Walden Pond—a place called DeSoto Falls, in the mountains of northeastern Alabama.

DeSoto Falls, Alabama's highest waterfall, a site of unusual beauty, an Indian gathering place for thousands of years and a state park (or so I thought) was for sale. The state, as it turned out, only owned one side of the falls and a developer was planning a trailer park for the other side.

Concerned that this would ruin one of Alabama's most outstanding scenic wonders, I organized a campaign that successfully halted the development and bought the threatened land. Many years later, I am proud to be playing a small role in preserving Walden Woods: a landscape of less scenic splendor but greater symbolic meaning.

Even if you never visit Walden Pond, it is important to save it because it is a unique symbol of the larger struggle between mindless materialism and a spiritual renewal. What's more, the threat to Walden Pond and Walden Woods is the same threat facing countless other special places in communities across America.

To understand the connection, think back to what your hometown looked like just ten or fifteen years ago. *Now* look at the changes. What do you see?

- Scenic country roads lined with garish billboards.
- Tree-lined streets replaced by flashing portable signs and endless commercial clutter.
- Acres of asphalt where groves of trees once stood.
- National parks and historic sites ringed by ugly strip development.

The truth is, America is getting uglier by the day. A wave of rampant, unmanaged growth is rapidly stripping our land of trees, spoiling our countryside, eroding what's left of our historic heritage and sense of place.

Today there is an urgent need to save America's special places. This is why I am supporting the Walden Woods Project, and why six years ago I helped organize Scenic America. Frankly, I was tired of seeing crass commercialism cheapening America and spoiling our land. Sure, growth is inevitable and often desirable, but it doesn't have to be ugly or environmentally destructive. I don't believe that we have to sacrifice the distinctive character of our communities or the beauty of our countryside for America to grow economically.

In recent years, we have devoted great resources to cleaning up air pollution, water pollution, even noise pollution. But until now we've devoted very little attention to the problem of visual pollution.

Visual pollution has many sources, but the most conspicuous is billboards. Most of us thought the billboard problem was solved twenty-five years ago, when, prodded by Lady Bird Johnson, Congress passed the Highway Beautification Act.

Intended to clean up the countryside, this act has become a classic failure, turned on its head by persistent industry lobbying, lax enforcement, and loopholes in the law.

In the early years of the program, thousands of billboards were removed. Indeed, four states—Hawaii, Alaska, Maine, and Vermont—have succeeded in removing all billboards, but elsewhere the removal program has come to a halt. According to the Federal Highway Administration, only 226 non-conforming billboards—those located in areas forbidden by the act—were removed nation-wide in 1990. At the same time, thousands of new and completely legal billboards were going up. According to Congressional Research Service estimates, almost fifty thousand new billboards were erected between 1986 and 1988. And in another report, the Department of Transportation's Inspector General said that "billboard operators have actually erected more signs than they have taken down since billboard restrictions were imposed in 1965."

The billboard lobby has become America's most persistent polluter. Today giant billboards—the largest number plugging cigarettes and booze—are going up all over America.

So, you might ask, what's wrong with billboards? Like subway graffiti, strangers passing in an airport, or the advertising on a matchbook, billboards become invisible after a while. Part of the landscape—ugly, but barely worth noting.

Well, look again and then imagine multistoried, multifaced billboards. Billboards towering over your neighborhood school, near your home, along your favorite country road, even looming over our beaches, parks, and historic sites.

Think it can't happen? Think again! It is already happening in many parts of America. Billboards are among the worst signs of an America gone to greed and seed. The billboard is advertising slam dunk. You can't turn the page; you can't change the station. They're the junk mail of the American highway. Billboard companies are selling something they don't own—our field of vision.

So what do billboards have to do with Walden Pond? A lot. Billboards along a scenic country road and an office park next to Walden Pond are both as out of place as empty beer cans in a mountain stream. All evoke outrage and angst. This is because our sense of identity as individuals and as Americans is linked to special buildings, neighborhoods, places, and views.

John Costonis, the dean of Vanderbilt School of Law, calls these places the "icons of our environment." Icons like Walden Pond and Walden Woods are invested with rich symbolic importance that contributes to our identity no less than our linkages to language, religion, or popular culture.

The "aliens" of our environment, like billboards and office parks in pristine settings, threaten our icons and, hence, our sense of belonging and our psychological and social well-being. Threats to our heritage can take the form of extinction, as when a landmark building is destroyed, or the form of contamination, as when a billboard mars a scenic vista or an office complex intrudes on an historic landmark.

John Muir said, "People need beauty as well as bread." But while we've been saving endangered species, we've been losing our sense of place. While we've been cleaning up toxic waste, we've been trashing our landscape. For all the improvements in environmental quality, people still ask: Is this all there is? Can't our communities be more distinctive? More beautiful? More livable? Fortunately, the public is beginning to realize that even if we eliminate air and water pollution, hazardous waste and toxic chemicals, climate change and ozone depletion, something basic and important will be missing from our lives unless we protect the character and beauty of our land.

By saving Walden Woods, we are actually saving our history and our sense of self. We are also making it more likely that people will recognize and protect the special places in their own hometowns. The reassurance we derive from protecting America's special places is important because it anchors our identity as Americans and pays homage to the past.

I've not yet been to Walden Pond, but I know it's worth fighting for and I plan to go.

▲ ▲ ▲

Edward T. McMahon co-founded Scenic America, which is devoted to protecting America's endangered scenic heritage. He is the author of eight books, wrote and produced a series of educational films for Random House and has written and spoken widely on the topics of land use planning and historic preservation. He was co-winner of the Peabody Award for his work on CBS Television's "60 Minutes." He is currently a Visiting Scholar at the Environmental Law Institute. He is a member of the Walden Woods Project Advisory Board.

> I love to look at Ebby Hubbard's oaks and pines on the hillside from Brister's Hill. Am thankful that there is one old miser who will not sell or cut his woods, though it is said that they are wasting. It is an ill wind that blows nobody any good.
>
> JOURNAL, JANUARY 22, 1852
> HENRY DAVID THOREAU

STING

PROGRESS, THE G.N.P.
AND THE NAMING OF THINGS

One day a man walked into the forest. He was a modern man—you
could tell this by the clothes that he wore, by the shining airplane that he'd left in the clearing, but most of all by the way
he walked. He walked in a decidedly modern way—brisk, efficient steps
never varying, his eyes remaining fixed in front of him despite the beauty
of the surrounding forest. He was a modern man, with a modern mission.

The central government had sent him to the forest to integrate the
people of the forest into the modern society. They were to become part of
the "Gross National Product," as the government so nicely put it. They
were no longer to be excluded from the benefits of "Progress." In short,
they were to become "consumers," worthy participants of the twentieth
century.

The first step in "integration" for the forest people was to be taught
the modern language of the modern society. This was our man's mission,
this is what he'd been trained to do—and this is why he was walking with
such assurance toward a small circle of huts, made of leaves and the
branches of trees.

The forest people came out to greet the modern man; they were, as always, curious and cheerful, and impressed by the man's easy confidence, his neat clothes and his airplane.

He began to explain (as best he could) why he had come—that he was to bring them the gift of a modern language, the language of progress, science, and commerce, an efficient, universal language to replace the myriad of dialects and the countless and confusing tongues of the forest people.

"One language, one society." He'd been taught to repeat this as an article of faith. The forest people, always eager to please, were having great fun parroting the phrase back at him, although they didn't have a clue what it meant.

One luggage. One sussiety.

One luggage! One sussiety!

Meanwhile, in another part of the forest, a different kind of lesson was taking place. An old man was teaching his son the names of things. The old man was a healer; he used the plants of the forest to cure the ailments of the tribe as he'd been taught by his father before him. "This root we use to cure a bad stomach, this one for a headache; this leaf will mend a wound, this one a snakebite. There is a balance for everything in nature, the forest is our library, it contains the answer to many riddles."

The younger man looked disheartened. "But father, there are so many names to learn. Just this morning, you've taught me that there are twenty-four types of potato, eighteen types of manioc, fifty varieties of ant, each with a different name. How can I learn them all?"

"Be patient, my son," said the father. "This work is important for our future. There are cures here in the forest for diseases we don't even know about. We can't rest until we have named everything; that is why we are here. The naming of things is our science, our medicine, our religion, our history. Without this knowledge, we cannot live in the forest. We would be lost. And without us, the forest would be in danger, too. For countless moons, our fathers have been the gardeners of the forest. The wealth of the forest is in the differences of the many, growing together."

Back at the village, the modern man had begun his lesson. On a blackboard he had drawn a tree. Beneath it, he'd written the word "TREE." The forest people looked at each other, eyes shining, suppressed smirks growing on their faces irresistibly turning into wide grins. And then, from the back, an irrepressible wave of laughter swept over them and out into the forest to mingle with the sound of the tree frogs. The forest people were laughing out loud, and the man grew flustered and angry. He turned to one of the elders. "Why are they laughing? What's so funny?"

The elder tried to explain. "They are laughing because out in the forest there are thousands of different trees, each with a special spirit, a special use, a special name. You want to take them away and give us one name, and all you're giving us in return is one word. How will we be able to tell them apart?"

The modern man looked out at the riot of diversity that was the forest, and said, rather meanly, "You won't need a thousand words for tree, because pretty soon, all the trees will have gone, except for the trees we plant. It will all be the same tree in straight lines, so we can add them to the Gross National Product." He pointed a finger at the forest. "One day, this unproductive and unruly chaos will be replaced by a modern forest, orderly, efficient, economic, one that looks good from the air with lots of straight lines. You can't stop progress. 'One tree. One word.' "

"ONE CHEE! ONE WUD!"

The forest people repeated the phrase with a little less enthusiasm than before. Then they learned the words "fish" and "bird" and "insect." This language might be totally useless, but it sure was easy.

While the lessons of progress were being conducted in the village, and the naming of things was taking place in the forest, not far from both, a tiny root was growing, an extremely rare species, undiscovered for thousands of years, hidden among millions of others, just waiting. I wonder whether it will ever be named, or will progress render that unnecessary?

I also wonder, if there is a balance for everything in nature, whether such a root or such a plant could be holding a priceless secret, a cure for cancer, a cure for AIDS? . . . A cure for progress? And the Gross National Product?

"For countless moons, our fathers have been the gardeners of the forest, and they learned that the wealth of the forest is in the differences of the many, growing together."

▲ ▲ ▲

Sting's records, with the Police and as a solo artist, have won several Grammys and loads of platinum record awards. He has lent his talents to Amnesty International, Band Aid, the Special Olympics, Live Aid and the S.O.S. Amazonian Awareness Campaign for the preservation of the Amazonian rain forest. He is co-founder and trustee of The Rainforest Foundation.

The world rests on principles.

LETTER TO H.G.O. BLAKE, DECEMBER 19, 1854
HENRY DAVID THOREAU

KURT VONNEGUT

TO HELL WITH MARRIAGE

I did not like my teacher of freshman English at Cornell University, nor did he like me, and I didn't give a damn because I was going to be a chemist. But things got so bad between us that he threatened to throw me out of the course, and he meant it, too. He was a prick. I had to get past freshman English before I could go on to nothing but important stuff: chemistry, physics, math. I was faced with typical university chickenshit, a nonsensical hurdle I had to jump. The Italian dictator Mussolini was at about the same time making members of his cabinet jump hurdles of fixed bayonets, getting boosts from a springboard, to show how fit for war they were.

The make-or-break assignment given to me by this dweeb who stood between me and a Nobel Prize was the composition of an essay on Henry David Thoreau, a man I had already thought a lot about, as it happened. I was a product of a hot-shit, overachiever, impossibly conceited high school in Indianapolis, where we read *Walden* and *Moby Dick* and *Life on the Mississippi* and *Leaves of Grass* and *The Devil's Dictionary* and *The Red Badge of Courage* and all kinds of terrific American stuff. So when I got back to my rooming house with this stupid assignment, I was not only enraged, but I didn't have to do any research! I was also a high-speed typist. Anybody who was anybody in my high school could type like crazy.

So off I went! It may have been the best thing I ever wrote. I'm glad I don't have a copy, because it would almost certainly prove that my literary skills have been in steep decline for the past fifty years! I handed the teacher that brilliant essay with all possible hauteur, turned on my heel, strode out of the building with my head held high, and broke my ankle while descending the broad flight of stairs outside. The tumble I took was sheer coincidence, and needn't interrupt the flow of my story. It does explain why I was on crutches when the teacher told me how good he thought my essay was. He asked me why I hadn't written anything worth a nickel up to then, and I replied that I was going to be a scientist, and that writing was a tiresome chore for me. Never mind that I was then flunking calculus.

What I wrote about Thoreau then, and what I'd said about him in high school, is what I have to say about him right now: that he was a sensualist, a voluptuary, and a debauchee. The big difference between him and Don Juan and Diamond Jim Brady and the like was that he achieved high levels of whoopee without throwing a lot of money around and persuading other people to cooperate. As he himself said: "Beware of all enterprises which require new clothes." Unlike so many fellow pleasure-seekers, Thoreau had the decency not to get married or reproduce. ("Oh Father, dear Father, come home with me now. . . .")

The most famous thing he ever said, arguably, was, "The mass of men lead lives of quiet desperation. What is called resignation is confirmed desperation." I take this to be a warning against marriage. You can't appreciate life and support a family at the same time. He goes so far as to say that you can't really appreciate it, even if you don't have a job, if somebody, simply anybody, not necessarily a wife or kid, is with you, to wit: "I never found the companion that was so companionable as solitude."

After a heavy injection of truth serum, I think a majority of us—men, women, and children alike—would hear ourselves babbling that we agreed with him that we knew exactly what he was talking about. Other people wear us out! To quote the greatest exemplar of total self-sufficiency yet again: "the man who goes alone can start today; but he who travels with another must wait till that other is ready."

So a pilgrimage to Walden Pond, for those who know anything about Thoreau, honors not only a playful and cunning naturalist, and perhaps our most accurate and direct user of the English language so far, and a witty moralist, but an ancestor of all the borscht-circuit comedians who have had such hilariously horrible things to say about friendships and family life ("Take my wife, *please*") and so on. One thing those comedians often say is something Thoreau never thought of saying, because he never lied: "Only kidding, folks."

It has been suggested, I forget by whom, that he may have died of malnutrition, since nobody in those days knew anything about vitamins and minerals essential to health. He died in 1862, with the Civil War going on, at the age of forty-five, eating ever simpler and cheaper meals, demonstrating, he supposed, that people didn't have to work as hard as they did for money, since it cost so little to stay alive. He could easily have made the same point without dying so young. During the Great Depression before this one, I know, there were people eating for ten cents a day, a nickel for a loaf of bread and a nickel for a pound of beans, but they had sense enough to grab fruit and vegetables, too.

There must be many people today who live as cheaply as Thoreau did, not because they have to but because they want to, who avoid human contact as he did, feeling; "Where a man goes, men will pursue him and paw him with their dirty institutions, and if they can, constrain him to belong to their desperate oddfellow society." I envy and admire them, and deeply regret that my own mind is not the perfect companion that theirs must be.

▲ ▲ ▲

Kurt Vonnegut has written many influential, best-selling novels. His most recent is *Hocus Pocus.*

I have never felt lonesome, or in the least oppressed by a sense of solitude, but once, and that was a few weeks after I came to the woods, when, for an hour, I doubted if the near neighborhood of man was not essential to a serene and healthy life. To be alone was something unpleasant. But I was at the same time conscious of a slight insanity in my mood, and seemed to foresee my recovery. In the midst of a gentle rain while these thoughts prevailed, I was suddenly sensible of such sweet and beneficent society in Nature, in the very pattering of the drops, and in every sound and sight around my house, an infinite and unaccountable friendliness all at once like an atmosphere sustaining me, as made the fancied advantages of human neighborhood insignificant, and I have never thought of them since. Every little pine needle expanded and swelled with sympathy and befriended me. I was so distinctly made aware of the presence of something kindred to me, even in scenes which we are accustomed to call wild and dreary, and also that the nearest of blood to me and humanest was not a person nor a villager, that I thought no place could ever be strange to me again.

WALDEN
HENRY DAVID THOREAU

JANET JACKSON

LISTEN

The social and environmental problems we face are enormous, and finding solutions is critical. We continue to search for righteous and qualified leaders to guide us, yet we often feel helpless in the face of the monumental challenges that confront us. As individuals, we don't know how to make a difference.

Yet there is something each one of us can and should do. We should listen, not only to our own hearts, but to the hearts of others, to the hearts of children. This is one of the most valuable lessons I have learned during my life. When I begin to dwell on problems which seem insurmountable, I am continually drawn back to the present, to my limited world, to the people who are important to me. They are the source of my strength.

But others are not so fortunate. There are many people who suffer from neglect, and this is particularly true in the case of children. So often, children are not given the respect and the attention they deserve. Because they are young, we underestimate the depth of their understanding, the intensity of their frustration over not being heard.

The agendas of the adult world are often too crowded to accommodate the urgent needs of our children. Consequently, kids are frequently treated as second-class citizens. If the neglect is severe enough, a child's need for respect and love may turn from anxiety to anger. He, or she, may lose interest in learning, may become irresponsible, or may turn to gangs, drugs, alcohol, or prostitution as an escape from loneliness and isolation. We hear a great deal about the damage wrought upon children by sexual abuse. Yet there is a more subtle form of abuse that is also destructive. To ignore is to abuse.

Children have such important messages to impart, and this is especially true in the area of the environment. If we listen to the children, we will enrich our lives and make the world a better place in which to live. Kids are deeply concerned about their safety; about the future of the planet. They are worried about the ozone layer, the extinction of animal species, the loss of the rain forests and the hazards of toxic waste, landfills, air and water pollution.

Our children's future depends upon finding solutions to these problems. Young people recognize this and want to help us make the earth a safer place in which to live.

Places like Walden Pond are important to children. Kids learn about Walden and about Henry David Thoreau in school and they want our assurance that the pond and the woods around it will continue to exist for them and for their children and grandchildren. They need places like Walden to discover who they are and how they fit into the scheme of life.

The Walden Woods Project receives a lot of mail from children throughout the country. Michael Churchill from Iowa sent the letter that appears on the following page.

Children hold the future of the world in their hands. And so many of them, like Michael, truly care about our environment. Although we can't cure all the world's ailments, in a practical and immediate way we can make a start by listening to the children. Listening means putting someone else's needs first. It's not always easy, but it is possible and it is practical. It is something all of us can do right now. And it's something we must do if we hope to give our children and their children a better world in which to grow.

▲ ▲ ▲

Janet Jackson is best known for her multi-platinum albums *Control* and *Rhythm Nation 1814.* Her seventeen-year career in music and television includes several other albums and appearances on the sitcoms "Good Times," "Different Strokes" and "Fame."

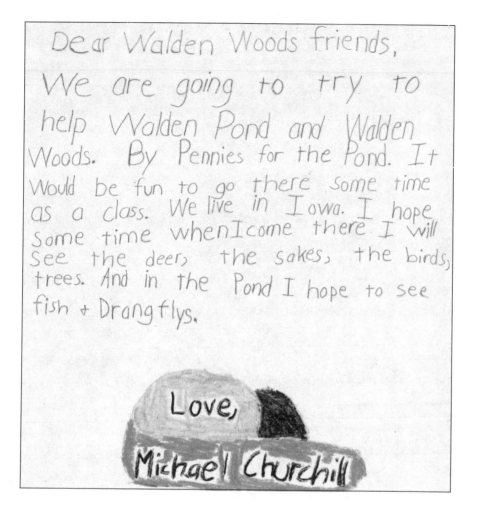

Dear Walden Woods friends,

We are going to try to help Walden Pond and Walden Woods. By Pennies for the Pond. It would be fun to go there some time as a class. We live in Iowa. I hope some time when I come there I will see the deer, the sakes, the birds, trees. And in the Pond I hope to see fish & Drangflys.

Love,
Michael Churchill

If some are prosecuted for abusing children, others deserve to be prosecuted for maltreating the face of nature committed to their care.

JOURNAL, SEPTEMBER 23, 1857
HENRY DAVID THOREAU

CESAR CHAVEZ

PESTICIDES, CHILDREN AND CANCER

Johnnie Rodriguez was five years old when he died after a painful two-year battle with cancer. Like all farm workers, his parents, Juan and Elia, are exposed to pesticides and other agricultural chemicals. Elia worked in the table grape vineyards around Delano, California until she was eight months pregnant with Johnnie.

Juan and Elia cannot say for certain if pesticides caused their son's cancer. But neuroblastoma is one of the cancers found in McFarland, a small farming town only a few miles from Delano in the great Central Valley, where the Rodriguezes live.

"Pesticides are always in the fields and around the towns," Johnnie's father told us. "The children get them when they play outside, when they drink the water or hug you after you come home from working in fields that are sprayed."

"Once your son has cancer, you hope it's a mistake, you pray," Juan said. "He was a real nice boy. He took it strong and lived as long as he could."

I keep a picture of Johnnie Rodriguez. He is sitting on his bed hugging his Teddy bear. His sad eyes and cherubic face stare out at you. The photo was taken four days before he died.

Johnnie Rodriguez was one of thirteen McFarland children diagnosed with cancer in recent years—and one of ten who have died from the disease. The rate of cancer in McFarland, with about six thousand residents, is eight times what is expected for a community of its size.

Jimmy Caudillo died of leukemia. He was not yet four. His parents, Jaime and Maria, work in table grape vineyards near Earlimart, where they live, about fourteen miles north of McFarland. Earlimart has twelve times the cancer rate expected for a town of its size.

Earlimart residents Gonzalo and Ramona Ramirez also work in the vineyards. Their daughter, Natalie, has Wilm's Tumor, a rare form of cancer. She lost one kidney to a malignant tumor. Now cancer threatens her remaining kidney.

Maria Robles's parents are also grape workers who live in Earlimart. She has leukemia. A bone marrow transplant left her weak and vulnerable to disease.

Felipe Franco is a bright nine-year-old boy who lives in Delano, located between Earlimart and McFarland. Felipe was born without arms and legs. His mother, Ramona, worked in the grapes near Delano until she was in her eighth month of pregnancy. She was exposed to Captan, known to cause birth defects and one of the pesticides our California table grape boycott seeks to ban. "Every morning when I began working I could smell and see pesticides on the grape leaves," Ramona said.

Like many farm workers, she was assured by growers and foremen that the pesticides that surrounded her were safe, that they were harmless "medicine" for the plants. Only after the boy saw specialists in Los Angeles did Ramona learn that the pesticides she was exposed to in the vineyards caused Felipe's deformity.

Ten million pounds of pesticides went on grapes in 1986 alone. More restricted-use pesticides are applied to grapes than any fresh food crop. Forty-four percent of them pose potential health hazards for humans. About one-third of grape pesticides are known carcinogens, like the chemicals that may have afflicted Johnnie Rodriguez, Jimmy Caudillo, Natalie Ramirez, and Maria Robles. Others include teratogen, the birth defect–producing pesticide that doctors think deformed Felipe Franco.

Farm workers and their families are exposed to pesticides from the crops they work, the soil the crops are grown in, drift from sprays applied to adjoining fields—and sometimes to the very fields where they are working. The fields that surround their homes are heavily and repeatedly sprayed. Pesticides pollute irrigation water and groundwater.

Children are still a big part of the farm labor force. Or they are taken to the fields by their parents because there is no child care. Pregnant women labor in the fields to help support their families. Toxic exposure begins at a very young age, often in the womb.

Pesticide poisoning causes eye and respiratory irritations, skin rashes, systemic poisoning—and sometimes death. Scientific studies show that the chronic effects of pesticide poisoning include birth defects, sterility, still births, miscarriages, neurological and neuropsychological effects, retarded growth and development among children—and cancer.

Farm workers endure skin irritations and rashes that no one else would tolerate. They continue to work because they desperately need the money. They don't complain out of fear of losing their jobs. They aren't told when pesticides are used. They rarely have health insurance. They are cheated out of workers compensation benefits by disappearing labor contractors or foremen who intimidate people into not filing claims.

In the old days, miners would carry birds with them to warn against poison gas. Hopefully, the birds would die before the miners. Today, farm workers are society's canaries. They and their children demonstrate the effects of pesticide poisoning before anyone else.

The unrestrained use of agricultural chemicals is like playing Russian roulette with the health of both farm workers and consumers. Hundreds of pesticides leave residues on food and most can't be detected by commonly used tests. Many can't be detected by any test at all. Many pesticides used on food such as grapes, even though they have government tolerance levels, can cause cancer in human beings.

The irony is that pesticides haven't worked. Crop loss to pests is as great or greater than it was forty years ago. Pesticides haven't changed anything because Darwinian evolution has favored pests of all kinds with an enormous ability to resist and survive. You can't fool Mother Nature. In time, insects can outfox anything we throw at them.

People thought pesticides were the cure-all—the key to an abundance of food. They thought pesticides were the solution; but they were one of the problems. The other problems are the huge farms, this mammoth agribusiness system; the pressure on the land from developers; the refusal to let the land lie fallow and rest; the abandonment of cultural practices that have stood the test of centuries, such as crop rotation and diversification of crops.

The problem is monoculture—growing acres and acres of the same crop; disrupting the natural order of things; letting insects feast on acres and acres of a harem of delight; and using pesticides that kill off their natural predators.

So we allow growers and chemical companies to continue in this mindless submission to pesticides. But at what cost? The lives of farm workers and their children who are suffering? The lives of consumers who could reap the harvest of pesticides ten or twenty years from now? The contamination of our groundwater? The raping of the land?

People forget that the soil is our sustenance. It is a sacred trust. It is what has worked for us for centuries.

Growers and chemical companies say, don't ban the worst of these poisons just because some farm worker might give birth to a deformed child. They say, don't imperil millions of dollars in profits today because, some day, some consumers might get cancer.

So they allow all of us, who place our faith in the safety of the food supply, to consume grapes and other produce which contain residues from pesticides that can cause cancer and birth defects. So we accept decades of environmental damage these poisons have brought upon the land.

The growers and chemical companies and regulatory bureaucrats say these are acceptable levels of exposure. Acceptable to whom? Acceptable to Natalie Ramirez, Maria Robles, and Felipe Franco? Acceptable to the families of Johnnie Rodriguez and Jimmy Caudillo? Acceptable to all the farm workers who have known tragedy from pesticides?

Do we carry in our hearts the suffering of farm workers and their children? Do we feel deeply enough the pain of those who must work in the fields every day with these poisons? Or the anguish of the families that have lost loved ones? Or the heartache of the parents who fear for the lives of their children, who are raising children with deformities, or who agonize the outcome of their pregnancies?

Do we feel their pain deeply enough? I didn't, and I was ashamed.

I studied this wanton abuse of nature. I read the literature and heard from the experts about what pesticides do. I talked with farm workers, shared their anguish and their fears. I spoke out against the cycle of death.

But sometimes words come too cheaply. And their meaning is lost in the clutter that so often fills our lives. That is why, in July and August of 1988, I embarked on a thirty-six day, unconditional, water-only fast in Delano.

The fast was first and foremost directed at myself, to purify my own body, mind, and soul. It was an act of penance for our own people—farm workers who, out of ignorance or need, cooperate with the production and sale of food treated with toxins.

It was also for those who know what is right and just. It pains me that we continue to shop without protest at stores that offer grapes; that we eat in restaurants that display them; that we are too patient with those who serve them to us. The fast was for those who know that they could or should do more—for those who, by not acting, become bystanders in the poisoning of our food and the people who produce it.

The misery that pesticides bring farm workers and the dangers they pose to all consumers will not be ended with more hearings or studies. The solution is not to be heard from those in power, because it is they who have allowed this deadly crisis to grow.

The answer lies with you and me. It is all men and women who share the suffering and yearn with us for a better world.

▲ ▲ ▲

Cesar Chavez, president of the United Farm Workers of America, founded and leads the first successful union of agricultural workers in U.S. history. The lowest-paid union president in America, he leads "The Wrath of Grapes," an international grape boycott, opposing the threat posed to vineyard workers and consumers by reckless application of pesticides.

Will mankind never learn that policy is not morality—that it never secures any moral right, but considers merely what is expedient? chooses the available candidate, who is invariably the devil,—and what right have his constituents to be surprised, because the devil does not behave like an angel of light? What is wanted is men, not of policy, but of probity—who recognize a higher law than the Constitution, or the decision of the majority. The fate of the country does not depend on how you vote at the polls—the worst man is as strong as the best at that game; it does not depend on what kind of paper you drop into the ballot-box once a year, but on what kind of man you drop from your chamber into the street every morning.

"SLAVERY IN MASSACHUSETTS"
HENRY DAVID THOREAU

TOM HANKS

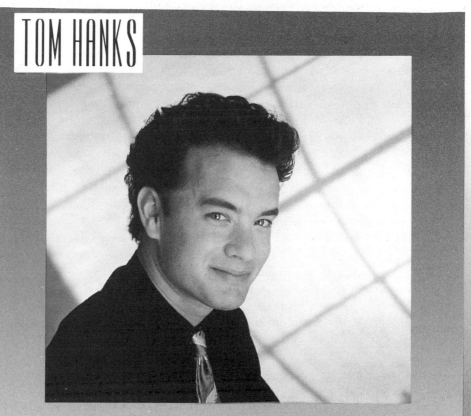

BABY, YOU CAN DRIVE MY HOVERCRAFT

In 1966, I believed my *Weekly Reader*.

I had faith in that mini-tabloid handed out to us in elementary school. It was full of information. It was full of news. And best of all, it was full of prophecy.

My *Weekly Reader* told me how I would be living in Our Future. Back then, Our Future would begin as soon as 1976. The thought of what life would be like in the year 1991 was the stuff of fantasy—in 2001, movie make-believe.

According to my *Weekly Reader*, luxury passenger trains would be zipping along the bottom of the Atlantic in huge vacuum tubes. Hundreds of people would get sucked from New York to London in just a few hours. Those trains would pass by underwater villages, marvels unto themselves, where the populace would live in total comfort and style. Dads would scuba-dive to work. Moms would walk to the supermarket through transparent tunnels. I wondered if I would be able to see the Sub-Atlantic Vacuum Train Tunnel from my bedroom window.

On the land, my *Weekly Reader* foretold of The Cities of Tomorrow, where tree-lined mono-railways would zip us off to scientifically designed workplaces where the air temperature would always be a fresh seventy degrees. Everything, from picnic tables to hovercraft, would be made out of space age materials, lighter than aluminum, stronger than tungsten steel, and cheaper to make than paper. The cities would be perfectly planned, from trash collection to police protection, and the public facilities would be so expertly organized and executed that everyone living everywhere would enjoy the same fair standard of living.

Massive farms would be supplying us with food from Outer Space, though not from other planets, as the *Weekly Reader* was very much fact-oriented and 1976 was still a little too close for interplanetary commerce. Instead, but just as amazing, astro-farmers would be taking NASA roto-tillers to the soil inside revolving space stations. The lesser gravity would make for squashes the size of coffee tables and leaves of kale and spinach as big as sleeping bags. Cows and chickens would grow fat and huge. Corncobs would stretch up to three feet. And all this through the wonders of applied science and practical know-how.

The best part of all was that up there, from perigee to apogee, the Future Farmers of America would be looking down at Mother Earth at Her most regal . . . all blue and white and green . . . all safe and orderly and clean.

Of course, we were just kids. My *Weekly Reader* was just a kids' tabloid. We didn't know then that you can't believe much of what you read in a tabloid.

In 1991, the living-under-the-sea scenario is still a fiction of science. You have to admit, though, maritime technology has achieved something when super-tankers the size of the Empire State Building, and filled to the rails with petroleum products, are churning up the waterways of the world. Of course, when you consider all the spills and wrecks and crude slicks that go along with the transporting of motor oil via the oceans, that same technology takes a beating. Add on the loss of life to millions of dolphins and porpoises (our friend Flipper, each and every one) just so we can order tuna sandwiches for lunch and you begin to wonder—who is in charge of this technology, anyway?

Certainly not the former editors of my *Weekly Reader*.

The City of the Future turns out to be no place at all. Dayton, Ohio and Toronto, Ontario, and a few other places that were smart enough to keep all their original trolley tracks and subway lines—they come close. Old-fashioned thinking helped them get honorable mentions in the Future Cities of the World Competition. But as for the kind of town we were promised back then, for most of us it ended up being something called the "Tri-State Area" or "L.A." or some other "Metropolis-minus-Superman," where the traffic requires radio updates every ten minutes and the public facilities are subject to cancellation due to tax cuts.

The space station farm idea is still a ways off. The cost will be more money than everyone in the world has in their pockets at this very moment. Instead of those huge peas and carrots, though, we do have microwave diet string beans almondine and low cholesterol Maui-style potato chips. But, damn it, none of them are manufactured three hundred miles above terra firma.

I couldn't wait for Our Future to get here. I was sure we would all share in the glories of better living through technology, bringing our pursuit of happiness to a triumphant end.

It all made so much sense!

So what happened?

What happened to Our Future?

Technology and know-how have given us some cool things that do make life easier and quicker. But the dynamic of that idea swings upon a vicious counterbalance. Instant spaghetti sauce that tastes "more tomato-ee" than the kind our grandmothers made is on one end of the easier/quicker scale, while atomic power towers that produce both electricity and death-glowing canisters of waste which never go away hang on the other end.

We all still drive cars powered by the internal combustion engine, even though the fossil fuels needed to keep those motors combusting are running out, fouling the air, and getting more and more expensive. And we have no other choice because, we are told, the economics of producing any other kind of engine for any other kind of car are unfeasible.

We have landfills that are bursting. I don't remember if we had to recycle in Our Future or not.

A piece of our sky called the "ozone" is depleting. Who would have thought the World to Come would be short on sky?

A great many of God's creatures no longer exist, and many more are threatened. I was sure all of Earth's inhabitants would enjoy Earth's inheritance.

Our Future wasn't supposed to be like this.

Instead, the five-passenger hovercraft would take us anywhere we wanted to go without ever being at the mercy of sig-alerts. If the hovercraft didn't have all the bugs out of it by 1976, at least the quiet and cool electric family sedan would take us to the beach and back without wasting petrol and blowing smoke into the sky at every stoplight.

And speaking of the beach, Our Future wasn't supposed to include plastic six-pack rings that choke pelicans or styrofoam milkshake cups that last a thousand years. No citizen of that City to Come would ever litter in the first place.

We would take care of our Tomorrowland. The beaches and oceans and skies and forests and even the boulevards would be clean and teeming with the wonders of nature.

> That is what Our Future held for us.
> Nothing would be "disposable."
> Nothing would be "economically unfeasible."
> Nothing would be impossible.
> Not in Our Future.
> I want Our Future back.

▲ ▲ ▲

Tom Hanks is a native of California, from the city of Oakland. As a Longboarder, he is a member of the Surfriders Foundation.

The universe is wider than our views of it.

WALDEN
HENRY DAVID THOREAU

JOHN DeVILLARS

"It's time to bring common sense to our common problems for the common good." That was Gifford Pinchot's call to arms for a generation of environmentalists a century ago. Now, it must serve as the rallying cry for our time and our generation. We should be emboldened by the same spirit that empowered Pinchot, John Muir and the other environmental leaders of the nineteenth century.

But we must also recognize that the challenges we face are far more daunting than anything imagined by those pioneers—or even by those who participated in the first Earth Day, in 1970.

In the next hour, six thousand acres of Central and South American rain forest will be cut, bulldozed and burned, which means that we have lost forever one hundred species in the course of a single day.

In Eastern Europe, as the Iron Curtain rises it reveals not a red menace, but the threat of green rapidly turning to gray: In Romania, 80 percent of the water undrinkable; in Czechoslovakia and Hungary, the air over capital cities so polluted that it chokes both human and economic health; in Poland, 65 percent of the rivers too contaminated for even industrial use and a quarter of the soil too contaminated for farming. And then there's the recent dispatch from the *New York Times*: "In the depths of a salt mine in Poland, men, women and children lie in bed bundled in coats and tugging at heavy blankets. In an upside down world, they have come to this underground clinic to breathe clean and healing air."

Sadly, we don't have to travel to other continents to witness such an assault on our environment. In America, 136 million people live in cities that fail to meet federal air quality standards. In America the Beautiful, we've created toxic ghost towns out of what were once healthy, thriving communities.

Listen to Luella Kenney—hers was one of the 249 Niagara Falls homes evacuated at Love Canal. She lost her seven-year-old son to a rare kidney disease. It was caused by dioxin levels in the Kenneys' backyard that were thirty-two times higher than what the federal government calls harmful. Twelve years later, Luella Kenney's tears have dried but her pain remains. "When I lost my son," she says now, "I lost my dreams." How many more moms and dads will lose their dreams as a consequence of the 180,000 abandoned hazardous waste sites that scar America's landscape?

How will filling and destroying 300,000 acres of wetlands each year affect our environmental lifeblood? What will be the effect of the 160 million tons of garbage Americans toss out each year? We already know that not nearly enough of our trash is recycled, that far too much of it spews into the air from incinerators and leaches into groundwater from landfills. When will we get serious and shift our energy toward recycling?

In Massachusetts alone, hazardous wastes have ruined 110 public water supplies and more than six hundred private water systems in nearly two hundred communities. Every day, we generate enough trash to fill 45,000-seat Sullivan Stadium one hundred feet high. And every year we spend nearly $100 million to dispose of it all.

"To know us go to our mountain tops and ocean shores," Walt Whitman said of New Englanders. But today, even in a cooling economy, those mountain tops and ocean shores are besieged. Each week, we lose an area the size of ten Boston Commons to new development—too much of it poorly planned and poorly located. We see the ravages of such shortsightedness every day: Travel to Cape Cod, where, to borrow from a Yankee of more recent vintage than Whitman— Yogi Berra—"No one goes anymore; it's too crowded." Or go to America's foremost symbol of the conservation movement, Walden Pond, where the developer's bulldozers stand poised to ravage Thoreau's legacy.

This isn't just environmental neglect, it's environmental abuse, and whether it occurs in the Massachusetts Berkshires or the cities of Poland, it affects us all. We're *all* downwind or downstream from someone: Belching Midwestern smoke-stacks poison Canadian and New England lakes; radioactive fallout from Cherno-byl victimizes much of Europe; twenty years after DDT was banned in the U.S., it once again shows up in the waters of the Great Lakes—transported by air from

Central America. Meantime, deforestation in Haiti and drought in Africa have prompted massive refugee movements—just a forewarning of the mass migrations that could result if the predicted doubling of the world's population over the next fifty years outstrips world food and energy resources.

What can we do about all this? Mostofa Tolba, director of the United Nations Environmental Program, has an answer. "Addressing the global environment crisis requires nothing less than a *radical* change in the conduct of world policy and the world economy," he has said.

Forty Nobel laureates and seven hundred members of the National Academy of Sciences have an answer. They sent a letter on global warming to President George Bush earlier this year. "Study is fine," they wrote, "but the time to act is now."

The pollsters tell us that ordinary Americans have an answer, too: 85 percent want Congress to pass tougher environmental protection laws. Strangely, however, not many in Washington seem willing to listen. The 1990 clean air bill moving through Congress hits a home run on acid rain but a foul ball on auto emission controls. The Office of Management and Budget says that guarantees of no net loss of wetlands and restrictions on offshore oil drilling might make good campaign rhetoric, but doesn't sit well in the boardrooms of the oil companies. Lobbyists on Capitol Hill dust off dire warnings from two decades ago to claim that more fuel efficient automobiles represent an economic peril, even as the Japanese and Germans put themselves profitably in the driver's seat for a cleaner future.

The U.S. State Department sends representatives to international conferences on carbon dioxide reduction and on international standards for toxic waste disposal—and it is the often lonely task of the American delegation to lead the charge *against* meaningful improvements.

But even if we had more enlightened leadership in Washington, government alone couldn't possibly get the job done. Ultimately, each of us as individuals controls his or her own destiny and each of us in some small measure controls the destiny of this earth.

Our planet has been likened to a spaceship. All of us travel together as passengers on that spaceship—and it is preserved only by the care, the work, the love we give to our fragile craft.

People all over this world are providing that care and work and love. It's marked in mass movements like the Green parties of Western Europe that are now driving political debate in France, Germany, and England. In Lithuania, the first mass protests were aimed against governmental policies on the environment. The first students in Tianenman Square marched to protest *environmental* policies. It was a third grade class in Lexington, Massachusetts that prompted me, as the state's secretary of Environmental Affairs, to put the toughest degradability standards in the nation on plastic six-pack rings. It was Gil and Jo Fernandez, an elderly couple in southeastern Massachusetts, who singlehandedly reintroduced the endangered osprey that now flourishes on the Westport River. It was Ed Cooper, a towering Roxbury native, who a decade ago started Boston Urban Gardeners; now eighty-six years old, he's still spreading its bounty to hundreds of inner city families.

This Sunday, Ed Cooper and the Fernandez family and those third graders, and thousands like them, will join the Earth Day march to Boston's Hatch Shell to celebrate what they've done—and call on the quarter of a million others who will assemble there to do even more.

One hundred thirty million people in more than one hundred nations will rally to the cause this Sunday—the largest demonstration of citizen activism in the history of the world.

I hope you will join them. Not just Sunday, but every day.

Nearly a quarter century ago, on a warm spring morning at the University of Capetown, South Africa, Bobby Kennedy spoke to a smaller audience than we'll see at Sunday's Earth Day celebration, but one equally challenged and inspired. His words remain as relevant to today's challenges as they were to those of the 1960s. "Few will have the greatness to bend history itself," he said, "but each of us can work to change a small portion of events. And in the total of all those acts will be written the history of this generation."

May what we write chart a healthy and sustainable future, not only for our generation, but for all the generations that follow.

▲ ▲ ▲

John DeVillars is managing director of Environmental Strategies, a Boston-based strategic and management consulting business. From 1988 to 1991, he was Massachusetts' Secretary of Environmental Affairs and chairman of the board of the Massachusetts Water Resources Authority. Mr. DeVillars has received numerous environmental awards, and is a member of the board of directors of a number of environmental organizations, including the Walden Woods Project Advisory Board. The preceding piece was excerpted from remarks that Mr. DeVillars delivered on Massachusetts high school and college campuses in the week leading up to the twentieth anniversary of Earth Day, April 22, 1990.

SHIGEYUKI OKAJIMA

THOREAU & QOMOLANGMA

March, 1988. I was at the base camp on the north, or Tibetan, side of Qomolangma (Mt. Everest, 8848 meters), at the foot of the Ronbuk glacier. This was my third visit to Qomolangma; the first was in autumn 1979, and the second in spring 1980. Because of my last two experiences, I had brought two books with me from Japan: *Proposal for Naturalization* by the Japanese ecologist Dr. Kinji Imanishi, and *Walden; or, Life in the Woods* by H.D. Thoreau. I wanted to think deeply about nature in this place.

Here at the base camp the sky was pure blue and clean and the air was fresh and crystal clear. The cold wind off the Ronbuk glacier carried with it the smell of the wilderness.

As we climbed, I continued reading these two books. As I was reading them then, I realized that Thoreau's theory might be accepted without too many difficulties by Japanese people. In this book he recognizes that people's ephemeral life and existence is not superior to nature, but is only a part of nature. As I am a Buddhist, it matches my basic thoughts surprisingly well. It probably matches equally well the thoughts of most Japanese people.

There are some poems from many years ago that tell us about the relationship between nature and people in Japan, expressed in a traditional way. People still read these poems by writers such as Saigyo[1] and Basho,[2] though they were composed hundreds of years ago. Underlying their poems we can feel the naturalism in which people could find relief from the bitterness of this world, which Buddhism could not redeem, in the touch of nature.

This is very close to Thoreau's theory, and it may be one of the reasons that Thoreau has been so popular for so long. However, the books of John Muir and Aldo Leopold are not widely read in Japan, even though their books are based on a view of nature close to Thoreau's.

Dr. Imanishi's book presents a strong argument against the neo-Darwinist theory of evolution. He expresses doubts about the rule, "Survival of the fittest." "If a life were born in the earth and many species were born from it, then they are all basically one family," Dr. Imanishi writes. "If species developed in the sea and moved toward the land, there must have been many places for them to live and survive. Even when more species were born, they would be able to find uninhabited places. There was no need for them to fight over living spaces as they could move a little aside from each other to make space for newcomers."

Dr. Imanishi thinks of nature in friendly terms. His thoughts seem to be based on traditional Japanese ways of thinking, like those of Saigyo and Basho. For the Japanese, nature is like one's mother; she is warm-hearted and takes away your pains when you are suffering. You can find this way of thinking in many parts of the East.

As I read through the books by Thoreau and Imanishi, I seemed to find something they held in common. It is quite interesting that two people, living in such different times and places, had such similar ways of thinking.

Now the destruction of the earth's environment has become one of the most important problems facing the world. The basis of this problem lies in the balance between human activity and the limits of how much nature can tolerate. Therefore, we need to look and think again about the relation between people and nature. At the same time, we should not forget that there are many people who have different ways of thinking—not only you and the people around you, but also people living in the tropical forests who still follow folkways handed down through many generations. We might find a good way of keeping "the relation between people and nature" through looking at history.

Does nature exist for people? Or does nature exist only for itself? Do we have the right to completely eliminate the cockroach or the mosquito? Hasn't the AIDS bacillus the right to survive?

If "biological diversity" is important, and if nature is not under the sway of mankind, then we must express doubt about exterminating any seeds, even though they may be harmful to mankind.

On a stormy, sleepless night, various questions were passing through my mind. Qomolangma stands with its grand features on a fine, clear day, telling me, "If the environment were destroyed, mankind might die but the planet would continue. It is nothing but your conceit to say, 'Save the Planet.' Remember that today's environmental danger is not to the planet but to the people who inhabit it."

The pond at Walden is a place for people to think in the way I was thinking on Qomolangma. So even myself, a Japanese who lives far from America, cannot stop thinking about how to preserve Walden Woods.

▲ ▲ ▲

Shigeyuki Okajima joined *The Yomiuri Shimbun,* a Japanese newspaper in 1969. Since then, he has traveled worldwide from the North Pole to the Amazonian rain forest, and climbed Mt. Everest, to write stories on the environment. In 1988, he received The Global 500 Award from the United Nations.

It is not that we love to be alone, but that we love to soar, and when we do soar, the company grows thinner & thinner till there is none at all. It is either the Tribune on the plain, a sermon on the mount, or a very private *extacy* still higher up. We are not the less to aim at the summits, though the multitude does not ascend them. Use all the society that will abet you.

LETTER TO H.G.O. BLAKE, MAY 21, 1856
HENRY DAVID THOREAU

---

[1]Saigyo (1118–1190) was a Buddist priest of the Heian period in Japan, who loved writing Japanese poems. He was once a Bushi (Samurai), but found the vanity of life in the fighting period of his time and became a priest. Later he traveled various places in Japan as he felt his heart was not rested in spite of his belief in Buddhism. While he was traveling, he was taught by the beautifulness of nature and wrote about the beauty in his poems. Saigyo is said to carry the hearts of Japanese poems most effectively, and many people have read his poems with appreciation.

[2]Basho (1644–1694), like Saigyo, was a Bushi, but later he became a poet. He changed the traditional Japanese poem style of "renga" to the short form of "haiku." He also traveled around Japan in writing his poems. Among his works, "Okuno Hosomichi" is a masterpiece of Japanese travel notes.

PRISCILLA A. CHAPMAN

AIR APPARENT

W ho will buy this wonderful morning?" sings Oliver Twist in the popular musical *Oliver!* "Such a sky you never did see! Who will tie it up with a ribbon and put it in a box for me?"

Oliver's questions are playful and tongue-in-cheek. We all think of blue sky as one of a few commodities that is still free, enjoyable for all, even penniless orphans like Oliver. "So what am I to do to keep the sky so blue?" he continues. "There must be someone who will buy!"

Maybe Oliver Twist had a premonition of what the Industrial Revolution, especially the invention of the combustion engine, would do to the air we breathe. When the federal Clean Air Act came before Congress for reauthorization in the late 1980s, it had become sadly clear that blue sky is no longer free. Unhealthy air had been recorded in more than seventy U.S. cities. The debate was about how many years should be allowed for cleanup, how much damage to human health and the environment is acceptable, and how clean the U.S. economy can afford to make the nation's air in the end.

Nineteenth-century poet Gerard Manley Hopkins wrote of "wild air, world mothering air" as a substance "that's fairly mixed with riddles and is rife in every least thing's life." In 1989 the U.S. Environmental Protection Agency said that about 110 million Americans live in areas with unhealthful air. A recent study confirmed that children who grow up in the smog of Los Angeles develop reduced lung capacity.

Ozone, the main component of smog, causes contraction of the lung passages and impairs breathing. Sulfur dioxide and nitrogen oxides also trigger respiratory attacks and are linked to increased infant mortality and premature death in adults. Hopkins referred to "this air, which by life's law my lung must draw and draw." It's frightening that we have no choice but to breathe contaminated air if we live in a polluted area. In Mexico City, where severely fouled air causes high numbers of respiratory attacks, and even kills birds in trees, officials may establish "fresh air booths," where people experiencing breathing problems can stop and revive themselves. As the plan is proposed, people will *pay* for fresh oxygen.

The harm from air pollution is not limited to humans. As a result of the "acid rain" caused by sulfur dioxide and nitrogen oxide emissions, many lakes and streams in North America are devoid of the tumultuous jumble of life that normally populates a freshwater ecosystem.

The water bodies become acidified and toxic metals are released. These conditions interfere with the vital life functions of fish, amphibians, and insects. Gills malfunction, reproductive processes fail, and the number of hatching eggs and spawning larvae declines.

Aquatic populations, from dragonflies to salamanders and frogs to trout and other fish, dwindle and finally disappear. Mammals that drink the altered water suffer organ damage. Birds and waterfowl that feed on the insects and fish lose their food supply. All over North America, biologists have observed a disappearance of salamander species and general decline in waterbird populations.

Forests in the United States and Europe have also suffered from air pollution. Yellowing needles, brown spots on leaves, reduced growth, dieback of the treetops, and tree death have been recorded in the San Bernardino Mountains of California, the Boundary Waters Wilderness of Minnesota, the Smoky Mountains of Tennessee, the Pine Barrens of New Jersey, and in Acadia National Park in Maine. Acid rain alters the chemical composition of soils and interferes with the ability of roots to take up nutrients. Ozone enters leaves through their stomata and reduces the rate of photosynthesis, the process by which a plant or tree produces its own food from water, sunlight, and carbon dioxide. Scientists seem to agree that air pollution subjects forests to stresses that make them more vulnerable to drought and insect attack. In Germany, where up to 70 percent of the Black Forest has been affected, the phenomena is referred to as *"waldersterben,"* or "death of the forest."

For most of us, saving forests, meadows, ponds, and wildlife means stopping the bulldozers in their tracks and preventing the conversion of natural areas to concrete and pavement. Heading off the developers is the first step, but it is also crucial to ask, will the natural ecosystems that evade the construction crews also survive acid rain, smog, global warming, and others threats from atmospheric pollution?

Part of the reason air pollution is out of control is that, for a long time, we accepted the idea that we could safely wave goodbye to unwanted emissions by sending them up, up, and away, out a tall smokestack. People forgot that winds and clouds move around the globe, although we see it every night when the weatherman on the six o'clock news activates his computer map. Air pollution often produces damaging effects hundreds or thousands of miles from the source. It took evidence of pollutants in remote wilderness areas, for which windborne transport was the only explanation, to convince some scientists and policy-makers that the problem of long-range transport had to be addressed. We now know that there is truly nowhere that qualifies as "away."

In 1990, Congress finally passed major amendments to the Clean Air Act, putting many new, more stringent requirements in place. The new law acknowledges long-range transport of pollution and approaches air quality as a regional, rather than local, problem.

Clean air will not immediately result, however. For starters, Congress gave cities that were originally supposed to have clean air by 1975, generous additional time to comply. For people living in the most polluted cities of the U.S. (and for many living downwind of those areas) dirty air will be legal for at least fifteen more years. Even if all goes well, some of the other programs required by the new law won't be implemented for ten to fifteen years. Economic and political factors may influence the resolve and vigor with which these new mandates are implemented and enforced. We will be well into the new century before we know whether the new requirements are strong and comprehensive enough to solve the problems we're now experiencing. There are many unknowns and some reason for doubt.

Under the new law, Congress basically allowed industries and individuals alike to keep doing what we've done in the past, as long as more pollution controls are installed. This technology-based approach will reduce emissions when measured per unit of time from a given source. But what if there are more sources— for example, more people driving more cars more miles? More factories, print shops, dry cleaners, sewage plants, incinerators? This approach may or may not result in reducing overall air pollution to non-damaging levels. Increased federal investment in energy conservation, efficiency, and renewable sources, and decreased investment in superhighway construction are likely to accomplish what the new Clean Air Act cannot.

Congress made one attempt, in the "Acid Rain Title" of the law, to set an actual ceiling on sulfur dioxide emissions from power plants. Utilities must obtain allowances for each ton of the pollutant emitted, and a maximum number of allowances are allocated. If a multimillionaire somewhere wants to purchase clean air and blue sky and put them in a box for Oliver, he could pose as a utility executive and buy up allowances from the government.

A major unknown in the future of air and atmospheric quality is what happens beyond the boundaries of the United States. Many countries are taking steps to reduce emissions from vehicles and stationary sources, but whether *all* nations—especially developing countries—will establish pollution limits remains an unanswered question.

Another unknown is what the rest of the world will do about carbon dioxide. This gas has not been implicated in direct damage to human health, vegetation, or wildlife, so it has largely been left unregulated. Now it is known to be one of the "greenhouse gases," which are accumulating in the upper atmosphere. Many scientists believe this buildup can prevent heat from escaping from the earth's surface and cause an increase in global temperature. The results could include melting of the polar icecaps, sea level rise, massive shifts in climate and rainfall patterns, and dislocation of agriculture, coastal communities, forests, and wildlife populations.

We have also learned that man-made gases such as chlorofluorocarbons are eating holes in the layer of ozone in the upper atmosphere. This upper ozone layer screens out the ultraviolet rays of the sun that cause skin cancer and damage vegetation. Ozone holes allow more ultraviolet radiation to reach the earth.

Throughout the 1980s, President Reagan delayed action on acid rain, citing the need for further study. The 1990s are becoming the global warming study period. Yet, with potential consequences so enormous and devastating, it would be prudent to begin reducing carbon dioxide emissions immediately.

A great place to start is automobile driving. Car commercials love to feature scenes of emerald green forests, healthy people fishing in woodland streams, and pastel sunsets gleaming on a crystal-clear horizon. They should be forced to show drooping trees, dead and deformed fish, smog-cloaked skylines, and people gasping for breath.

Overuse of cars implicates most of us in consequences we're fond of denouncing: We contribute money to the very oil companies that cause ecologically devastating oil spills. We increase America's dependence on foreign oil. We add credence to arguments for allowing oil drilling in fragile, irreplaceable areas like the coastal plain of the Arctic National Wildlife Refuge. Besides polluting, we deprive ourselves of exercise and waste time while attached to a steering wheel. The withering trees by the roadside show that the Wasteland is coming because we, the Fisher Kinglets, are too weak and incapacitated to walk or take the train.

I'm as bad as anyone else: I drive 125 miles to an environmentalist meeting on saving the North Woods of New England from development. Does this make me an environmental advocate or an environmental menace? I wonder if I'm doing more to save the forests than the hydrocarbons and other pollution my car spews out will do to destroy them.

"Look at the stars, Look, look up at the skies! / O look at all the fire-folk sitting in the air" wrote Hopkins in "The Starlight Night." Now it's often hard to see the stars through the smog. As a child, I thought of air as synonymous with the whole universe. It was a shock to learn that the atmosphere is really very thin, that the substance that keeps life going only extends a few miles upward. We must regard it as we would the last tract of primeval forest or an endangered species habitat.

"Wilderness" is defined in law as "an area where the earth and its community of life are untrammeled by man, where man himself is a visitor who does not remain." Most of us still cherish the existence of wild places that are too inaccessible for humans to colonize, dominate, and despoil. But if atmospheric pollution is not curtailed, there will be no place on earth that has not been transformed by human activity.

So what are we to do to keep the sky blue? The hope is that millions of us will begin to make the right choices about life-styles: recycling rather than disposing. Replacing inefficient light bulbs. Turning down the air conditioner. Taking the train or walking. The sea erodes the beach one grain of sand at a time. We can dismantle the threat of global transformation through air pollution by individual decisions and actions that will cumulatively redirect economic and environmental policy made by the world's leaders, whom we ourselves empower.

▲ ▲ ▲

Priscilla Chapman is executive director of the New England Chapter of the Sierra Club, a nationally based nonprofit conservation organization with more than 650,000 members.

> Most men, it appears to me, do not care for Nature, and would sell their share in all her beauty, for as long as they may live, for a stated and not very large sum. Thank God they cannot yet fly and lay waste the sky as well as the earth. We are safe on that side for the present. It is for the very reason that some do not care for these things that we need to combine to protect all from the vandalism of a few.
>
> "HUCKLEBERRIES"
> HENRY DAVID THOREAU

DAVE MARSH

THE BOLL WEEVIL SONG

First time I met Boll Weevil, he was sittin' in the square
Next time I saw Boll Weevil, he had his whole family there

Leadbelly

ike all city boys, my versions of natural treasure tend to be
almost ridiculously overspecific: a scrubby field for playing ball,
my grandfather's raspberry patch, the enormous oak that divided the road on the way to school. Best of all, I remember a weeping
willow in the backyard of one of my boyhood neighbors, for the beauty of
its hanging limbs, for the shade they offered and the shelter they provided
for all manner of plots and explorations, and for the pain those limbs could
cause when they were cut free and made into switches by an angry parent
or a neighborhood bully.

This was a world of lawns and shrubbery, each serving as a tiny,
mocking memory of the prairie and forest that had been displaced by the
Autoworld in which we lived. Autoworld is no metaphor—there was a
Pontiac Motors assembly line barely two blocks away, and past that, a brake
factory in one direction, a foundry in the other. General Motors made trucks

and buses on the other side of town. This was the landscape of my childhood, all asphalt and asbestos, but it was an environment as truly as Walden is one, and when GM decided it needed another parking lot and came one day to tear down those ticky-tacky houses, my friends and I were stunned and mournful.

My father, who'd better than doubled the money he'd paid for the house fifteen years before, felt no such remorse. He was glad to get us out of the city and into a suburb. Mainly, I think, he didn't want his kids to go to mixed-race schools, but he also was a farm boy, born and bred, as uncomfortable on paved surfaces as I've always been around tractors and harrows. My father had come to the city in the first place only because the possibilities for a second son on a family farm were limited—would have been narrow even if the eldest son had not repelled anybody who represented a threat at the point of a pitchfork. Dad counted it lucky that he wound up on the railroad, where he could at least work outside; his brother wound up losing the farm and worked instead in Midland, at Dow Chemical, where, for all I know, he poured napalm. They went back to nature annually, with all their similarly displaced friends, on the weekend look-out for pheasant, deer, and rabbit.

City boy I am, but my father's relatives were farmers and we spent a lot of time on their places, mostly summer and fall. In the fifties and sixties, any drive over fifty miles in the state of Michigan would have taken you into the sticks, and if you drove the seventy or eighty miles into the tip of the Thumb where we went, there were dirt roads and cultivation all around. So I grew up as a city boy who knew what he was missing, from the taste of fresh, warm milk only moments out of the cow to the dirt and dust that sticks down your T-shirt and roughs up the back of your throat after an afternoon spent tumbling in corncribs and haylofts.

That split Midwestern existence, town in the weekdays and farm from Friday night through Sunday afternoon, set me up perfectly for life in New York City, where from Memorial Day to Labor Day, everybody who can afford to (and many who really can't) harks to some crowded country plot, from the Jersey Shore east to the Hamptons, and north past Cape Cod to Maine. As I write this, one of my grown daughters is at the Cape, the other driving out to Sag Harbor; all three of us swore last weekend that we missed the Jersey Shore where they'd spent their childhood, and only their mother, who grew up down there but now reveres our Connecticut carriage house, disagreed.

Those addresses smack of privilege. Decker, Michigan, the hamlet my father called home, did not. Yet, in many ways Decker served the same purpose. It may surprise you, because I know it shocked me, to realize that we are only a generation or two divorced from a time when almost everybody in urban America, black and white, had some sort of connection to the land, and generally *not* as a renter of expensive waterfront property or an interloping hunter, backpacker, or fisherman, but as a place of homestead.

There is enormous tension in this fact, at least for me. The city boy, looking at what is left of the countryside from his sunbaked curb, must acknowledge that it does not feel especially natural (it certainly does not feel right) to be so cut off from our relationship to land. Yet my daughters know the countryside only in passing, far less well than I did, and I grew up listening to my father's stories about men who lived for weeks in the woods with not much more than a handful of shotgun shells—and thinking them improbably exotic, rather than matter-of-fact anecdotes about another era and way of life. Today, I speak of milking a cow (with a machine!), and my kids act like I've dropped in from another century. Which doesn't make any less significant my memory of standing in a corn row in the August heat and listening to the leaves rustle with growth.

Mine is a boll weevil generation, alien to the land, and the ones that have arrived since are the same, only more so. All of us just lookin' for a home—not a house, or a shelter, but a home-place, a place not to own but to belong to, to belong in.

This is not only because there are too many people in too little space. Perhaps the central myth of this era is scarcity. Properly managed, there is plenty to go around, though it seems to me that the world properly managed is not easily imagined. We are stuck with thinking that current conditions are eternal, even though people from Hanoi to Managua to Leningrad (not to mention the earth's own prodding plate tectonics) have done their best to show that this is a ridiculous fallacy.

One way to limber up our ideas is to redefine the environment. Too often, we act as if the earth ends where the sidewalk begins, a notion not only absurd but dangerous. And not only dangerous because it allows us to cavalierly poison the trash, but threatening because it encourages us to cavalierly trash our own best instincts and memories, including matters as trivial as milking cows and hearing corn grow or, for that matter, listening to that willow whip slice the air. We are all entitled to regret what has been lost and squandered, even if it has been gone for so long that we can no longer quite put our finger on what it is that's missing.

So even now, I mourn that little clump of houses in Pontiac, not because it was pristine or beautiful but because some of us had a life there, and it was wasted to no purpose. General Motors didn't really need that parking lot, it turned out, because it decided to start putting together its machines in Missouri and Mexico. But that was half a dozen years after I was uprooted, when it was too late to change anything, including my implacable hatred of all such corporations and their disdain for communities and environments. My version of *Roger and Me* would take this for its epigram: A boll weevil cut loose will ravage your crops, just looking for a home.

Thoreau, I think, was himself a spiritual boll weevil. He belonged to both Walden and Concord, and part of his relevance to moderns is that he wrote as a man in search of a home for his heart. He found such a place at Walden, but when his sojourn there was complete, he returned to Concord, with all its moral and physical pollution that his assiduously developed senses demanded he acknowledge, because being alone is one thing but being lonely is another. He was most certainly not a hermit; he intended to engage mankind and, so far as he could, change it.

So Thoreau returned to town as the tax protester and community moralist of "Civil Disobedience," an essay whose ideas still shake the world. Yet he remained essentially a naturalist, even during his night in that most perfectly urban environment, the town jail. "I saw that if one stayed there long, his principal business would be to look out the window," Thoreau wrote in "Civil Disobedience." Jail did not diminish him at all, because he was at home there, too, as long as (to use the phrase employed by a great contemporary boll weevil) he was doing the right thing. Restored by his time spent where there were no cobblestones, Thoreau lived in the confidence that heaven was under his feet even when all visible signs of it had been paved over.

Even in Autoworld, this would be recognized as a street-smart perception. But I wonder if my grandchildren will be able to put their finger on its elusive melody.

▲ ▲ ▲

Dave Marsh, author of the best-sellers *Born to Run* and *Glory Days,* lives to rabble-rouse. To that end, he compiled *50 Ways to Fight Censorship,* and edits *Rock & Roll Confidential,* a newsletter about music and politics.

> There is a solid bottom everywhere. We read that the traveller asked the boy if the swamp before him had a hard bottom. The boy replied that it had. But presently the traveller's horse sank in up to the girths, and he observed to the boy, "I thought you said that this bog had a hard bottom." "So it has," answered the latter, "but you have not got half way to it yet." So it is with the bogs and quicksands of society; but he is an old boy that knows it.
>
> WALDEN
> HENRY DAVID THOREAU

CARRIE FISHER

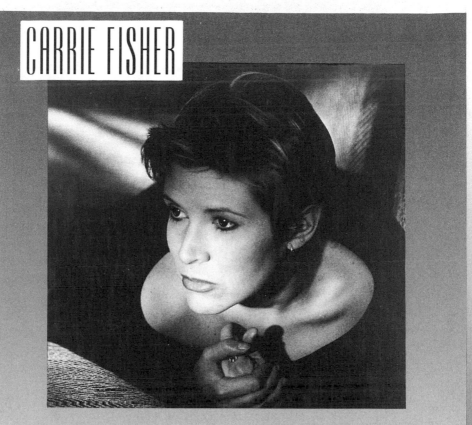

READING BY LAMPLIGHT

Alex Daniels was last seen in the novel Postcards from the Edge. *A former drug abuser, he is currently in his sixth year of sobriety. We met with him to discuss environmental issues on the set of his hit series* Would-Be Hero—*a spin-off of his first classic,* Rehab!—*which he is producing for the Fox network.*

I know that this is supposed to be this whole pro-ecology save-the-planet thing, but really—I mean, the world is designed to go downhill, isn't it? It's round. Living on the planet is hard enough. Can we really be expected to save it, too? I mean, I'm an ambivalent-type person enough as it is, to say the least. I don't know how I get out of bed in the morning, but somehow I find myself in the middle of the day having done it, and I regret it every time.

Hey, I'm the same as the next guy—I'd rather be mad about how smoggy it is than why I'm not making more money or don't have a girlfriend. But I think people worry about this stuff partly so they seem sensitive and concerned and then will get laid more. I figure that's how Ed Begley, Jr. got that nude chick from *The Grifters*—he picked her up in an electric car wearing aftershave that wasn't tested on tortured animals or something. I don't know, I would think it would be embarrassing to pick up a girl and take her to a screening in a golf cart, but maybe that's just me.

Look, I want to be correct, but it seems so complicated. There's so much to worry about, where would you even begin? Acid rain, for starters. What is it, does anyone know? I know it's something bad, like maybe metal went into the air and now it rains down. It sounds like it would burn, and probably cause pock marks, but no one seems to really know.

Or take global warming. Why is that bad? You know, like when you describe a warm person, it sounds kind of affectionate. Like, hey, come to Earth, we're a warm planet.

Or this so-called greenhouse effect. What's so bad about a greenhouse? They're a good thing. Greenhouses were designed to make plants grow and make vegetables get bigger and create exotic plants. So I try to look on the bright side—maybe we'll end up with some new flowers out of this. Who knows? I do know that I wouldn't want to be in New York with many more scrambling people and the greenhouse effect. The summers there were bad enough before, but now—well, it's boiling hot for virtually six months now, with bums asking you for money on top of it. Although in that kind of heat, it makes it easier to say no.

And the hole in the ozone. Where is it? I figure it's over Alaska—you know, where that kind of a tear is likely. They just seem more vulnerable up there. But, hey, I don't want to live in Alaska so I'm probably okay. I mean, Eskimo women aren't really my type, no offense—broad noses and bulky parkas. Anyway, if there's just one hole, maybe that's not so bad. But how big is it, and what's the shape, and can't we stuff it with something? A big doily? How about moving the people out from under the hole to a place where there isn't a hole? And how do you notice a hole in the ozone in the first place? Does that mean there's like an area of the sky that isn't blue? Is it like a rip? What's the deal?

I think in a lot of ways they're just trying to scam us. You know, like George Bush's son and that whole S&L thing. George Bush's son fucks up, and suddenly there's a tear in the ozone. I say it's a cover-up. I don't want to imply that there's no basis, but let's just say I think they exaggerate it so we're not as focused on, say, Nancy Reagan's affair with Frank Sinatra, you know?

The thing is, there's a lot of these sensitive journalist-types that control this information, and they want to seem like heroes, you know, and get their Pulitzer Prize or whatever by noticing the tear, and then they get to be the guy that the girl goes out with that noticed the tear in the ozone, or named the greenhouse effect. "Have you met my boyfriend? He's the one that coined the phrase 'greenhouse effect'—Arnie 'Greenhouse Effect' Klein." So I just think that a lot of these things are dating techniques for journalists and I know they're probably getting laid because they're oh so sensitive and they don't wear leather shoes and they don't eat violently killed meat. Well, what are we supposed to do, go to a restaurant and ask, "How was this hamburger killed?"

And this animal testing issue. Why do they test cosmetics on animals? It's not like they have long eyelashes, or look good in a lip gloss. Am I wrong, or don't that many animals have lips? Nails yes, lips no. Animals would look silly in makeup, but I guess if it looked good on an animal, it would look *great* on a human. Maybe that's the thinking.

Then there's all this talk about waste. There's always been waste. We're basically living in a trash dump that's been collecting since Christ. What did they do in the eighteen hundreds? What did Jane Austen do? Or Leo Tolstoy. Or Poe. You know what I'm saying? Henry James didn't separate his aluminum cans from whatever they need to be separated from, and now we're paying the penalty for these literary greats who didn't bother to watch where they threw stuff. Okay, they didn't know, but now we have to suffer for all this after-the-fact enlightenment.

Enlightenment can be a bummer. I mean, who wants to know extra stuff if it just makes you feel bad? So now we know that the air is filled with smog—I love when they make those announcements that the air is not acceptable today. What can you do when the air is not acceptable? Keep oxygen in your house? Who do you protest to? Can you make a couple of calls to some politicians who are out trying to get laid in secret so that it doesn't ruin their image? Anyway, we know that the air is deadly, the beaches are strewn with AIDS-riddled needles, and the birds are covered in oil.

On the other hand, if God hadn't meant for forests to be destroyed and air to be polluted, he wouldn't have given us brains that would invent cars and paper. Still, it would be a damn shame if something like junk mail were the reason that they were destroying the forest in the Amazon, and then we were left with nothing to breathe and all this shit to read. You know, this really shallow breathing as we're reading all this crap about how we could save thirty cents on cat food somewhere. But hey, the way I look at it is, evolution has always had its casualties. Does anybody really miss the Tyrannosaurus Rex? I don't think so. The world just looks lived-in.

And maybe smog does a good thing that we can't tell yet, besides making the sunsets prettier. You know, like killing certain kinds of germs and not just causing cancer. Maybe it's preparing us for something. Anyway, people will always die of things. You could just as easily die of a tree falling on you in Walden Woods as pesticide poisoning. I mean, my arteries are probably filled with all kinds of gicky plaque, but I'm waiting for that laser that'll just Hoover it all out. I mean, they're gonna come up with a pill or a laser for everything, aren't they? I figure ten more years, right? We'll look back on all this and laugh. I don't know, maybe I'm just rationalizing, but if I didn't rationalize, I'd be even more depressed than I already am.

I mean, I live in a world with shopping malls and Fotomats and even though I can get my film developed in an hour, what are the pictures of? Freeways and liquor stores and people looking distressed. Sure, I'd rather have lived in a more contemplative time where things took longer, where I wouldn't have minded the waiting so much 'cause things were lit by lamplight. And yeah, I'd have liked living in a cobblestone kind of village where everybody knew your name and pies cooled on windowsills and the big deals were on a smaller scale. I wish I were the type that liked to listen to the wind in the trees and get all worked up about finding a bird's nest instead of watching "The Simpsons." I'm a corrupted guy, I admit it. Corrupted and contaminated and not quite the type to get back to basics any time soon. I blame my parents, really—if they'd have sent me to summer camp, maybe I'd know how to get all worked up about some disappearing wilderness. Why wasn't I raised to yearn for the great outdoors? I'll tell you why—'cause it's not so great anymore. At best it's pretty good.

Besides, what good is paradise if you can't live in it? If it's just some great thing that you've pretty much missed out on? I mean, if time really is money, who can, in all good conscience, go fishing? I mean, one just feels delinquent, no? Sure, I'd like to sit in the shade on the shore of a rustling stream and watch the tall ships move out onto the horizon carrying their cargo of silks and spice. But who's going to pay me to do that? Phil Rizzuto? David Geffen? I tend to doubt it.

Anyway, I do stuff. I feel bad about it sometimes when I see those birds covered in oil on TV, and I figure feeling bad is a beginning, and I'm aware of the problem now, and soon I'll take that next step—wear a button, or not order meat, or look at a woman wearing fur with disdain. Timing is everything. I feel like I've got the makings of some environmental heroics in me, and I'm just letting it come out at its own pace. I'll do a fine thing. I just have to let myself know when it's the exact right time to do it.

I mean, I don't want to just save *anything*. When I protest, it will be for something so unconscionable that no high-minded, fine-faced soulmate will be able to resist me as I overcome her mild protestations and remove her 100 percent cotton blouse in my golf cart parked behind Mrs. Gooch's health food store where we have gone to stock up on supplies for our ecologically sound camping trip/love fest in the finally saved Walden Woods. We will finish each other's sentences and separate each other's trash. She will turn me around. I know just what I'll say to her.

"What took you so long?"

It will be easy and natural, and I will regard everything I did before this transformation as essential, knowing that what I was, I was only in order to be more fully not that now.

I wait for this, and forgive myself in the interim. As I said, it's hard enough to be me, much less me drinking carrot juice in an electric car.

▲ ▲ ▲

Carrie Fisher has excelled as an actress (she played Princess Leia in the *Star Wars* films), author (*Postcards from the Edge, Surrender the Pink*), screenwriter (*Postcards from the Edge*), and television producer "Esme's Little Nap," starring her mother, Debbie Reynolds). She is a member of the Walden Woods Project Advisory Board.

It is never too late to give up our prejudices.

WALDEN
HENRY DAVID THOREAU

BILL McKIBBEN

THOREAU COUNTRY—THE WILD, WILD EAST

Somewhere along the Thorofare River in Wyoming's Teton Wilderness there is a spot twenty-one air miles from a road. It is impossible to find a place in the lower forty-eight more remote than that—nowhere in the canyons of Idaho or the Montana woods or Minnesota's lake country or California's desert. That claustrophobic fact comes from a book called *The Big Outside*, by Dave Foreman and Howie Wolke. It's the first attempt in more than fifty years to systematically inventory all the wilderness left in the United States, and it is overwhelmingly depressing. Even by the generous definitions of the federal government, which will count as wilderness any untrammeled tract of five thousand square acres—that is, an hour's walk across—only 10 percent of the lower forty-eight is "wild," and this remnant is being methodically reduced by agencies like the United States Forest Service, which has announced plans to build 100,000 miles of road into previously untouched areas. On the public lands as a whole, wilderness—and with it grizzlies, bison, wolves, condor—disappears at a rate of at least two million acres each year. That's a Yellowstone annually. In other words, if Thoreau was right about wildness being the world's salvation, then we're up a creek without a paddle, or would be if we could find a creek.

Still and all, there are a few nice surprises left on this continent, and one of them is this: If you take a map and look for places where the improved roads are still few and far between, you'll see New Mexico, Idaho, Wyoming, New York—New York? New York! And Maine, and bits of New Hampshire and Vermont, and even Massachusetts. In the northeast corner of the country, in the first states settled by Europeans, there is still an awful lot of undeveloped country, including a great swath of forest that cuts from the Adirondacks east to Maine's North Woods. Large stretches are wilder than they were when Thoreau wandered through them, as farms have grown in and the scars of the largest-scale logging have started to heal. "It may not be wilderness with a capital W," says Michael Kellett of the Wilderness Society. "A lot of it has been logged over once or twice. But it's wild, and it's remote."

And it's big. "I was up in an airplane the other day going over one new proposed wilderness," says Adirondack conservationist George Davis. "It seemed to go on forever. It's a western-sized piece of land. They have a lot of wilderness acres out West, but it's mostly high up. You're out there on the rocks and ice, but you can still see Fort Collins down below. Here in the East you don't have to go very far to get a sense of real isolation."

All of which is to say, there's still time for a real tribute to Thoreau—the Thoreau National Wilderness, we could call it, its heart in the Maine woods with fingers reaching down through New England to the Berkshires and Connecticut and across Champlain and the Hudson to the vastness of the Adirondacks— maybe even, since this is all on paper, up into the wild lands of Quebec and Ontario. We're so used to thinking of the East as overcrowded and polluted—a megalopolis. And it is, too much of it. But half a day's drive from Boston and Hartford and New York are mountains and woods that are drawing back the moose, that ring with coyote calls, that once more know the eagle—that could, if we acted wisely, support again the wolf and the mountain lion and the lynx.

Needless to say, though, like every other environmental opportunity, this one is almost past us. Have you noticed how with each crisis some activist says, "the next ten years will be crucial"? The Wilderness Society's Kellett says, "You shouldn't have to go to Colorado to find wild land. If we nurture it, it's here. But we've got a window of maybe ten years."

These northern forest lands, forming their piny arc of perhaps thirty million acres, are mostly in private hands, the property of huge timber firms. Their logging—and especially the clearcutting and herbicide-spraying that have grown increasingly popular—often harm the woods, destroying both scenic vistas and wildlife habitat. But the biggest threat at the moment is different—it's that the loggers will start *selling* their great tracts of land to developers, who will break them up for vacation homes and retirement communities and end forever the unbroken wilderness sweep unique in the East.

This threat results from shifts in relative land values, a prosaic topic that nonetheless can turn deep dark forest into Creek Hollow Acres Manor Homes virtually overnight. These vast wooded parcels, sold as timberland, can command perhaps two or three hundred dollars per acre. For many centuries they had little other (monetary) value—they were too cold, too bug-bitten, too far away from the cities and the oceans, too hard to farm. They were de facto wilderness. But then came the interstates, and the New England boom years, and a hell of a lot of Bostonians and New Yorkers who were willing to go farther north for summer homes or ski chalets. Subdivided and sold to these people, that same land could all of a sudden fetch maybe a thousand dollars an acre. "If it's got any water frontage, you're talking hundreds of dollars *per foot,*" says Paul Bofinger of the Society for the Protection of New Hampshire Forests.

At the same time the timber industry has been facing stiff competition from the flat, warm, nonunion forests of the southeast. "You can see what the problem is," says Bofinger. "Any landowner, be they corporation or private family, has to look at what they're getting for their investment. It's hard to justify growing trees, which are a relatively low-value crop, on high-value land."

Which is one way of looking at it, but not Thoreau's way. "Is it the lumberman, then, who is the friend and lover of the pine, stands nearest it, and understands its nature best? . . . No! No! It is the poet; he it is who makes the truest use of the pine, who does not fondle it with an axe, nor tickle it with a saw, nor stroke it with a plane, who knows whether its heart is false without cutting into it." We need lumbermen, of course, or you'd have to read *Walden* on chiseled stone. But do we need clearcuts, copters spraying herbicide, enormous stands of "even-aged" plantation trees? It is even less obvious to me that we need vacation home developers, destroying the very things—"pristine wilderness," "wooded beauty"—they market. Neither industry will disappear, of course. But if we had different conceptions of "value," perhaps they could shrink—be as tightly controlled as they are in New York's Adirondacks, so that all the other things we need could prosper too. Even more than Thoreau, we understand our practical need for diverse and healthy ecosystems; with his guidance, we've slowly come to understand the needs of our hearts and spirits for a wild world. And maybe we've even gone beyond Thoreau—begun, haltingly, to realize that the pine tree exists not for the lumberman *or* the poet, but for the pine tree.

Here's the real question: Will the current surge of interest in protecting the natural world translate into a real change of values and attitudes, so that the $10 billion it might take to really protect the North Woods would start sounding like the bargain it is? Or is it wisest to assume people will go on thinking of the woods as mainly a source of lumber and pulp, and of lakes as places to water-ski?

The plight of a lonely herd of caribou summarizes the gulf between the positions. A couple of years ago the state of Maine tried to reintroduce the animals, transplanting a group from Canada into Baxter State Park, home of mighty Mount Katahdin and the northern end of the Appalachian Trail. It's too early to say for sure if the animals will make it, but many biologists feel they need more room. That's one reason the Wilderness Society has called for a Maine Forest Reserve, several million acres around the state park where human activity would be strictly regulated. At least for the moment, however, most residents of the state of Maine, northern New England, the United States, and planet earth would probably agree with a lumber industry spokesman who said, "Caribou do not particularly like people. If you're suggesting we need to exclude people from parts of Maine, that's not something most people would want." And so the human charge north will likely continue, ringing once-remote lakeshores with vacation homes and cutting roads through forests.

But it's always possible that attitudes really will change, and change fast enough so that politicians will take the necessary steps to preserve the land. It's started to happen in Brazil—maybe Boston will catch up some day. And if that happened, the northeastern wilderness could prosper. Blessed with ample rain and snow (though currently it reeks of acid), the land is more forgiving than the arid West, where scars last centuries. It's not like the California desert, where you can still see the tank treads from General Patton's war games. It will never, not in human time, be the northern woods Thoreau explored, where nature still had the guts to say to him, as he climbed Katahdin, "I cannot pity nor fondle thee here, but forever relentlessly drive thee hence to where I *am* kind." Murch Brook will never swim with the living river of trout he saw, and the virgin woods have all but vanished. But wild enough! Wild enough. Saving Walden Woods is noble calisthenics. Saving the northern woods—that's a real milepost on the road we must travel.

▲ ▲ ▲

Bill McKibben has written hundreds of articles for *The New Yorker*. His writings about nature have also appeared in *The New York Review of Books, The New York Times* and other national publications. His book, *The End of Nature,* has been translated into seventeen languages. He is a member of the Walden Woods Project Advisory Board.

JOHN NICHOLS

CONSCIENCE AND COMMUNITY

I thought I might begin by admitting that if for some terrible reason I was thrown back into high school today, I'm not so sure I would know how to graduate.

I think back to my own checkered high school career, and I am continually amazed at how I ever managed to escape it all in one piece. There were seventy-two students in my graduating class, and I was the sixty-ninth person in that class of seventy-two. I usually flunked two courses per annum from my freshman year on, and I was always going to summer school, getting tutored, taking makeup exams in the fall to see if I would move on to the next class. Finally, my senior year, I didn't even have a graduating average. I had to be voted a diploma by a special faculty committee, which no doubt wanted me *out* of there so it wouldn't have to worry about me any more.

To tell the truth, I think the only reason that I graduated at all was because I was a jock. I played football and ice hockey, and I ran the mile and the low hurdles in track. And I actually got accepted at a decent college, even though I was almost a D student, and I think that acceptance was based primarily on the fact that I was an athlete.

In fact, I remember this, during my first weeks in college. I had reported three weeks early to play football. But when my academic advisor found out I was on the gridiron, he threw a royal fit. He ordered me to quit football immediately, get a tutor, and spend all my time on studies the first semester so that I would be eligible to play hockey when the winter season rolled around. "We accepted you to play *hockey!*" he exclaimed. "And if you play football I'm sure you'll flunk out by the end of the first semester!"

And he was almost right. Yet I ignored his advice, played football, somehow came up with a seventy average, and played hockey that winter, and moved on to track in the spring. I wasn't much interested in academics, and in fact I almost blew it all in the spring when I wound up getting a forty on my final exam in English! I loved to write stories, but I hated grammar and composition. And it might interest you all to know that even though today (and for the last twenty-three years or so) I have made my living as a writer, in high school I was actually placed in remedial reading and writing classes because they felt I was such a moron.

Well, somehow I graduated college. But when I got out into the cold, cruel world, I had no idea what to do with my life. Certainly, I didn't want to settle down, get a job, make money, have a sensible career. I thought I might be a cartoonist—I loved to draw—or a guitarist—I loved rock and roll, blues guitar, folk music—or perhaps I'd be a writer.

And so I floundered around for a while, drawing a comic strip, playing my guitar in little New York dives, and writing books. Everybody in my family thought I was nuts, wasting all that education to be a bum who would never earn a nickel. But somehow a miracle happened, and I published first one novel and then another. And believe me, nobody was more surprised than myself when these things happened. The odds against earning a living as a writer in this country must be a million to one, but somehow I stumbled into that as a career, and I have been doing it ever since. And it continually surprises me that somehow people take me seriously. To tell the truth, I'm forty-five now, but I often feel like I'm eighteen. I keep wondering when I'm going to grow up and become an adult like everybody else in the world. I still spend a lot of my life feeling like a child.

Perhaps that has been the bane and torment of my life. But it has also supplied a lot of magic to my days. I always had a dream of doing something that most people told me was impossible, and, as luck would have it, I suppose I have realized that dream. When I look back on the past twenty-three years, I'll admit I'm not sure how it all came about. Most of the books I wrote during that time were never published. In fact, I think I've written about thirty-five books, but only nine of them have been published.

So most of the work I've done you'd probably say has been a failure. Certainly, a lot of my life has been a life of rejection. Until the past five years or so, I began each new year wondering how I was going to earn a living. But somehow I just kept plodding along, and sooner or later things seemed to fall into place.

I'm not exactly sure what the moral of that story is for a group of seventeen and eighteen year olds, except that if you have a dream that everybody else in straight society tells you is crazy, you should ignore them and just persist with what you feel you have to do. Even if it never works out, at least in the end you know that you tried. Me, I always figured I would rather live like a bum than exhaust myself in endeavors I didn't want to do.

This means that early on in my life I quit worrying about earning money, having material things, a nice car, fancy house, all of that. I never figured those things would make much difference to me. Certainly it was clear to me at an early age that if I wanted (or needed) to live in the fast lane, I would never survive as a writer. So I put those things out of my head, and persisted in my literary endeavors.

I never discovered a clear path in my writing, however, until I came to Taos. I moved here in 1969, and it occurs to me that may be the year in which many of you were born. I came to Taos from New York, and I'll admit I was kind of a burnt-out case. I hadn't sold a book for four years, I was going broke. I wouldn't sell another book for four more years, so the future didn't look very bright. I managed to find a house real cheap, the same house I live in today, but I couldn't buy a refrigerator, so for months I kept my milk and juice and other stuff in the Pacheco Irrigation Ditch, which runs in front of the house.

But almost immediately Taos became a special place to me, and I want to talk a little about that today. About the way this town, its people, its land, its cultures and history, its battles and all its problems and its triumphs, have molded my life and my spirit, and given to me the most treasured gift that I have ever received.

Mostly, I guess, Taos has taught me to survive in a way that feels special, hopeful, and fullfilling.

I remember when I first moved into my house in Upper Ranchitos, there was a huge junkpile out by the garage and the outhouse. I thought, oh golly, that's sure ugly, I better get it out of here. So I started carting it off to the dump. While I was doing this, my neighbor, Tom Trujillo, came over and said, "What are you doing with all that junk?" I said, "I'm getting rid of it, it's a terrible eyesore." He said, "Well, if you don't want it, give it to me." I asked, "Why would you want all of this crap?" He just smiled and said, "Well, you never know when it might come in handy."

So I said, "Sure, go ahead, take whatever you want."

Just about that time, I remember, the sink drain in my kitchen clogged up, so I called a plumber. The plumber came over with a Roto-Rooter and stuck it into the drain and broke off the head of the Roto-Rooter. Then he said, "Well, I'm sorry, I guess I can't help you." And he split, and sent me a bill for forty dollars! I was outraged, I refused to pay the bill, and instead I ran into town and bought myself a couple of plumber's wrenches. I started taking apart some pipes, and digging up other pipes, and I discovered that one pipe was terribly corroded and would have to be replaced. Then I remembered I'd seen a long length of pipe in that junkpile, and I went running out, yelling at my neighbor, Tom Trujillo, saying, "Stop, don't take any more of that stuff, I think I *need* it!"

And I grabbed the length of discarded pipe and fixed my kitchen sink!

I think that was the first survival lesson I learned in Taos, namely: A junk pile can be worth its weight in gold.

The next survival lesson I learned in Taos was how to fish. I mentioned that when I got here in 1969 I was pretty burnt-out, tired, and on edge. My soul needed a bit of a recharge. So one day, after making a wood run over in Carson, I stopped at the lower part of the Pueblo River to cool off, taking a little swim. And while I was lolling in the water, these two old geezers came up the river, fishing for trout. They had fly-rods, and were going flickety-flickety-flick into all the riffles and back eddies behind rocks. And one of the guys had an enormous brown trout stuffed into his front shirt pocket. It was bent double, the tail hanging down; to me it looked like a whale! And right at that moment I had a vision, a lightning bolt came out of the sky, and a voice in the thunder said, "Nichols, why don't you dedicate your life to learning how to fish like that?"

Immediately, I bought a rod, asked about the proper flies to use, and started fishing for trout. And for a while I didn't do so hot. In fact, I'll admit I even went to another neighbor, Bernardo Trujillo, and asked him: "What is the secret to catching fish?" He said, "Well, one way they used to do it was to go up to the high country lakes, take a cider jug, pour in a lot of lime, pour water on the lime, cap the bottle tightly, throw it into the lake, and, when the bottle exploded, you could simply wade in and scoop up the trout."

I was pretty chicken, however, so I simply kept on trying with flies. I would get on a bike early in the morning and ride around Ranchitos Road to Ranchos, then out Route 3 to the Rio Chiquito, and up the Rio Chiquito to where I first tried to catch trout on flies. And finally, after weeks and weeks, I caught a fish on a fly, and it was a wonderful experience. I took that fish and laid it in the basket of my bicycle on a bed of grasses, and put snow atop the fish, and more grasses, and I pedaled home feeling as if I had just captured the Holy Grail!

I had many experiences like that when I first came to Taos: fishing, gathering wood for the winter, building a chicken coop, putting a horse in my front field, learning to irrigate, gathering apples, mud plastering an adobe shack to make a watertight room that I could work in. These were daily endeavors that I suppose the average Taoseno takes for granted, but for me they were a whole new rhythm of life that I still very dearly cherish. These efforts built a connection in me to land, to water, to community, to culture, to a kind of human wholeness that I had not known before.

So right from the start, Taos gave me a gift of learning how to live that became very special to my life. And this gift was given to me by neighbors like Tom Trujillo and Bernardo Trujillo; and by neighbors like Eloy Pacheco, who taught me about working on the *acequias* in the spring. He also showed me how to maintain the *compuerta* so we could get water in our ditch for the summer irrigating. Friends like George and Jeri Track and their family out at the Pueblo taught me how to find wild raspberries up on U.S. Hill and they shared their lives and knowledge about this valley with me. My pal Candido Garcia took me deer hunting in the hills above the Rio Chiquito on horseback, and although we never shot a deer we sure had a wonderful time riding around in the snow and singing *ranchera* tunes . . . which must have scared off every animal within a hundred miles!

Then one day some of my neighbors came to me and said, we have got a big problem here in Taos, and there's going to be a meeting, and I should come to the meeting. So I went. This meeting was about a conservancy district and a large dam that was planned east of Talpa, called the Indian Camp Dam. Many people in town thought the project would be good for progress in Taos, but many others felt that the kind of progress it would bring might destroy a way of life they valued, and so they wanted to fight it. At that meeting, which occurred in 1970, I met old-timers like Andrés Martínez and Paul Valerio and Bernabé Chavez, and J.J. Garcia, and Jacob Bernal, and many others who had made up their minds to fight against the Indian Camp Dam because they felt the taxes and the commercial progress would hurt more than it would help this valley.

In that meeting, and during the long eight-year struggle that followed, I learned that you never really get anything for free in life. You almost always have to struggle real hard, and always against "impossible odds," to preserve and protect things that you believe in—you can't take anything wonderful for granted.

I learned a lot about Taos, its history, this community, by working with the Tres Rios Association in its effort to defeat the conservancy district and the Indian Camp Dam. I remember dozens of meetings where old-timers—*viejitos*—would stand up and talk about the land, the water, this community, its history, the *roots* that exist here, and why it was so important to preserve these things. I remember many afternoons when I would drive around the valley with Andrés Martínez, and he would point out old houses where certain people lived, and orchards (still surviving) where he had picked apples as a child. He explained the history of different *acequias* in the valley. He took me over to Carson to visit Pacomio Mondragón's sheep camp near Tres Orejas in the spring, and I watched them do the lambing and the shearing, and heard the scare guns firing out on that lonely mesa to keep away the coyotes.

And I listened to people like Bernabé Chavez talk about his childhood in Carson, and what it had been like to run sheep on the mesa, and how so many people out there had eventually lost their land because a project to build a dam in Carson failed.

And I remember when Jacob Bernal stood up in Tres Rios meetings and talked about the community, the old days, the people who had kept the culture solid, a culture that needed to be protected against the negative effects of "progress."

After that, it seemed I was forever attending meetings in this town. I supported people at the Pueblo who were struggling to win back their Blue Lake Land. It wasn't my land, but it was my kind of idea; it related to the preservation of land, culture, history that had become important to my life. So I was glad to lend my support. It seemed an impossible task, and it took the Pueblo seventy years to get back that land, but in the end they triumphed.

Well, of course it never ended, they never will end—all the struggles in this town. And if you care about how you live, you have to work for the life and well-being of *all* the land and *all* the neighbors around you. Because all of us, in a community, are connected to each other. The naturalist John Muir once wrote, "Whenever we try to pick out anything by itself, we find it hitched to everything else in the universe."

And so I found that if I wanted to irrigate my fields in the summer, I would have to insist on the rights of everyone else to irrigate their fields during the growing season. And if I wanted to fly-fish for trout on the little rivers or on the Rio Grande, then I would have to join all struggles to maintain the health and the prosperity of those waters. And if I enjoyed the camaraderie of Pacomio Mondragón's sheep camp out on the Carson Mesa, then I would have to help all sheep ranchers maintain their grazing territories and their permits and their water rights, on the mesas or in the surrounding forests. In short, if I wanted to live in this vital community, I would have to join all the efforts of my neighbors to maintain a healthy balance between forces that hope to develop and change the valley, and other forces wishing to preserve and protect the values that for centuries have made our valley a powerful and beautiful place to live in.

We live in a country whose material culture most often teaches us to be selfish, to look out just for our own interests, to be concerned about Number One. We are trained not to care very much about things beyond our own personal concerns. We are taught that the way to be a success in life is to make a lot of money, buy a big house, have air-conditioning and washer-dryers and the latest model car, a color TV, a VCR. But I have never felt these things offer that much reward, or that pursuing them will result in personal fullfillment.

One reason I feel so deeply connected to Taos is that it is a community which still has strong roots into a different kind of tradition. It is a community which boasts many people whose roots are tied into the values and beliefs of a less selfish system. Over the years, I have met and worked with people whose ideals transcend purely selfish pursuits. They see the preservation of land and communal culture as something worth fighting for.

And they have been willing to dedicate much time and energy, for no financial remuneration, to struggle for what they believe in. Yes, it's an endless fight, but for them it has been one of the most rewarding aspects of their lives.

A few weeks ago I went to yet one more big community meeting in the Garcia Middle School. The gathering seemed very much like that first big meeting about the Indian Camp Dam to which I went sixteen years ago. This meeting was not about the dam, or a conservancy district; it concerned the highway bypass they are planning to build through the last, best agricultural land in Ranchitos.

Dozens of citizens stood up and spoke. Most of them were against the highway bypass because they felt it would further destroy a way of life they cherish. There was my friend Andrés Martínez, now eighty-seven years old, reading his speech with a magnifying glass, complaining about loss of fertile land and water rights. There was my youthful neighbor Andy Vigil talking about those same things. There was Ben Tafoya from Cañon, speaking about the value of the land, the history, and the community that he felt the highway project threatened. There was Romolo Arellano from Arroyo Hondo speaking on behalf of a culture and a way of life that needs to be respected. And there was Manuel Trujillo, another of my neighbors, determined to preserve agricultural and ethnic traditions for his children.

I was moved by all these speakers engaging in yet another battle to maintain the integrity and the quality of life that remains in this valley. And I was reminded once again, as I am reminded so often here in Taos, that if we truly care about the world around us, we must be prepared to spend a good part of our time defending it.

It is an obligation. It is a responsibility to have a social conscience, if we truly care about how things turn out.

That is the heart of any message I have to share with you all today. I know it's about the only advice I care to give my own children. I have no desire at all for them to be rich or famous or the owners of property, or anything like that. My only hope for them is that they care about the world, the community they live in. I hope they care enough to dedicate a good part of their time to social concerns. I hope they develop an idealism that cares about humanity as much as they care about themselves.

A few years back, I climbed Tres Orejas Mountain on the other side of the gorge with my friend Andrés Martínez. I mentioned he's eighty-seven now; back then he was only eighty. He told me that as a child, in the early 1900s, he had herded sheep all around the mountain, but he had never climbed it. So we tackled the job together. I was worried at the start that his heart might give out; but he scrambled up ahead of me so fast that by the time we reached the top I was afraid *my* heart would collapse!

On top of the mountain we could survey the entire Taos Valley around us. There was Pedernal to the west, the Jemez Mountains and Picuris Peak to the south, there was Llano and Ranchos and Taos across the gorge, and Taos mountain. And Chiflo and Ute Mountains up north, and Cerros de Taos closer by, and San Antonio in the northwest. And the Rio Grande Gorge ran down through the center of it all. Andrés and I studied this scene for a while. It was extraordinarily beautiful, this place where we all live. And finally Andrés said, "I thank God for giving me this day, for letting me see it all like this."

I, too, am very grateful for being allowed "to see things like this." I am also very grateful for old-timers like Andrés, whose idealism is still so intact that at the age of eighty-seven he is still fighting for what he believes in. And I hope that when I am his age, and my children are his age, we will still be involved in many struggles no matter how impossible the odds—because I know it's worth it. And it is the only way to keep a balance in this crazy world of ours.

▲ ▲ ▲

John Nichols, author of *The New Mexico Trilogy,* originally delivered the preceding piece as a commencement address at Taos (New Mexico) High School in 1986.

Time is but the stream I go a-fishing in. I drink at it; but while I drink I see the sandy bottom and detect how shallow it is. Its thin current slides away, but eternity remains. I would drink deeper; fish in the sky, whose bottom is pebbly with stars. I cannot count one. I know not the first letter of the alphabet. I have always been regretting that I was not as wise as the day I was born. The intellect is a cleaver; it discerns and rifts its way into the secret of things. I do not wish to be any more busy with my hands than is necessary. My head is hands and feet. I feel all my best faculties concentrated in it. My instinct tells me that my head is an organ for burrowing, as some creatures use their snout and fore-paws, and with it I would mine and burrow my way through these hills. I think that the richest vein is somewhere hereabouts; so by the divining rod and thin rising vapors I judge; and here I will begin to mine.

WALDEN
HENRY DAVID THOREAU

WALLACE STEGNER

QUALIFIED HOMAGE TO THOREAU

Before I get around to saying why I think that Walden Woods absolutely must be preserved from subdivision and development, let me confess that, much as I admire Thoreau's hard-mouthed intellectual integrity and his knotty grappler's mind, I have some reservations about him. There are writings of his that I admire more than *Walden*—the essay "Walking," for example, which is superb from first line to last, and "Civil Disobedience," though this latter is as explosive as dynamite caps, and should not be left around where children might find it and play with it. Reading *Walden*, I am alternately exhilarated and exasperated, as some of the author's contemporaries were with the man himself. In one paragraph he may say something that has been waiting a thousand years to be said so well; in the next he is capable of something so outrageous that it sets my teeth on edge.

With the Thoreau who observed and participated in nature, the Thoreau who loved wildness, and the Thoreau who trusted physical labor so long as it was not a compulsion, and who mistrusted material ambition, I am completely in accord. It is Thoreau the moralizing enemy of the tradition to which he owes all his own authority who puts me off. Especially in the first chapter, "Economy," he reveals himself to be a Wordsworthian romantic, and a self-absorbed one at that, with an underdeveloped social sense, a limited patience with his fellow men, and an independence that frequently amounts to pig-headedness.

Like any zealot, he is intemperate. The individualism that in moderate doses would be bracing sometimes becomes shrill and toxic. At times he sounds perilously like his spiritual descendants of the 1960s, who trusted no one over thirty and believed that they existed outside of, and were exempt from, the society they were protesting. What I miss in him, as I missed it in the more extreme rebels of the 1960s, is the acknowledgment that their society shaped them, that without it every individual of them would be a sort of Sasquatch, a solitary animal without language, thought, tradition, obligation, or commitment. It is culture, tradition, that teaches us to be human, teaches us almost everything, including how to protest and what to protest about.

I never hear Thoreau admitting this—in fact, he often specifically denies it, and his denials raise my temperature. "How about a little well-deserved humility?" I feel like asking him. It is like arguing with a television screen, but it eases the mind.

The fact is, it is precisely Thoreau's repudiation of the dead hand of the past that makes him so excruciatingly American. He is a caricature of our ahistorical weakness. He pretends to believe that all experience is not merely fruitless, but damaging. "Men think they are wiser by experience, that is, by failure," he remarks in the "Economy" chapter. "I have always been regretting that I was not as wise as the day I was born." And further, "Age is no better, hardly as well, qualified for an instructor as youth, for it has not profited so much as it has lost." (Here come the spontaneous, blind-leading-the-blind Free Universities of the sixties.) And finally, in a foreshadowing of the "no one over thirty" proscription, "I have lived some thirty years on this planet, and I have yet to hear the first syllable of valuable or even earnest advice from my seniors."

No benefit from his experience at Harvard College, then? Who taught him to read Latin and Greek? Who directed him to the Bhagavad Gita? And what was clogging his ears during the seasons when he lived in Emerson's house as a member of the family?

Extreme statements have their value as shock; they stimulate response and debate. As an outline for action, which is more or less how they are proposed, they can be poisonous. Nobody, in fact, can fully mean such things, and Thoreau reveals that he doesn't, either. While denying authority to any elder, he reveres the elders of literature and philosophy, he quotes us Homer and Shakespeare and the Indian mystics. Denying that there are philosophers any more, but only professors of philosophy, he undermines himself and disparages the people who have been his tutors and friends. Denying the validity of experience, he constantly (and properly) cites his own to bolster his beliefs.

Civil disobedience came easier to Thoreau than to most people because he never cared much for the civil aspects of life in the first place. His antisocial stance is very American, like his independence, but it is less a philosophical position than a temperamental dislike of influence and control. He has a loner's aversion to society, a need for private space. Instead of working to improve the world, he said, one should try only to make oneself "one of the world's worthies." As a companion, he was rather chilly. Emerson said he would as lief take hold of an oak limb as Henry's arm.

Even his prose style and his literary tastes trouble me. His style is didactic and apothegmatic to a degree. ("The mass of men lead lives of quiet desperation." "In the long run, men hit only what they aim at." "Trade curses everything it handles; and though you trade in messages from heaven, the whole curse of trade attaches to the business.") Being a Transcendentalist, a product of his tradition and his times, he finds every natural object or act emblematic of some larger Truth. The sentences which report these truths are declarative and dogmatic, and when read aloud they tend to have the same tune. They suggest a mind impervious to interruption or diversion, the kind of mind that cannot discuss, but only assert. He adds insult to injury, and offends the storyteller in me, by expressing contempt for fictions of all kinds; and yet he frequently invents little fables and parables from which he plucks meanings like a man cracking and eating walnuts. It is the moral that interests him, not the story, and in that he differs temperamentally from me.

This sounds like a litany of offenses, a list of reasons why Walden Woods should *not* be preserved as a memorial to Thoreau. It has no such intention, but so long as we are running through it, let us make one addition. It is that Thoreau's experiment in spartan living fudged its declared restrictions, and that the lessons Thoreau drew from it are therefore less persuasive than they sound.

The land on which he built his cabin was not his; he squatted on it in a most American way. On this borrowed ground, for a few dollars' worth of old boards, bricks, mortar, and sand, and by the application of his own labor, he made himself a shelter that satisfied all his limited needs. His demonstration of how little it takes to live, and live healthily and well, stirs the mind. So does his demonstration of how far personal independence will take us. Over the past 140 years thousands of people, singly or in couples, have taken off to places where they can escape the rat-race, own their horizon, live close to nature, and subsist on fish and mooseburgers. Thoreau was the model for most of them, probably.

But notice the moral he draws from his Walden experience (experience being synonymous with failure, as he said): "I thus found that the student who wishes for a shelter can obtain one for a lifetime at an expense not greater than the rent he now pays annually." So? Maybe, if there is land out there free for the stealing or squatting on, and if we can find some complaisant freeholder who doesn't mind our cutting down his trees for lumber or firewood and thus, as

Thoreau says, "improving the property." Maybe, if there are people, presumably some of those who live lives of quiet desperation, who will lend us the wheelbarrows, shovels, axes, hammers, and hoes we need; and if we know of friendly attics where chairs may be had for the labor of taking them away. And if our own independence allows us to sponge on those we scorn or pity.

Maybe it is the morality of property and ownership that makes this seem less than admirable to me. But I wish Thoreau had felt these squattings and borrowings as acts that entailed some sort of obligation. I am reminded of the hippie girl from the Haight-Ashbury district of San Francisco who some time in the sixties was stopped by a policeman from picking flowers from a bed in Golden Gate Park. She was angry. "They're not your flowers," she told the cop. "They're God's flowers." She might have been quoting one of the more extreme passages of *Walden*.

Thoreau does not strike me as a completely dependable guide to conduct. He refuses to pay the social dues that everybody owes. One reason for his continuing popularity is that he seems to offer an excuse for not doing what many overburdened people don't want to do. But for me, at least, his formula for plain living and high thinking has a flaw in it from the beginning. His economy is uncomfortably close to that of the desocialized hoboes of "The Bum Song":

> For we are three bums, three jolly old bums
> We live like royal Turks.
> We have good luck in bumming our chuck,
> God bless the man that works.

Nevertheless, having said all this, and assuming that it is all true, I have not diminished Thoreau's stature by a millimeter, or reduced the significance of Walden Woods by a milligram. Walden must be preserved and made into a shrine, not just because it is a pretty wood surrounding a little pond in suburban Massachusetts, or because any pretty little wood or pond saved is a step gained on a bearable future, but because this little pond is a glowing spot in the American memory, and because Thoreau made it so by living a couple of years on its shore.

Transcendentalist that he was, he made Walden Pond into a symbol of American possibility, and his own living routines into a paradigm of the American experience. If, as Robert Frost has said, the land was ours before we were the land's, Thoreau was one of those who showed us how to make ourselves the land's. His deeper and deeper penetration into Walden's secrets, his closer and closer participation in the pond's life and the pond's seasons, are a miniaturized and syncopated parallel to our invasion, use, and gradual understanding of the continent. His personal independence was the shadow of American cultural autonomy, his rebellion from Concord echoed America's rebellion from Europe.

He could be wrong, as I have surlily tried to demonstrate; but when he was right he was often spectacularly right, and he was, right or wrong, American to the marrow. His withdrawal from obligation and domination, his loner streak, were paralleled in thousands of lives across the whole history of America's frontiers. He did not invent the antisocial stance he sometimes took, but he gave it and all the cultural tendencies that surrounded it their most telling expression. The rebels of the 1960s found him unerringly, and overstated their case as he had overstated his.

But it was in his love of wildness, his perception that "in wildness is the preservation of the world," that he spoke his nation's mind at its best and highest reach. There is little of that in *Walden*—he was learning it there, but did not formulate it until later—but Walden is the proper place to commemorate it, for how do you make a significant human monument in the midst of the Maine woods?

No, Walden is the place for Thoreau's monument as surely as Washington is the place for the temples we have erected to Jefferson and Lincoln. This little lake within sight of the tracks and sound of the train whistle should be part of the American iconography. But we need no marble columns. The pond itself, and the creatures that find life in it and in the woods that surround it, are the most fitting monument for the man who took so much from them, and gave it back in unforgettable terms to his countrymen.

When it is dedicated, I will go there and walk the shore arguing with Thoreau's ghost. But I will go there.

▲ ▲ ▲

Wallace Stegner, the Pulitzer Prize winner for *Angle of Repose* and the winner of the Blackhawk award for *Wolf Willow*, is also editor and author of numerous other works. As keynote speaker at the Trust's 1982 Annual Meeting, he told his audience that he spent his childhood and youth "in wild, unsupervised places, and was awed very early, and never recovered."

> The greater part of what my neighbors call good I believe in my soul to be bad, and if I repent of any thing, it is very likely to be my good behavior. What demon possessed me that I behaved so well?
>
> *WALDEN*
> HENRY DAVID THOREAU

"I look down into the quiet parlor of the fishes, pervaded by a softened light as through a window of ground glass, with its bright sanded floor the same as in summer; there a perennial waveless serenity reigns as in the amber twilight sky, corresponding to the cool and even temperament of the inhabitants. Heaven is under our feet as well as over our heads."

WALDEN
HENRY DAVID THOREAU

PHOTO CREDITS